WAR AND NATURE

Globalization and the Environment Series

Series Editors

Richard Wilk, Department of Anthropology, 130 Student Building, Indiana University, Bloomington, IN 47405, USA, or wilkr@indiana.edu

Josiah Heyman, Department of Sociology & Anthropology, Old Main Building #109, University of Texas, 500 West University Avenue, El Paso, TX 79968, USA, or jmheyman@utep.edu

This AltaMira series publishes new books about the global spread of environmental problems. Key themes addressed are the effects of cultural and economic globalization on the environment; the global institutions that regulate and change human relations with the environment; and the global nature of environmental governance, movements, and activism. The series will include detailed case studies, innovative multi-sited research, and theoretical questioning of the concepts of globalization and the environment. At the center of the series is an exploration of the multiple linkages that connect people, problems, and solutions at scales beyond the local and regional. The editors welcome works that cross boundaries of disciplines, methods, and locales and span scholarly and practical approaches.

Books in the Series

Power of the Machine: Global Inequalities of Economy, Technology, and Environment, by Alf Hornborg (2001)

Confronting Environments: Local Environmental Understanding in a Globalizing World, edited by James Carrier (2004)

Communities and Conservation: Histories and Politics of Community-Based Natural Resource Management, edited by J. Peter Brosius, Anna Lowenhaupt Tsing, and Charles Zerner (2005)

Globalization, Health, and the Environment: An Integrated Perspective, edited by Greg Guest (2005)

Cows, Kin, and Globalization: An Ethnography of Sustainability, by Susan A. Crate (2006)

Global Visions, Local Landscapes: A Political Ecology of Conservation, Conflict, and Control in Northern Madagascar, by Lisa L. Gezon (2006)

Globalization and the World Ocean, by Peter Jacques (2006)

Rethinking Environmental History: World-System History and Global Environmental Change, edited by Alf Hornborg, John McNeill, and Joan Martínez-Alier (2007)

The World's Scavengers: Salvaging for Sustainable Consumption and Production, by Martin Medina (2007)

Saving Forests, Protecting People? by John W. Schelhas and Max J. Pfeffer (2008)

Capitalizing on Catastrophe: Neoliberal Strategies in Disaster Reconstruction, edited by Nandini Gunewardena and Mark Schuller (2008)

World in Motion: The Globalization and the Environment Reader, edited by Gary M. Kroll and Richard H. Robbins (2009)

War and Nature: The Environmental Consequences of War in a Globalized World, by Jurgen Brauer (2009)

WAR AND NATURE

The Environmental Consequences of War in a Globalized World

JURGEN BRAUER

ALTAMIRA
PRESS

A division of
ROWMAN & LITTLEFIELD PUBLISHERS, INC.
Lanham • New York • Toronto • Plymouth, UK

Published by AltaMira Press
A division of Rowman & Littlefield Publishers, Inc.
A wholly owned subsidiary of The Rowman & Littlefield Publishing Group, Inc.
4501 Forbes Boulevard, Suite 200, Lanham, Maryland 20706
www.altamirapress.com

Estover Road, Plymouth PL6 7PY, United Kingdom

British Library Cataloguing in Publication Information Available

Library of Congress Cataloging-in-Publication Data

Brauer, Jurgen, 1957–
   War and nature : the environmental consequences of war in a globalized world / Jurgen
Brauer.
      p. cm. — (Globalization and the environment series)
   Includes bibliographical references and index.
   ISBN 978-0-7591-1206-3 (cloth : alk. paper) — ISBN 978-0-7591-1929-1 (electronic)
   1. War—Environmental aspects. I. Title.
   QH545.W26B73 2009
   363.7—dc22   2009017974

∞ ™ The paper used in this publication meets the minimum requirements of American
National Standard for Information Sciences—Permanence of Paper for Printed Library
Materials, ANSI/NISO Z39.48-1992.

Printed in the United States of America

CONTENTS

FIGURES AND TABLES

Figures

Tables

Acknowledgments

In the years it took to research and write this book I have benefited from the work of my research assistants Mr. Ihsan Tayfur, Ms. Sapna Patel, Mr. Matthias Spoerle, Ms. Amanda Cox, and Ms. Manja Jonas. Also at my home institution, I thank Ms. Dar Scarff and her Interlibrary Loan staff as well as my academic colleagues, biologists Charlotte Christy, Judith Gordon, Bruce Saul, Emil Urban, and Donna Wear, chemists Tom Crute and Donna Hobbs, and political scientist and lawyer Raymond Whiting.

Outside of Augusta State University, I thank Saleem H. Ali, Jay E. Austin, Carl E. Bruch, Nils Petter Gleditsch, Rebecca Ham, Reg Hoyt, José Kalpers, Karl Kranz, Jeanne Mager Stellman, Jeffrey McNeely, Judy Oglethorpe, Steven Price, Don Reisman, Jamie Shambaugh, Jeremy Speck, F. Joseph Spieler, Jason Switzer, Amanda Watkins, Arthur H. Westing, and Alison Quito Ziegler for comments, reviews, interviews, and research materials they shared with me. I also thank a cadre of anonymous peer-reviewers who critiqued the developing manuscript.

Further, I thank colleagues for comments offered at various conferences and university seminars at which I presented portions of the material gathered in this book. These included visits to Middlesex University Business School in London, Afyon Kocatepe University in Turkey, the Allied Social Science Associations annual meetings in New Orleans, a Phi Kappa Phi honor society presentation at Augusta State University, a World Bank/European Union meeting at the University of Uppsala, and an international conference in Larissa, Greece. A month-long lecture tour in South Africa, generously funded by South Africa's National Research Foundation and undertaken after much of the basic research was completed, allowed me to see how the finished product might "play." Lectures were given at the University of Cape Town, the University of the Western Cape, Stellenbosch University, the Nelson Mandela Metropolitan University (Port Elizabeth), the University of Kwa-Zulu Natal (Durban), and the University of South Africa (Pretoria). Public lectures based on this material were given in Sydney, Australia, and at the Augusta, Georgia, chapter of the Sierra Club.

For their support to give birth to this book after an altogether too long period of gestation, thanks go to Professors Josiah Heyman and Richard Wilk, editors of AltaMira's Globalization and the Environment (GATE) series, and to Jack Meinhardt, the acquisitions editor for the press.
I offer a special thank-you to my colleague Professor J. Paul Dunne, at whose home in Bristol, United Kingdom, I was able to spend some quiet weeks in early 2009 to prepare the book's final manuscript. Finally, a special thank-you of a personal nature also goes to Luca, Sandro, and Stefano.

The usual disclaimer applies: all helped to improve the work; none but the author are responsible for the shortcomings that remain.

JURGEN BRAUER
Bristol, U.K.
April 2009

Preface

" All plants must travel," writes British naturalist, author, and broadcaster David Attenborough. "The lives of plants, like our own and those of all other animals, culminate in the production of more individuals of their own kind which will try to claim space for themselves and so extend the dominion of their species. And to do that, plants—at some stage in their lives—have to travel." [1]

Establishing dominion, and the travel upon which it at first relies, is facilitated by geography. For this, the University of California, Los Angeles, physiologist and geographer Jared Diamond has made the perhaps most celebrated case of recent years. Proximate causes of change, he writes, such as those brought about by war, disease, and metallurgy—or *Guns, Germs, and Steel*, as the title of his most well-known book has it—rely for their propagation on ultimate causes. And a key ultimate cause for the ease with which species travel and propagate lies in the extensive east-west axis that connects Europe and Asia across nearly one-half of the globe's Northern Hemisphere. [2] Other continents, especially Africa and the Americas, also are vast, of course. But their primary axis of orientation lies north-south, imposing stringent climatic restrictions on species travel. For example, traveling north from Tierra del Fuego at the southern tip of South America individuals of a species would need to fend off established species as they moved northward. At the same time they would need to adapt to an ever hotter, ever more humid climate, and conquer considerable changes in altitude as well. Then, crossing the equator, they would have to reverse course, now adapting to an ever colder and flatter environment on their way to the Bering Strait on the west coast or the Hudson Strait on the east coast of the North American tectonic plate. In contrast, a species at home in Lisbon or Madrid might feel equally at home in Istanbul, or Baku, or Beijing, all clustered around 40 degrees north latitude.

Given evolutionary time, however, all species will travel, foiled only by geological obstacles, habitat conditions, and by the species that already are there. To professional geographers and biologists, then, the ongoing post–Cold War debate about globalization must in a way seem puzzling. After all, for nature, globalization is the way of life. Attenborough's dictum that "all plants must travel," might as well read "all species must travel." And as they do, they come in conflict with locally established species, the domestics. What sets the human species apart is our willingness not only to fight other species for living space, but to fight among ourselves. To be sure, an owl may control a considerable stretch of aerial territory, or a damselfish a patch of coral, and defend this from encroachment. But there are no groups of owls or groups of damselfish flying or swimming on other owls or damselfish as humans march on one another. Even among social animals such as termites, wolves, and dolphins one does not observe this behavior. It is largely a human trait.

This book is about our wars—humans' wars—and the environmental consequences they entail for the rest of nature.[3] By way of introduction chapter 1 first addresses some related themes. These ask, for example, what natural resources are consumed by the world's state and nonstate armed forces, review the environmental effects of nuclear testing and nuclear war, explore whether freshwater scarcity or climate change contribute to the probability of war breaking out, and how specific resources such as petroleum, timber, or gemstones may tie in to global production and consumption patterns. Globalization after all is not only about the worldwide diffusion and steady expansion of our species but also about the modern ease with which goods, services, people, and ideas move through and interact in the web we have spun and by which our species hangs together.

While nuclear war would affect the entirety of the globe's environment, seemingly minor local wars also relate to the theme of globalization. For example, the civil war in Sri Lanka that began in the early 1980s would perhaps have stalled soon had it not been for the funds supplied by the Tamil diaspora located in Canada, the United Kingdom, and elsewhere. So-called conflict diamonds extracted in Sierra Leone or opium harvested in Afghanistan would not have generated warlords' financial wherewithal were it not for global consumer demand. And the rush to tap Sudanese or Kazakh petroleum and natural gas resources threatens to reconfigure in a serious way power relations among the United States, the European

Union, Russia, India, and China. (Potential) war, nature, and globalization are entwined in myriad ways.[4]

The bulk of the book, however, deals with the environmental consequences of non-nuclear war. Yet to know war's environmental effects, one must measure them. This, it turns out, is no easy task. Although soldiers risk their lives in war, and although journalists and humanitarian relief workers may risk theirs as well, rarely will a scientist be put in that position for the mere chance to observe and measure the effect of bombing Guam's shorelines, Vietnam's forests, Kuwait's desert, Serbian nature parks, Afghan mountains, or urban Baghdad. There are exceptions, and for complex reasons, as chapter 1 details, but on the whole environmental measurement in war is fiendishly difficult. The chapter concludes with a synopsis of the treatment of the environment in international law of war, a topic not otherwise dealt with in this book.[5]

Chapters 2 and 3 summarize research covering two major international wars. The Vietnam War of the 1960s and 1970s (chapter 2) was a long war taking place in an environment of tropical forests, commercial tree plantations, and mangrove stands. In contrast, the 1991 Persian Gulf War (chapter 3) was of relatively short duration and took place in an arid desert environment (mostly in Kuwait), with downwind and downcurrent effects on the Persian Gulf marine environment of a neighboring country (Saudi Arabia). The Vietnam War used weaponry and methods of war-fighting that were comparatively crude. In Kuwait computer-programmed, satellite-directed, precision-guided munitions were fired off naval vessels stationed far from areas of active combat; but in Vietnam fleets of high-altitude, long-range B-52 bombers carpet-bombed vast swaths of forests, cratering the soil and injuring or killing millions of trees. Explosion-generated shock waves flung fragments of bombs, soil, and vegetation as high-velocity projectiles into the surrounding stands, injuring wildlife that was left bereft of whatever medical care might have been afforded human victims. In contrast to the B-52 raids, forest defoliation missions were flown at low altitude directly overhead of the intended targets. A variety of factors, such as the spray technology, spray mixture and density, prevailing wind direction and wind speed, determined the noxious clouds' final landing areas. How the resulting litter of defoliated leaves might have affected local soil ecology would then depend on factors such as the porousness of the soil and the slope of the terrain. Seasonally determined rainfall, from sprinkle to downpour, might then carry various quantities of leaf litter, at various stages of decomposition, into local waterways and thence to areas possibly far away from the original release point. A war such as that in Vietnam is likely to have affected nature differently than the Persian Gulf War (or other high-tech wars since then). Is it possible that today's technology of war affects nature somehow more benignly than in previous decades?

Chapter 4 examines the environmental effects of (ill-named) civil wars. Of course, there are civil wars aplenty, and so one must select one's cases. The chapter examines two, namely those for which the largest variety of scientific material is available. One concerns Central Africa: the Rwandan civil war and its effects on neighboring countries, especially the eastern Congo (that is, the eastern part of the Democratic Republic of the Congo). The war started in 1990, and peaked in 1994; in its effects on the Congo, it has not been settled even today. The other case concerns south-central Asia: the decades-long Afghan conflicts (from the overthrow of the Afghan king to the Soviet invasion and the U.S. war on Taliban forces there) and its environmental repercussions on Pakistan. The Soviet invasion of Afghanistan was an international war, and heavy military equipment was brought to bear. The Taliban were, in some degree, an armed resistance. Once the Soviets left, tables turned, and the resisters were resisted. Then, in 2001, the country experienced a period of aerial bombardment by the United States, the Taliban were defeated, democracy was declared, and today the country is again in a state of internal war.

Obvious exceptions notwithstanding, the weapons used in civil wars fall mostly into the small arms category, such as bladed weapons and firearms. Generally low-tech, they are at times no more than agricultural implements. Yet the environmental and humanitarian effects of such arms and wars can be devastating, for example when they result in refugee streams. The most widely recognized case is that of the Rwandan war, which spewed millions of people into eastern Congo and western Tanzania where, to better control and assist them, they were at first herded into geographically highly restricted refugee camps. But in the absence of instant international aid supplying fuel and food, survival demanded forays into the forests, first to collect loose firewood and to break off easy-to-reach branches, later to cut whole trees and to dig up tree stumps. In a matter of weeks large forest areas were denuded of vegetation, driving ambulatory wildlife into its own refugee crisis and sessile flora into death. Animal migration routes were disrupted, bushmeat was hunted, and waterways polluted with human waste and wasted humans. Qualitatively and quantitatively, these sorts of effects of war may be very different from those we might expect to observe as a consequence of the Vietnam or Persian Gulf Wars.

Chapter 5 collects the evidence from the case studies. Certain patterns and hypotheses emerge, some of them unexpected and surprising. For example, the thesis that war's effects on nature are unambiguously detrimental turns out to be too simple. Just as war imposes costs on nature, war also bestows benefits. The Korean War of the early 1950s resulted in a demilitarized zone that today is a haven for wildlife seen nowhere else on the peninsula. The minefields scattered about the world from Angola to Cambodia limit human resettlement, creating refuges wherein wildlife thrives. In the 1980s, in Nicaragua, forests offered protection to armed forces, which led to their protection of the forests. Indeed, it is likely that it is not humans' wars but the economic development that comes with our peace that remains the greatest threat to nature. Jeffrey McNeely, chief scientist of the International Union for Conservation of Nature and Natural Resources (IUCN) writes: "While war is bad for biodiversity, peace can be worse . . . market forces are often more destructive than military forces."[6]

Other themes addressed in chapter 5 include the environmental effect, in civil war, of mobility and firepower—the jeep and the gun—of conservation neglect in civil war, of the role of refugees and returnees, and of the possibility that the conduct of at least some civil wars may be more harmful to the environment than that of major international wars. The chapter also reviews the role of business and global consumer demand in war's environmental destruction, and attention is paid to the potentially positive role commerce can play in righting wrongs. Although globalization is often maligned, we can learn how to make it a force to be harnessed for the common good.

Chapter 5 concludes with a reasonably practical agenda—a way forward—not only to help collect scientific evidence from future wars but an agenda of what the world's environmental and conservation organizations can and should do in this regard. Although to prevent war and to protect nature is of course a job for all of us, it is, after all, their self-adopted brief and mission to protect nature, in peace as in war, and we rely on their expertise and leadership.

Notes, references, and an index conclude the book.

From nature's point of view, both human peace and human war can be destructive. If the pro-environment community were to pay more attention to the destructive effects not only of peace but also of war, and if the pro-peace community were to pay more attention not only to the destructive human effects of war but also to its destructive nonhuman effects, then the two groups might benefit from each other's efforts. Although many people espouse pro-environmental and pro-peace views, they tend to do so without noting the direct link between the two. Even though this book emphasizes nature more than war, I hope it helps to make the connection.

Notes

1. Attenborough (1995, p. 11).

2. Diamond (1999). The bulk of the Eurasian landmass lies between 20 and 70 degrees north latitude, with some regions reaching farther north nearly to the pole. To the south, the Malaysian peninsula in southeast Asia nearly touches the equator.

3. One can separate war's environmental from its ecological effects, but the word *environment* has become so generic that it is best simply to speak of the environmental effects of war. When a precise biological meaning is needed, this will be made clear in the text. *Environment* is defined as the conditions, circumstances, and influences surrounding the development of organisms, sometimes taken more strictly as the abiotic physical and chemical habitat; and *ecology* as the study of the relation between environment and organisms.

4. Tamils: Human Rights Watch (2006). Conflict diamonds: first report by Global Witness (1998). Fuel: in 2005, 2006, and 2007, the Harriman Institute at Columbia University, New York, held annual symposia on this topic. See its website for details.

5. The literature on the environment in international law of war, and of war in international environmental law, is vast. Still the single best starting point is the edited volume by Austin and Bruch (2000).

6. McNeely (2000, p. 369). Other versions of McNeely's paper have appeared as McNeely (2002; 2003).

Globalization, Nature, and War

1.1 Natural Resource Consumption by Armed Forces

Every bullet made, every barrack built, and every battleship set to sail consumes natural resources. No one knows how much. Even approximations are difficult to make. Between 2 and 3 percent of measured annual world income is expended on military pursuits, at times more, at times less, in some states much more, and in others much less.[1] Because military expenditure, as conventionally measured, understates the actual outlays, as a rule of thumb the upper edge of the range, 3 percent of world income, will be a safer assumption,[2] and more so—perhaps much more so—if the world's very numerous nonmilitary and nonstate armed forces were to be included.[3] A large part of that expenditure goes toward paying the wages and salaries of the members of the state and nonstate, military and nonmilitary armed forces (the "military" for short). No one knows what that amount is worldwide, but it must be subtracted as it reflects the use of human, rather than nonhuman, resources that the military absorbs.[4] Much of the remainder is spent on the acquisition of new equipment and infrastructure and on training, operations, and maintenance of existing assets such as bases and weaponry as well as on payment for services provided by contractors. For contractor services, again one would need to subtract payment for human resources. For example, if a contractor is paid to ship heating oil to a military base, the pay that ultimately goes to the contractor's employees does not consume natural resources but the resources consumed in the process of shipping the heating oil, let alone the oil itself, do constitute a natural resource use by an armed force.

No one has done these sorts of calculations. For convenience, let us say that as a first approximation 3 percent of world income is spent on military-related consumption of natural resources. For illustration, if the world had a forest of 1,000 trees and grew one hundred new ones to be harvested in a particular year, three of those would go for military purposes and ninety-seven for nonmilitary, civilian purposes. The stock of trees, a renewable natural resource, would remain unchanged. Likewise, if the world had 1,000 trees and grew no new ones (as if they were a nonrenewable resource), then the stock would fall to 900. Of the net loss, three trees could be ascribed to the military and ninety-seven to civilian activity.

More specifically, in 2005 for example, world total primary energy supply (TPES) produced from all sources reached 11,468 million metric tons of oil equivalent (MTOE), almost all of which was consumed. (A negligibly small amount went into primary energy stocks.) Three percent of that would equal 344 MTOE for the military. As the United States accounted for nearly half of world military expenditure and as it was fighting two energy-intensive wars overseas, and as the United States is a high energy-use and relatively energy-inefficient society to begin with, it is probably safe to say that military-related energy use, let alone that of all armed forces, is above the 344 MTOE figure just computed. In terms of orders of magnitude, the same can be said with regard to the use of other natural resources and the consequent stresses placed on the environment in the process of extraction, use, and disposal.[5]

To put this number in perspective, if in 2005 world military-related energy use amounted to 344 MTOE, all of Latin America's 449 million people that year had to make do with just 500 MTOE and all of Africa's 894 million with 605.[6] On the one hand we thus may say that world military forces absorb only 3 percent of world total primary energy supplies but, on the other hand, they absorb more than one-half of all of Africa's needs and more than two-thirds of all of Latin America's. Another perspective is offered by the insufficiently appreciated fact that vast amounts of primary energy are lost in the process of energy transformation to usable energy and transfer to end-users. In the United States, for example—and again for 2005—of available primary energy inflows of 97.9 quadrillion British thermal units (QBTUs), only 42.8 QBTUs, or 43.7 percent, ended up as usable energy for residential, commercial, and other purposes, the remaining 56.3 percent being lost in the energy conversion and distribution processes.[7]

A related consideration, before the energy-use thread is picked up again, therefore deals not with raw material inputs into military preparedness per se but with resource-use inefficiencies, waste generation, proper materials use and waste disposal, pollution, pollution prevention, and natural resource conservation; that is, with general economic, environmental, and public health and safety issues. This is not so much a point regarding globalization as one that globally affects every local military base and arms production site. In the past, the expediency, if not to say the excuse, of war or preparing for war, made it comparatively easy to shush those who opined that the risk soldiers face in war not unnecessarily be added to in peacetime. Shushing those within military organizations is one thing; shushing those on the outside is another. In nondemocratic societies, protesters, troublemakers, and dissidents could be effectively silenced, of course. But even in democracies, it proved difficult during the Cold War years to speak of public health and safety concerns alongside military preparedness for national security. If not nationally, at least locally the military was almost always given the benefit of the doubt, and not only because the military dollar supported local economies. A culture of consent absolved the military from environmental stewardship. But with the end of the Cold War came base closures and defense production-related layoffs, as did questions regarding the environmental legacy of war preparation. In an excellent book, Robert Durant writes of the difficulty that military organizations faced when abandoning a "Cold War ethic of sovereignty, secrecy, and sinecure in favor of a post–Cold War ethic of accountability, transparency, and resource reallocation" toward prevention, clean-up, remediation, and restoration.[8]

In the United States, post–Cold War efforts initiated by the George H. W. Bush administration and continued by the Bill Clinton and George W. Bush administrations, certainly led to improvements. But the nature of these improvements can be questioned. As Durant points out, the downsizing of the U.S. American military sector alone would imply commensurate reductions in military-related resource absorption and environmental stresses. Thus, the achievements that were in fact made must be seen against the background of a smaller military, just as the current environmental position must be measured against the rising U.S. military effort since 2001. Improved fuel efficiency of military vehicles, for example, should be in the military's, that is, Congress's or the taxpayers', own interest. In principle, a dollar wasted could be a dollar saved and shifted into higher military preparedness and fighting effectiveness. In practice, as Durant's book recounts in much detail, innumerable and interminable squabbles between and among officials and officers at the Pentagon, the president's office, and Congress degenerate into fights among vested interests, inhibiting and slowing the greening of the U.S. military.[9]

Whereas the environmental footprint of the U.S. military and other militaries is thus real enough in terms of resource consumption and stewardship (or lack thereof), the absence of the military is unlikely to result in a reduced footprint, however. To see the reason for this, take the opposite position—more military effort—and note that war or warlike conditions tend to suppress economic activity, at home and abroad. This implies a fall in income and expenditure and hence a fall of the energy and other natural resource usage inherent in civilian production and consumption. During the 1990s Balkan wars, for example, a United Nations Environment Programme study noted a cleaner environment in the former Yugoslavia and attributed this to the fall in economic activity due to the economic sanctions that preceded the wars there. Of course this does not mean that to save the environment, humans should fight more wars. That would be an absurd conclusion to draw. Instead, the point is that because of substitution effects—fewer guns, more butter—the absence of war, or the absence of preparations for war, will not necessarily result in reduced environmental stresses. From an environmental point of view, war preparation and war are just other forms of production and consumption.[10]

1.2 Nuclear War and Nuclear Weapons Testing

1.2.1 Nuclear War

Some forms of war or war-related production and consumption can carry particularly deleterious effects, however. Without doubt, the most frightening of these is the specter of nuclear war and the prospect of "nuclear winter." During the Cold War in the mid-1980s, hundreds of scientists affiliated with the Scientific Committee on Problems of the Environment (SCOPE) of the International Council of Scientific Unions carried out a series of studies on the likely environmental and human consequences of nuclear war. Because of the use of two atomic weapons on Japan in World War II and because of nuclear weapons testing, some data were available to be fed into mathematical models to simulate physical and atmospheric effects of, and ecological and agricultural responses to, large-scale nuclear weapons detonations. The number of explosions, their total yield, the location and height at which explosions are triggered, and a large number of other factors determine the initial and delayed effects.[11]

The effects may be categorized as local, regional, and global in scale. Thus, the physical effects of the quasi-instantaneous thermal (heat) radiation and the follow-on explosive shock wave are circumscribed by factors such as the bomb's yield, its release height, the topography of the terrain and the matter that this terrain contains. For example, because of Hiroshima's relatively flat terrain, the blast wave and the subsequent fires resulted in an almost circular pattern of destruction. In contrast, in Nagasaki the blast and subsequent burn pattern extended along the axis of the valley in which the city lies. Region-wide effects come from the downwind fallout pattern of radioactive dust particles. Surface bursts—ground-level explosions—generate large clouds of soil and debris as the bomb's explosive force is reflected off the land surface. The larger, heavier particles that are lofted into the air, containing perhaps half of a bomb's radioactivity, tend to precipitate early. Lighter particles will stay aloft longer and are carried farther, and their radioactive effects therefore disperse more widely. In contrast, the explosive force of an airburst—such as for Hiroshima and Nagasaki, with bomb release heights of 580 meters and 500 meters, respectively—does not contact land surfaces as much.[12] This generates a smaller dust cloud with smaller particles and smaller radioactive regional fallout. Instead, the radioactive effects are transported over very large regions of continental size, or even globally. Radioactivity is carried by small particles into the upper troposphere (to about 14 kilometers above sea level) and stratosphere (to about 50 kilometers above sea level). In the troposphere—the part of the atmosphere where weather patterns form—air currents move horizontally and vertically; in the stratosphere, air flow is mostly lateral. Together, this ensures thorough mixing of irradiated particles and also that they stay airborne for periods of weeks, months, and years, thus having the potential to affect climatic change. For example, depending on factors such as the number, yield, height, and location of atomic bombs exploded, smoke and debris injection into the atmosphere could be of such volume, thickness, aerial extent, and length of time as to engender a "nuclear winter," that is, an atmospheric debris cover leading within days to dramatic and prolonged surface temperature drops as sunlight is blocked. A fall in primary productivity among sun-energy dependent autotrophs (i.e., plants and algae) and subsequent food shortages and large-scale privation and starvation for other organisms follow. Earth's biosphere would be substantially altered.[13]

A nuclear bullet cannot miss. Once it is exploded, there is no turning back, and whatever may be done amounts to damage mitigation. Nature's restorative capacity, including humans' capacity to mitigate damage, will be limited as food production and the intricate local, regional, and global physical and social infrastructures serving its distribution are going to be curtailed. Unlike any other form of war, a major nuclear exchange has virtually no optional environmental qualities about it. All depends on the size of the nuclear bullet, and in light of the subsequent growth in yield, efficiency, and number of atomic weapons, it is worth emphasizing that the Hiroshima and Nagasaki bombs were small nuclear explosions. For example, already by 1954—not even ten years after Hiroshima and Nagasaki—a United States nuclear weapons test called Bravo, part of its Operation Castles test series at the Bikini Atoll, on which more later, had a TNT-equivalent yield of 15,000 kilotons, 1,000 times the yield of the Hiroshima bomb.[14]

The Cold War has ended and, with it, the world's total nuclear arsenal has shrunk. Some states have given up their nuclear weapons (e.g., South Africa) and others have given up programs to develop them (e.g., Brazil). At the same time, however, others have labored to increase the yield, efficiency, and "chunking" of the remaining weapons into smaller parcels, for example for tactical (battlefield) rather than strategic use or to fit them onto smaller carrier devices. In addition, new states have joined the nuclear club, and the prospect of nuclear proliferation in additional states is a serious ongoing concern. Forty or more states now are in possession of fissionable material, although not necessarily (yet) in the purified form needed for nuclear weapons. In all, the nuclear weapons–use risk has shifted from global exchange to include regional-scale and battlefield exchanges (and possibly to terrorist uses).[15] It is therefore useful to learn from a recent study that the global environmental risks even of regional-scale nuclear war remain substantial. Directed at major cities, an airburst nuclear war between Pakistan and India of one hundred Hiroshima-yield weapons (i.e., about 15 kilotons each) might result, simulations predict, in "1 to 5 million tons of carbonaceous smoke particles" that could persist in the atmosphere for a decade and induce "substantial global-scale climate anomalies." These would have follow-on effects on "surface land temperatures, precipitation rates, and growing season length." For example, in the first year or two, the growing season in the southeastern United States and southeastern Australia would drop by thirty days each, in southern Africa by ten days, and over much of Europe and southwest Latin America by ten to twenty days. (Isolated regions such as the Nile River Valley of Egypt would see an expanded growing season of about ten days.) In all, worldwide agricultural productivity would decline in this hypothetical, computer-simulated, limited nuclear war that expends only one-third of Pakistan's and India's estimated combined number of nuclear weapons (their yield, though, is unknown; hence the assumption in the simulation of fairly low-yield weapons).[16]

1.2.2 Nuclear Weapons Testing

What is not hypothetical are the known effects of nuclear weapons testing. Worldwide, over 2,000 such tests have been carried out. Between 1945 and 1992, the United States for example conducted 1,149 nuclear detonations in 1,054 tests (24 tests jointly with the United Kingdom).[17] The majority of the testing (928) and detonations (1,021) took place at the U.S. Nevada Test Site. Of all 1,054 tests, 839 were underground, 210 atmospheric, and five underwater. Since 1963, all were underground and all were conducted in the United States (including Alaska). Prior to that, and most notoriously for the United States, 106 detonations were undertaken in the Marshall Islands (Bikini and Enewetak Atolls), Christmas Island, Johnston Atoll, and elsewhere in the Pacific Ocean (e.g., submarine vessel–related firing tests) and Southern Atlantic Ocean. The United States, the United Kingdom, and the Soviet Union ended atmospheric testing in 1963, France in 1974, and China in 1980. (Nonatmospheric testing continued, however, and a number of those tests resulted in the release of radioactive material into the atmosphere, as will be described shortly.) Importantly, the United Kingdom conducted atmospheric tests also in Australia as did France near Reggane in Algeria—even after Algerian independence—and in the Mururoa and Fangataufa Atolls in French Polynesia in the South Pacific. Although no atmospheric tests were conducted in Latin America, the Middle East, South Asia, or in non-Soviet Europe, fallout of radioactive material nonetheless has been detected everywhere on Earth in soil, water, and polar ice.

All organisms are naturally exposed to some degree of radiation. Earth's atmosphere is bathed in cosmic-source radiation, and radon gas emanates from Earth's surface. Anthropogenic sources include medical devices such as X-ray imaging and of course nuclear weapons tests. Whereas many radionuclides created by nuclear combat or test weapons explosions decay quickly into harmless particles, the concern about the others arises from their long half-life—that is, from their damaging persistence in the environment. Radiation harms tissue, notably by stimulating cancerous growths and contributing to diseases such as leukemia and thyroid cancer.

There is no doubt as to the human medical (and social) effects from radiation fallout. Apart from Japan, of course, they have been documented in, for example, the Marshall Islands, French Polynesia, and the Semipalatinsk test site in northeastern Kazakhstan (then part of the Soviet Union), as well as in the continental United States. The United States government has accepted responsibility and offered compensation to affected Marshall Islanders. Scientifically there is no dispute about the causal chain of events:

> Following the deposition of fallout on the ground, local human populations are exposed to external and internal irradiation. External irradiation exposure is mainly from penetrating gamma rays emitted by particles on the ground. Shielding by buildings reduces exposure, and thus doses to people are influenced by how much time one spends outdoors. Internal irradiation exposures can arise from inhaling fallout and absorbing it through intact or injured skin, but the main exposure route is from consumption of contaminated food. Vegetation can be contaminated when fallout is directly deposited on external surfaces of plants and when it is absorbed through the roots of plants. Also, people can be exposed when they eat meat and milk from animals grazing on contaminated vegetation. In the Marshall Islands, foodstuffs were also contaminated by fallout directly deposited on food and cooking utensils.[18]

The uptake of radioactive material is stronger through terrestrial than through marine foodstuffs. Among the former, the effect mediated by iodine-131 through the "pasture-cow-milk-man food chain" is particularly strong, with radiation doses amplified tenfold, hundredfold, and more (and more so through goat's than through cow's milk). The primary effect on populations within the immediate fallout region lies with elevated risk of stomach and colon cancer (due to ingestion of contaminated foodstuffs) and with higher bone marrow and thyroid cancer risk for populations farther downwind. Other radionuclides of special concern include strontium-90 and caesium-135. One scientific review reports estimates of fallout-related excess thyroid cancers in the United States—primarily among persons who were under age twenty in the years 1951 to 1957—on the order of 49,000 cases. These are due to atmospheric testing in the continental United States (i.e., mostly the Nevada Test Site). The estimate rises to 54,000 cases when effects of radiation fallout from worldwide testing are added. For perspective, these excess cases are anticipated in addition to baseline estimates of some 400,000 cases likely to occur in the absence of any radioactive fallout—that is, about a 12 to 14 percent increase.[19]

Apart from the size of the explosion, the nonhuman effects of a nuclear test strongly depend on whether it was triggered underground, underwater, at the surface, or at altitude. In atoll-based testing, the physical effects on parts of the atolls are unquestioned. In French Polynesia, for example, explosions triggered in sealed shafts 500 meters to 1,100 meters underground resulted in the creation of cavities due to rock vaporization and rock melting in the immediate blast vicinity. Farther away, rock shearing and deformation occurred as a shock wave first became plastic and then elastic as it traveled away from the blast center. The propagation of the blast wave can create rock fissures in the boundary zone from rock to open water. The inner blast cavity then fills with sea water seeping in through the fissures. Gradually, radioactive products are leached out from the surrounding rock and become suspended in the water column, and, depending on the hydrology of the atoll, eventually can find their way to the overlying lagoon or open ocean. As radioactive material decays in time, the degree of danger and damage depends on the transition time from cavity to open water, lagoon water, or surface areas. Studies found that "although direct venting of gaseous radionuclides to the atmosphere probably did not occur, in about fifteen cases there is conclusive evidence of the release of tritium, strontium and caesium to the top of the volcanics within a few years of the test. This indicates that either the full volcanic cover was significantly damaged by the explosion, or the integrity and/or initial permeability of the volcanic cover above these tests was significantly different from that anticipated." In particular, it appears that temperature changes associated with each explosion led water to move vertically from the volcanic into the carbonate rock layer above it and from there to travel into the surrounding ocean and atoll lagoon. Tritium and plutonium levels in the French test lagoons are elevated. Toward and at the surface, the blasts caused fractures at the atoll rim, surface settlement and submergence, and submarine slope failures (landslides). Colonization of the newly submerged areas by coral growth has been noted, but it is not expected that the atoll rim will be reestablished. Long-term changes to atoll hydrology are expected to be "negligible."[20]

Nonetheless, the studies on French Polynesia conclude that dangers to current and future human populations on account of the underground tests are minimal, below one-tenth of natural background doses. Even if a catastrophic collapse of one of the blast cavities at Mururoa should occur and release remaining radionuclides into the ocean, the maximal additional dose is estimated to be around 3/1,000 of natural background radiation (in the initial year, and less thereafter due to decay). Based on site samples, the impact of the underground tests on native plants and animals likewise is thought to be extremely small:

> The [IAEA-IAC] Study concluded that it is unlikely that the residual radioactive material will have any effects on healthy populations of living organisms on or near the Atolls. Overall, the additional doses, due to the

tests, to the vast majority of native marine organisms are less than, or about the same level as, the doses due to natural background radiation. Aside from the Colette sandbank, in which plutonium containing particles from atmospheric safety trials were found, the highest doses in the vicinity of Mururoa and Fangataufa atolls to marine organisms are at least 200 times lower than those that could have detrimental effects on populations. For the Colette sandbank, it is possible that some individual creatures living in the sediment could receive absorbed doses from particles containing plutonium that would be sufficient to produce effects in microscopic volumes of tissue. However, there would be no harmful impact on the wider eco-systems.[21]

In the Marshall Islands, to return to U.S. testing, all nuclear weapons tests there, conducted between 30 June 1946 and 18 August 1958—twenty-three in Bikini Atoll and forty-three in Enewetak Atoll—were airbursts, surface, or underwater explosions—that is, explosions with atmospheric release. None were underground. Human effects have already been referred to.[22] As regards the nonhuman effects, a report published in 2008 in the *Marine Pollution Bulletin* reviews Bikini Atoll coral biodiversity five decades after nuclear testing ended there.[23] It is the first report to make use of prenuclear testing coral survey data. Its authors therefore are able to establish some facts about one aspect of the long-term near-shore marine impact of the tests. In brief, of 126 coral species described in pretest data, forty-two were not recorded in post-test data. Of these, fourteen "may be pseudo-losses due to inconsistent taxonomy between the two studies or insufficient sampling in the second study [but] twenty-eight species appear to represent genuine losses." Seen at other Marshall Islands atolls, they may be locally extinct at Bikini. However, twelve species new to Bikini were discovered as well, and "overall coral species richness at Bikini Atoll appears to have remained approximately the same over a fifty year period." Of the apparently locally lost species, sixteen were lagoonal specialists. Sampling locations outside the lagoon showed comparable pre- and post-nuclear testing coral biodiversity. The lagoonal losses are understandable as the weapons tests were carried out within the lagoon—the 15,000 kiloton (TNT-equivalent) Bravo surface test on 28 February 1954 leading to the complete vaporization of three islets—and caused considerable repeat disturbances of the lagoon, such as substrate removal, extreme blast shock and water wave action, sediment displacement and redistribution, super-heated surface water temperatures of up to 55,000°C, and long-term loading of radioactive material in invertebrate tissue and in sediment. Whether future years will see natural or artificial recruitment of these lagoon coral specialists remains to be seen.

The surface areas of Bikini remain polluted with radiologically significant radionuclides and human population resettlement is not recommended. Surface application of potassium-based fertilizer and scraping and removal of top-layer soil and coral rubble are potential remedial actions, but are extremely expensive and environmentally disruptive and a matter of continuing dispute between the Republic of the Marshall Islands and the United States of America. One report on the floral cover of the Marshall Islands states that on Bikini Atoll postnuclear natural recolonization progressed to such an extent that "some scientists voiced concern when it was proposed to scrape the land to remove residual radiation before human reoccupation, although this option was favored by the islanders. The scientists prefer the use of potassium fertilizer, which they say would be absorbed by plants in preference to Cesium-137. The concern is that scraping would destroy the plants and the bird nesting habitats."[24]

In sum, it bears repeating and emphasizing that the regional and global differences in the simulated or actual nuclear war and nuclear testing effects described here are consistently and entirely due to whether radioactive material is released into the atmosphere, an environmental and ecological concern not dissimilar to, although in scale vastly different from, the use of lead munitions and of depleted-uranium munitions.

1.3 Need and Greed As Causes of War

Apart from questions related to military resource absorption in preparing for war and of the environmental effects of nuclear testing and nuclear war, another area of study has reversed the direction of causality. Instead of asking what are the effects of potential war on nature, the question is, what are the effects of nature on war? More specifically: do environmental stresses caused by resource scarcity, high population density, energy needs, or human-induced climate change lead to armed conflict?[25] Primatology suggests that population density by itself does not necessarily lead to increased incidence of conflict, let alone violent conflict. Instead, one line of inquiry on the relation between and among population density, environment, and conflict suggests that environmental stress is more likely to result in voluntary migration, which is cheaper than fighting over contested economic resources. But, another research line says, where population densities have reached a saturation point and migration is no longer a viable escape route, violent conflict caused by resource stress may ensue. Yet plenty of land areas with extremely high densities of human populations exist, such as in continental Europe, and conflict there is now for the most part solved peaceably. Violence is not the necessary outcome, and it would appear to depend on the policy responses to crisis situations that a polity's institutional and governance structures permit, a theme to which this section returns repeatedly.[26]

If not population density per se, does resource scarcity cause war? Of many, one example pertains to the possibility of war over the availability of freshwater. Especially in the Middle East where the Jordan River basin is shared among Lebanon, Jordan, Israel, and the occupied Golan Heights and the West Bank territory, and where the Euphrates and Tigris River basins are shared among Syria, Turkey, and Iraq, it has often been feared that water abstraction by upstream users will unduly rile downstream users. But the empirical evidence does not support a general contention of water wars between and among states. One study surveying 412 international crises between 1918 and 1994 found only seven that related directly to freshwater access. The main reason for this finding is that, contrary to public perception, freshwater is not scarce. Instead, the main problem is that freshwater sources rarely coincide well with the location choices of growing human populations. Water is expensive to transport, and water transport infrastructure is not well maintained, leading to tremendous loss by leakage. Also, water tends to be inadequately priced. Although intrastate water conflicts are numerous and may perhaps rise in number and intensity in years to come, on the international level disagreements over water mostly are settled peacefully and formal cooperation among riparian states is common. Among many other examples, the United States and Mexico, the states along the Danube River in Europe, and those along the Mekong River in Asia routinely cooperate to jointly manage their transboundary freshwater resources.[27]

None of this is to say that, given sufficient deprivation due to environmental stress, an inflection point may not be reached. But it is to say that the conflicts that do emerge mostly relate to access rights and resource management rather than to resource scarcity. Rather than estimating demand and supply and some feared imbalance between the two to be resolved by violent conflict, economists highlight that proper resource pricing creates tradable values that eliminate any "imbalances." Seeming liabilities can be converted into solid assets. The point is well made by quoting an example from the preface of the aptly named book *Liquid Assets* by Franklin Fisher and co-authors on Jordan River water:

No matter how much you value water, you cannot rationally value it by more than the cost of replacing it. Hence, the availability of seawater desalination places an upper bound on what water can be worth on the seacoast. In the case of Israel and Palestine, such desalination now costs roughly $0.50–$0.60 per cubic meter on the Mediterranean coast. Hence, water in the cities of that coast—Haifa, Tel Aviv, and Gaza, among others—can never be worth more than $0.50–$0.60 per cubic meter . . . the water of the Mountain Aquifer [at the northern end of the West Bank], however, is not on the coast but rather underground and some distance inland. Such water has its own costs. The cost of extracting it and bringing it to the cities of the coast is (very roughly) $0.40 per cubic meter. It follows that ownership of Mountain Aquifer water can never be worth more than about $0.20 per cubic meter.[28]

Given the quantities involved, this amounts to about $20 million a year, a trivial amount for an economy the size of Israel's. Thus, Fisher et al. caution not to focus on quantities of water, but instead to think about its economic value. Even if the water quantities in question are increased by a factor of ten, the annual water value would be $200 million. This is not a small amount, to be sure, but as David Philips points out, the "month-long hostilities between Israel and Lebanon in July-August 2006 are estimated to have cost approximately US$20 billion."[29] It is much cheaper to trade water than to trade blows. For politics to wrest the water question away from economics is not helpful.

Like pollution at military bases or the use of toxic materials at arms production sites, conflicts over freshwater are appearing globally but almost always in a highly local context. In contrast, the topics of world energy demand and supply are, like that of nuclear war, generally regional (natural gas) or global (petroleum) in nature. For example, the question of whether the perceived need for petroleum is somehow responsible, at least to a degree, for U.S. engagement in wars in the Middle East always springs up: is it "blood for oil"?[30]

With a population of 300 million people, the United States of America is not small. At 500 million people, the twenty-seven countries of the European Union pack an even larger population count. But even if the numbers are combined, this amounts to only 12 percent of the world population. If one includes all of the Organisation for Economic Co-Operation and Development (OECD) countries (about thirty "rich" countries), the total jumps to roughly 1.2 billion people, or 18 percent of the world population. In 2005, the OECD countries consumed almost half of the world's total primary energy supply (TPES) and produced slightly more than half of the world's economic output (measured in so-called international dollars, or PPP$).

Enter China and India. At well over one billion people each, they hold more than double the OECD's combined population. Whereas the OECD has an 18 percent share of the world population, China and India have over 37 percent. China and India consume about 20 percent of the world's energy and produce about 20 percent of world economic output (see table 1.1). But they use only 0.94 units of energy per person, whereas the OECD uses about five times as much, namely 4.73 units per person. At $25,870, the average OECD person also earned about five times as much as the average Chinese and Indian ($4,750).

Energy input and economic output go together. The more work the machines do, the more we can consume. Because one cannot reasonably expect Chinese and Indians to stay relatively poor so that "OECDans," and U.S. Americans in particular, can drive hefty vehicles, it stands to reason that China's and India's demand for energy supplies will increase. But if it increases, say, five times as much, the energy demand by China and India alone will equal the current world total. Total demand would zoom to 20,522 MTOEs, an increase of 180 percent over the demand in 2005. China and India and the United States, to engage in a more direct comparison, are already on equal energy and total economic footing, both consuming about 20 percent of world energy supplies and producing about 20 percent of world output. But, per person, U.S. Americans generate almost eight times as much income because they consume about eight times as much energy. Suppose, then, that China and India aspire not to OECD's standard of living but to U.S. standards. Demand would go up to

Table 1.1.   Some Indicators of World Energy Use, 2005

Indicator	World	OECD	U.S.	China	India	China/India
Population (mn)	6,432	1,172	297	1,311	1,095	2,406
GDP (PPP$ bn)	54,618	30,321	10,996	8,057	3,362	11,419
TPES (MTOE)	11,434	5,548	2,340	1,735	537	2,272
GDP/Pop. (PPP$ '000s)	8.49	25.87	37.02	6.15	3.07	4.75
TPES/Pop.	1.78	4.73	7.88	1.32	0.49	0.94
GDP/TPES	4.78	5.47	4.70	4.64	6.26	5.03
Pop. share (%)	n/a	18.22	4.62	20.38	17.02	37.40
GDP share (%)	n/a	55.51	20.13	14.75	6.16	20.91
TPES share (%)	n/a	48.52	20.47	15.17	4.70	19.87

Source: www.iea.org/textbase/nppdf/free/2007/key_stats_2007.pdf.

27,338 MTOEs, or 240 percent of 2005 levels. The worldwide economic recession of the late 2000s notwithstanding, petroleum already has traded at close to US$200 per barrel (in 2008), and if people were to switch to natural gas and other sources such as coal, thermal, hydro, wind, solar, or nuclear energy, the extra demand exerted on those markets would drive their prices up as well, at least in the short term.

It is clear that the historic economic power shift from the West to the East implies another kind of power shift, and with it a battle for energy sources. Although it is well known that China is engaged in places like the Sudan in Africa, it is less well appreciated that current energy hot spots lie in Central Asia, in places like Kazakhstan and Turkmenistan. Unlike Saudi Arabia and Iraq, unlike Angola and Nigeria, unlike Venezuela and Ecuador, even unlike Norway and the United Kingdom, all of which have direct access to the sea, Central Asia is landlocked. To get to shore-based oil and gas terminals, thousands of miles of oil and gas pipelines will need to cross geologically rough terrain. Unlike oil, which is easily stored and moved about on tankers and is truly a global commodity, natural gas needs to be converted to liquified natural gas, LNG, for seaborne shipment. At present, this is still so expensive that natural gas remains essentially a pipeline-restricted commodity.

Pipelines will also need to cross dicey political borders. Russia has already shown that it is willing to use its power as a producer and as a transit country to hold natural gas recipients hostage to higher prices. It was not pleased at prospects of Kazakhstan selling directly to China, and it wants to prevent Turkmenistan from selling to India via Afghanistan and Pakistan (the so-called TAPI line). Another gas pipeline under discussion would run from Iran through Pakistan to India (the IPI line). One wag called this the line "from hell to hell through hell." That is unkind, but the point is well taken.

There are other ways to fight the coming energy battle than that implied by this unsettled and unsettling political constellation. Apart from the stopgap measure of more exploration, one can think of two ways in particular: conservation and proper pricing. Like freshwater, energy is wasted on a royal scale. But even if we all were good Danes or Swiss or Irish, who press nearly twice as much economic output from a unit of energy input than do U.S. Americans, conservation alone will not bring China and India up to OECD or U.S. American living standards. Conservation alone may hardly keep pace with the energy demand growth implied by world population growth. Thus there is but one direction to go: price energy properly, especially with regard to its environmental effects. This automatically will lead to the allocation of substantial amounts of money to research and develop alternative and possibly limitless and nonpolluting energy sources.

Meanwhile, the suggestion has been made that climate change, in large part adversely affected by humans' injudicious use of fossil fuel energy, may lead to armed conflict among humans, for example via the pathway of "environmental refugees."[31] Changing weather patterns may lead to monstrous hurricanes and floods that overwhelm protective infrastructure, as was the case for the region of southern Louisiana and Mississippi in the United States in 2005, and for the city of New Orleans in particular. Hundreds of thousands of people fled the region, and many still have not returned. Despite bumbling responses by government authorities, almost all of these refugees could be accommodated in some fashion, and violence, while it did break out sporadically, was small-scale. But in Mozambique or Bangladesh or Ecuador, where the absorptive capacity of refugee-receiving regions is smaller, future disasters may lead to sustained violence among humans. But is it climate change or is it the lack of emergency planning and preparedness that is the issue to be addressed? Weather-related natural catastrophes such as earthquakes, volcanic eruptions, and horrific storms have created environmental refugees since the dawn of time. Even if the frequency, duration, and intensity of these events have increased, whether or not this results in violence is largely a matter of emergency preparedness and policy responses.

That climate change is happening has not seriously been doubted in the scientific community for many years now. That there will be effects on the length of growing seasons and the location of water and prime food production areas also is not doubted. What may be doubted are the consequences as regards specific geographic regions and the nature and quality of local, regional, and global policy responses. Thomas Schelling, for instance, points out that investing in climate change abatement today amounts to an income transfer from parent to offspring generations, even as the likelihood is that offspring generations will be richer than we are today and hence that they could better afford that investment. An intergenerational bequest for tomorrow places a limit on our ability to effect an intragenerational income transfer today. Thus, our generation's investment in climate change abatement today crimps income transfers from currently rich to currently poor people. Yet global economic development is the very thing that can mitigate and even reverse the effects of a lack of environmental sustainability. For example, Schelling says, malaria kills a million people a year, but not anymore in the United States where it used to be common. Measles kills a million children a year, but not in the developed countries. Singapore and Malaysia, he says, were nearly identical in development and in climate in the 1960s but now are equal in climate only. Developed countries are "substantially immune to climate," as most of our economies, unlike those of developing nations, rely on the service sector, not on agriculture.[32] Schelling is pointing to a tension between global environment and global economic development in that we may be sacrificing the very development today that may help bring about sustainability in future. It is no coincidence that, with one notable exception—the United States under the G. W. Bush administration—Kyoto-like climate change control agreements are championed foremost by highly developed economies that can best bear the cost of adjustment. These economies were no environmental angels during their own development phase.

That being "middling and dirty" may for some developing countries be a transitional phase on the way to becoming "well-off and clean" may be argued, especially when population and energy-use growth may leave far less room for error than may have been the case for previous generations, but the larger point here is that on the question of nature and war, the challenges posed by nature in terms of population densities, resource scarcity, energy needs, and climate change convert into local, regional, and global conflict only when policy is inadequate. Little there is in the nature of nature per se that inevitably would make humans fight.[33] Like the specter of nuclear war and nuclear winter, environmental stresses definitely are not to be lost sight of but are best treated under the rubric of prevention.

There is one exception to the statement that the nature of nature per se would not inevitably make humans fight. If freshwater and petroleum are examples of resource need driving (manageable) conflict, does resource greed play a role in war? Research conducted by economist Paul Collier and co-authors has helped to establish the notion that natural resources can serve as focal points for war. As natural resources tend to be randomly distributed, stationary, and peripheral relative to the location of capital cities, several temptations arise. One is for central government to neglect the broader development of the income-generating and tax-revenue generating capacity of the economy in preference to access to easy rents gained from natural resource extraction. By the same token, resource rents are attractive "honeypots" for corrupt politicians or, indeed, secessionist or rebel groups. Political scientist Michael Ross correctly cautions that natural resource wealth does not inevitably lead to war. But Collier points out that even if

> rebellion is not motivated by these rents it is greatly facilitated by them: from the proceeds leaders can purchase arms and pay recruits. Warfare is a costly business: whereas thirty years ago rebel groups largely had to depend upon a friendly government for finance and armaments, now rebellion has been "privatized"—markets in natural resources and armaments have developed to the extent that rebel groups can be self-sufficient. Rebel groups gain access to natural resource rents in several ways. One is to run protection rackets against the companies or people who are the exporters. Another is directly to operate extractive businesses. Yet another is to sell concessions to mineral rights in anticipation of subsequent control of the territory. The prolonged viability of UNITA in Angola and the RUF in Sierra Leone; the violent gangs of the Nigerian Delta; and the success- ful rebellions of Laurent Kabila in Zaire and of Denis Sassou-Nguesso in Congo Brazzaville, were all assisted by one or the other of these methods of natural resource financing.[34]

If researchers have emphasized that the "pathways by which resources lead to armed conflict [work] through their effects on economies; through their effects on governments; through their effects on people living in resource-rich regions; and through their effects on rebel movements,"[35] they have tended to somewhat neglect how natural resources such as tim- ber, diamonds, or fish tie in to economic production patterns and consum- erism around the globe. Resources are not just extracted. They are then shipped for usage and consumption elsewhere. Important for the theme of globalization is the unwitting complicity of consumers everywhere in these wars. While a film such as *Blood Diamond* and the international campaign to limit the trade in conflict diamonds have helped to make some buyers of diamonds aware of the possibly bloody origin of the gemstones, few consumers appear to have extended this awareness to other goods. Timber harvested in Liberia or in Burma ends up in consumer products; coltan (columbine-tantalite) extracted from the eastern Congo ends up in virtu- ally every mobile phone; rising world prices for tin, gold, and opium make harvesting all these resources ever more attractive to help finance local war; and near-shore unsustainable fishery rights to serve global consumption are sold for a pittance, enriching conniving and corrupt governments (or rebels) while leaving local fishermen and their families hungry.[36] This, in turn, can have cascading effects on human conflict and security and can also result in stunning follow-on consequences for terrestrial wildlife. A

2004 research report in *Science* documented with thirty years of data for Ghana in West Africa how a decline in fisheries pushed human populations to seek their sustenance through bushmeat hunting, with dramatic adverse effects on mammalian inland biomass.[37]

The theme of local wars and global consumption is taken up again in chapters 4 and 5. For now, turn to the effects of the actual fighting of (non-nuclear) war and begin with the issue of how to measure war-related damage to nature and natural resources.

1.4 Measuring the Environmental Consequences of War

We live in an age of measurement. Measurement is a way of record keeping, of keeping score. It aids and corrects our memories. It permits us to recognize change that accrues slowly over time. It allows us to develop and test models of cause and effect. The idea is to separate putative from real effects, and proximate from ultimate causes. In 1995, eight children in Henderson, Minnesota, noted what appeared to be an unusual number of limb deformities in frogs they had collected for a school assignment. Local people postulated proximate explanations. For example, they asked if increased ultraviolet (UV) radiation due to stratospheric ozone depletion could explain the deformities. Research and measurement that covers a large number of locales may eventually lead to the identification of one or more ultimate, often hidden and unexpected, cause or causes. In the case of the frogs, research established that some sixty species across forty-six U.S. states showed sometimes severe deformities in up to 80 percent of the local amphibian populations. UV radiation did explain some but not all of the observed deformities. Another explanatory factor was water pollution, primarily from pesticide runoff. But again this explained only some of the observed deformities. The key factor was fertilizer and cattle manure runoff. Both contributed to algal blooms and the consequent growth of a specific parasite, *Ribeiroia ondatrae*. This parasite lodges itself in amphibian larvae and inhibits limb development, hence the observed deformities.[38]

Measurement is important. But who is to measure what in the first place? UV radiation and stratospheric ozone depletion involve atmospheric chemistry; pesticide pollution of water engages the biochemist; the parasites are the provenance of aquatic biologists. A number of scientific specialties were needed to solve the puzzle. One way, then, to assess environmental damage in war is by partitioning such damage into physical, chemical, and biological components. Another possible classification of environmental damage in war addresses the needs of environmental law and law of war. Relatedly, a third classification of damage is by intention of the attacker: direct intentional damage, incidental damage, and indirect unintentional damage. For reasons to be explained, none of these is entirely suitable for our purpose, and hence another classification must be developed. Deciding how and what to measure and classify is one thing, but for the case of war-related environmental damage the collected data are often poor, as shown in subsection 1.4.1. Subsection 1.4.2 examines some of the reasons why this is so. Suggestions for data collection improvements are discussed in chapter 5.

1.4.1 Classifying War-Related Environmental Damage

Systematic thinking about the effects of war on the environment is rare to find in the literature. One approach classifies war's effect on nature by intention. Lanier-Graham proposes three categories: (1) intentional direct destruction of the environment during war; (2) incidental direct destruction, that is, collateral environmental destruction incidental to war aims; and (3) induced destruction, that is, medium or long-term consequences directly attributable to war.[39] The first category refers to the deliberate attack on cultivated and uncultivated lands and resources with the objective of environmental destruction for its own sake. The setting of oil-well fires by Iraq during the 1991 Persian Gulf War serves as an illustration. Examples of the second category include soil disturbance, as when troops dig trenches or when heavy equipment and battle tanks are ridden across fragile surfaces. Riding heavy war machinery on desert surfaces can break the desert's thin sheet of encrusted sand. This disturbance of desert cover can uproot scant indigenous plant cover, crush and compact desert soil, and leave behind a top layer of loose sand for release by wind erosion that possibly contributes to increased occurrences of dust and sand storms. In Lanier-Graham's classification, such dislocation of vegetation and churning of soil would be categorized as direct but collateral damage, damage incidental to the primary military objective of digging entrenchments or moving battle tanks into position. Damage in the third category, induced destruction, may occur as a result of human population shifts. Afghans fleeing to Iran and Pakistan, or Rwandans to the eastern Congo, northern Burundi, and western Tanzania, can be expected to exert undue environmental stresses. Lack of sanitation and proper waste disposal can result in enormous amounts of untreated trash, and lack of shelter and fuel can result in deforestation. Induced destruction refers mainly to long-term wildlife consequences of war, probably the most important category of war-related environmental damage done. Lanier-Graham's classification is, however, of limited scientific use inasmuch as it attempts to enumerate the consequences of intentions rather than to measure gradations of damage. Put differently, nature does not care about human intentions.

A related way of classifying war-related environmental damage is from a legal point of view. Environmental damage can infringe on property and other rights. A party suffering environmental damage might be able to hold liable the party alleged to have caused it (and in that regard the question of intent might be important). Thus, Arne Willy Dahl, judge advocate of the Norwegian Armed Forces, classifies war-related environmental damage into six categories:

1. destruction of the human environment
2. destruction of the cultivated environment
3. destruction of the natural environment of economic importance
4. destruction of the natural environment of noneconomic value
5. general environmental degradation
6. environmental manipulation as a tool in warfare.

Arguing that parties in war might legally take aim at the first and second items—destruction of population shelters, infrastructure, and denial of cultivated environment—Dahl thinks about legal instruments that would relate to items three to six but, tellingly, only inasmuch as environmental damage might affect humans. Dahl's classification is not useful when one is interested in war's effects on nature per se, irrespective of whether it is economically useful to humans or not. In any event, first one needs to ferret out what the effects are before reshuffling them to fit legal needs.[40] (See section 1.5 for a synopsis of the environment in international law of war.)

A third, scientific approach categorizes the environment into physical, chemical, and biological components. This has its uses for the specialists carrying out the fieldwork. Scientists working in the isolation of their expertise provide valuable findings, insights, and clues, but this is not good enough to assess war's total effect on nature. For example, the exclusion of one species on account of war opens up habitat for another. Thus, at some point disciplinary boundaries must be transcended and an overall environmental assessment be made. A useful way to compile a joint assessment of physical, chemical, and biological effects of war-related environmental damage is

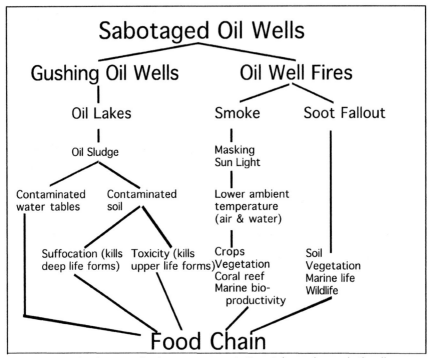

Figure 1.1.   Major threats to the desert ecosystem in Kuwait from sabotaged oil wells.
Source: Alsdirawi (1994, pp. 120–121).

provided in figure 1.1. Developed for the case of the Persian Gulf War of 1991, the figure traces possible pathways by which sabotaged oil wells might have come to affect the food web in the Kuwaiti desert. This provides a useful cross-disciplinary view, but a major shortcoming is that this approach cannot provide an integrated, ecology-wide assessment of damage done.[41]

A fourth way to classify environmental damage in war is by ecological severity. As if the designations were synonyms, descriptors such as environmental "damage," "depletion," and "degradation" are generally used in the literature without attempt at definition or clarification. Authors also tend to write about environmental disturbances associated with war without specifying whether or not the observed differences amount to damage. For example, one set of authors compared satellite images of the Kuwaiti desert before and after the 1991 war, but the reader is not informed about whether the noted changes amounted to damage. Even when quantified damage is reported, authors often fail to provide a standard of reference by which one could evaluate environmental damage. The standard may be arguable, but that is better than not to have a standard at all. To state that "80 percent of the forest was damaged" provokes one response. To say that after forty years of regrowth the forest recuperated to its former aesthetic beauty and ecological function evokes another response because the second statement provides the standard of restitution over time.[42]

Table 1.2 offers a standard of gradations of damage. It lists forms of environmental changes in qualitative order of severity. The first refers to the observation of environmental differences from time t to time $t+1$ and notes dissimilarities not associated with damage. The second consists of four grades of disruption that may reflect damage. If full natural or human-assisted restitution can be expected, the disruption is time-limited. Called disturbance, this refers either to habitat (abiotic) disturbance (e.g., earth removal or water diversion) or to biotic disturbance (e.g., killing of a living thing while leaving the physical habitat undisturbed). In either case, disturbance implies that space opened up can be recolonized by individuals of the same or of different species. Full recovery and restitution is possible and expected. In contrast, environmental degradation is a disturbance such that only partial restitution is possible or expected. Even so, in time a different ecosystem of comparable richness is expected to emerge. If, instead, the new ecosystem is impoverished relative to the previous one, this is referred to as depletion. The absence of any possible restitution at all is called destruction.[43]

This is not a perfect scheme. Comparable richness of ecosystems is the critical term around which definitions of impoverishment and restitution must be built. This is a task for ecologists. Unlike the other classifications, however, the scheme gets one started on the road of evaluating war-related environmental damage. To measure and to detect is not enough. The damage must be set in context. This is a problem that bedevils a good bit of the literature and its reporting. An egregious example concerns media reporting of findings from a United Nations Environment Programme (UNEP) mission to Bosnia-Herzegovina following the 1990s Balkan wars. This study detected radiation emanating from depleted-uranium (DU) munition fragments seven years after the war. But detection implies neither damage nor danger. The press failed to appreciate that measurement today can pick up dosages far below those that might cause health concerns. For Bosnia-Herzegovina, the detected DU-radiation turned out to be harmless.[44] Measurement without gradation cannot be usefully interpreted. What is needed is a combination of physical, chemical, and biological measurement and a scale of the degree of war-related environmental disruption, as proposed in table 1.2.

Table 1.2.   A Severity Classification of Environmental Damage

1. Environmental difference
2. Environmental disruption
    2.1 Environmental disturbance
    2.2 Environmental degradation
    2.3 Environmental depletion
    2.4 Environmental destruction

Notes:

difference	no damage
disruption	various gradations of damage
disturbance	transitory damage
degradation	only partial recovery of the original ecosystem expected but an ecosystem of comparable richness will emerge
depletion	an ecosystem of comparable richness will not emerge
destruction	complete devastation

All environments degrade. Weathering and erosion are natural, long-term processes that degrade habitat and induce changes in species composition, abundance, and distribution. Species emerge or invade, others die out or are locally displaced. One would still regard both the old and the new ecosystem as of comparable richness, in part because the changes are on time scales that permit adaptation. Depletion is different in that it drives on the idea of ecosystem impoverishment. This is usually related to the compressed time scales that anthropogenic intervention, including war, imposes on an ecosystem, such as depletion in the case of overfishing. Assessment might take place with measures such as net primary productivity or species diversity indices. Destruction is ultimate depletion, a disruption so severe that only the barest of life (if any at all) is expected to survive in the affected habitat.[45]

Consider two examples. During Germany's occupation of Norway in World War II, German troops killed about half of the then 95,000-strong reindeer population. By 1960, the reindeer population had regrown to 90,000. For the individual animals involved, the killing was a catastrophe. Ecologically, it was a disturbance, as reindeer populations can and did regrow.[46] Among beleaguered people, self-damage of one's homeland is a long-standing tradition. In 1672, the king of the Dutch ordered dikes opened to flood the marching routes of advancing French troops. The Dutch thus repelled the attack even as their lands were flooded with salt-water. To Lanier-Graham, this is intentionally caused damage. To Dahl, the land was withdrawn from economic use for a time. From an environmental perspective, the Dutch farmland was disturbed, but not degraded or depleted or destroyed, as it eventually recovered.[47]

Environmental disturbance, degradation, depletion, and destruction need to be viewed in the ecological context and time scale of the affected physical entity. If a coral reef is affected during war, fundamental changes in its ecosystem might result in a depletion of certain fish and invertebrate species. Yet the depletion of some species opens an ecological niche for others. If over time a comparable richness emerges, one would speak of a disturbed coral reef environment. It might be feared that this classification provides cover for those who would damage nature in war: make the long term long enough and some form of life reemerges. The ecological standard becomes a political excuse. This line of argument would be unfortunate. But what other standard of reference to use is unclear. Scientific contributors to the literature have not provided one, and until an improvement is offered, table 1.2 provides a provisional scale of war-related environmental damage with which to assess what damage war may impose on nature.

One exception is Green Cross International. Its 1998 study on the Persian Gulf War concludes by constructing an environmental risk assessment model. Specifically, environmental risk is computed by assigning values to three factors. These are:

1. The impact from war or ongoing nonwar activities on a particular resource, say freshwater sources, desert topsoil, or coral reefs. This is quantified by extent and magnitude in terms of short, medium, and long-term effects. The codes used for quantification are simply 1, 2, or 3 (low, medium, high) and are assigned by a study team.
2. The value of the resource is expressed as a combination of its intrinsic ecological value and its resource value for humans and also is coded in the 1, 2, or 3 manner just described.
3. A value purporting to measure human exposure potential is assigned (again, 1, 2, or 3).

Once these and other value assignments are made, a final risk index is computed. The higher the index number, the more urgent the need for intervention. Unique in the literature, it is an effort not merely to measure war's impact on nature and follow-on risk, but to scale it. Ranking the resource risk indices by magnitude then suggests priorities for policy and remedial attention.[48]

Exceptions notwithstanding, the literature generally also fails to distinguish between renewable and nonrenewable resources affected by war, what the degree of resource-specific depletion might be, and if, for renewable resources, the degree of depletion may have dropped below a threshold for full recuperation, thus leading to species or resource extinction (destruction). For example, it is not enough to note that perhaps 30,000 birds perished due to oiling in the Persian Gulf War. One must ask "30,000 out of how many?" and if the remaining stock can recover.[49] On the whole, the literature also fails to ask whether or not destruction of a cultivated environment may not be seen as an upgrading rather than a degrading of the natural, nonhuman environment (see chapter 5). Clearly, this is a literature that needs some sorting out.

1.4.2 The Data: Finding Out What Really Happened

Finding out what really happens to nature in war is no easy task. Research-based assessment, to be credible, tends to be dangerous, complex, and costly to conduct. As a result, it is usually incomplete. Early assessment, before the data are in, is consequently speculative and often grossly unreliable. And much of what is reported is anecdotal, mediated, and biased.

ASSESSMENT: DANGEROUS, COMPLEX, COSTLY. Data collection on war-related environmental effects can be dangerous. One unnamed Guatemalan ecologist is cited as follows: "Because of the continuing violence in many areas, few ecological studies have been done in [the] last thirty years: we don't even know what we have left to save." As in other instances, one of the victims of war is our ability to measure its effects. Reportedly, investigators were threatened and killed in El Salvador in the 1980s. During the African civil wars of the 1990s, there were numerous confirmed instances of threats to and killings of local and expatriate staff of conservation organizations. To limit danger to researchers, the U.S. military in Vietnam, even though it assisted with fixed-wing and helicopter overflights, restricted ground access to active battle zones. In Kuwait, heavy land mine contamination effectively curtailed research access needed for the conduct of desert soil studies.[50]

When air, water, and soil samples are taken they can be deliberately contaminated by border officials or inadvertently corrupted. During the Iraqi invasion of Kuwait, large quantities of scientific instruments were systematically destroyed. In Canby's phrase, Kuwait "had lost the means to measure the damage." For example, Iraq removed a fisheries and oceanographic research vessel, the *RV Abhath*, belonging to the Kuwait Institute of Scientific Research (KISR). A personal account is given by Jassim Mohammed Al-Hassan, professor of biochemistry at the Faculty of Science at Kuwait University:

> Within a few days after occupying Kuwait, the Iraqi government sent their University Presidents, Deans, Heads of Departments, and Professors to supervise the looting of Kuwait University [KU]. They removed everything from KU, including laboratory equipment, library facilities, computers, personal belongings of staff, as well as furniture and floor carpeting. . . . The author's Department and laboratories, which were well equipped for biochemical research and environmental investigations had their contents transferred to various Iraqi universities as indicated by the labels the Iraqis left on each laboratory.[51]

In addition to the difficulty of securing scientists' physical access to the field and to get them and their samples and data out alive, assessment of war-related environmental damage is subject to a variety of other constraints. Not least, these include that the number of qualified scientists worldwide to study highly specific ecological aspects of war is small, and that the difficulty of obtaining funds to field missions, obtain measuring instruments, and pay for laboratory time and follow-up studies is great. Table 1.3 lists some of the sets of studies conducted with respect to the Persian Gulf War. All refer to actual data collection efforts, not to modeling and forecasting of what-if scenarios. They cover atmospheric studies, bird life, coastal and marine habitat, and other aspects of nature. The list illustrates that to dispassionately understand war's effect on nature, a massive, comprehensive set of studies involving all scientific disciplines must be carried out. To do so is difficult, complex, and costly. It is for this reason

Table 1.3.   Scientific Missions Regarding the Persian Gulf War of 1991

- Three missions by the International Council for Bird Preservation (March 1991; April–May 1991; November–December 1991)
- A Greenpeace mission (MS Greenpeace, sailing the Persian Gulf, 8 August –1 October 1991)
- A NOAA mission (Mt. Mitchell, February–June 1992; 140-plus marine scientists from fifteen nations)
- Several U.S. National Center for Atmospheric Research missions flown in 1991 over Kuwait and Saudi Arabia
- Three IUCN missions (in August 1991; 1992; 1993)
- Two missions by the Japanese research vessel Umitaka Maru (15–26 December 1993 and 25–27 December 1994)
- Two volumes of field research reports from the Senckenberg Research Institute in Frankfurt-am-Main involving about forty scientists from six EU countries (1994; 1996)

Note: See chapter 3 for a complete listing and discussion.

that the Persian Gulf War of 1991 is the only war for which a massive research effort to comprehensively study war's environmental effects was ever financed.

ASSESSMENT:INCOMPLETE. In light of the danger, complexity, and cost of conducting comprehensive scientific studies, it is not surprising that in most instances our knowledge of war-related environmental effects on nature is incomplete or altogether lacking. Even in the best case, that of the Persian Gulf War, there are astonishing gaps. The most serious is that we know little about the effect of the war on Kuwait's desert surface and almost nothing about the effects on Iraq's territory.[52] Given the importance of soil for plants, the primary producers without whom terrestrial life is impossible, this omission is stunning.

Even if multiple studies are conducted, they can be incomplete for other reasons. First, scientific assessment may require pre-event data. Postwar studies without baseline data often are meaningless. Second, even where pre/post data exist, this is frequently limited to only one or the other aspect of nature. Knowing what happened to a particular species is informative but not necessarily useful for an ecology-wide assessment. Many ecosystems possess redundancy. If one species is affected, its ecological function may be taken up by others. A single-species study would likely be an incomplete study. Third, already discussed, even if data are available, it is often presented without an attempt at ecology-wide assessment as to the severity of the damage incurred. A fourth reason concerns the lack of long-term studies to generate follow-on data. Ecosystems can be resilient in the face of disruption. To describe the Vietnam War or the Persian Gulf War as ecocides may be correct with regard to the short-term impact of war on individuals in affected populations of species. This does not tell us, however, about ecosystem resilience and restitution—nor about delayed vulnerabilities—over a longer span of time.

In almost all the instances examined in this book there are no or only insufficient baseline data to which to compare war-related environmental effects. Counting species fatalities is of limited use without accurate baseline data.[53] The only exception regarding availability of prewar data across a reasonable range of environmental dimensions concerns the case of the Persian Gulf War, for which scientists were able to resample previously sampled sites and compare the results. But prewar data were not available in like degree. For example, for many bird species, knowledge of their distribution, migration, and breeding sites was lacking. Similarly, little was known about marine mammals in the Gulf. Lack of baseline data frustrates the study of almost all civil war situations in Africa, Asia, and Latin America.[54]

Even with baseline data in hand, what one may be able to establish may be limited. For instance, to learn that a member of the rare mountain-gorilla species *Gorilla beringei beringei* has been shot during the Rwandan civil war is not, by itself, a particularly useful datum. To conduct comprehensive, multispecies counts would be correspondingly more expensive, and likely prohibitively so. An alternative, to examine the "literature on comparable habitats" to estimate possible species extirpation, runs not only into the problem that comparable habitats rarely are truly comparable but also that species populations can rapidly explode and crash for reasons unrelated to armed conflict. Causality may be difficult to establish. Moreover, species counts tend to focus on so-called charismatic megafauna, such as gorillas, and to ignore microorganisms and hence overlook the potential for long-term damage or restoration. One may revert to count key food web or indicator species, species that occupy lower rungs in the food web and that may allow one to draw some conclusions about the habitat in question, but this requires that such knowledge has been well established beforehand, a condition not often found in the developing world, where most of today's wars take place.[55]

The problem of incompleteness is compounded by lack of long-term follow-up data. Short-term disturbances may even out over ten or twenty years. Alternatively, it may appear in the short term that no damage was done at all when lasting damage may crop up with a ten- or twenty-year delay. As Greenpeace notes with regard to certain pollutants released during the Persian Gulf War, even if nothing much can be measured today, "the population and environment will still have been exposed." An example of both types of problems is provided by the U.S. nuclear weapons testing on Bikini Atoll: coral biodiversity has recovered (short-term damage reversed) but radiation-induced cancers in humans (and presumably other mammals) have shown up only with very long time lags. Forecasting long-term damage on the basis of short-term data is perilous. Carl Bruch writes that a "number of methodologies have been used for assessing environmental impacts, but experience has shown that the long-term reliability of most environmental assessments [is] problematic at best." For instance, despite draconian predictions of long-term catastrophic consequences of the Persian Gulf War, "the desert ecosystem (including the marine environment) has proven to be remarkably resilient."[56]

ASSESSMENT: GROSSLY UNRELIABLE. One consequence of the listed difficulties is that scientifically credible assessment often cannot be undertaken. In the absence of data, some appear to follow Perry Robinson's line: "But one can speculate; and . . . speculate one must." Regrettably, egregious examples are provided by otherwise well-respected persons. Thus, Frank Barnaby wrote a highly speculative piece on the environmental effects of the Gulf War. Almost completely devoid of scientific data, it instead brims with what could happen, what may happen, what is likely to happen, and what will happen to the environment—once the data are in. Initial reports out of Kuwait amounted to little more than counting the number of oil well heads destroyed, guessing the number of gallons of crude oil spilled, and comparing this to the *Exxon Valdez* oil spill in Prince William Sound in Alaska in 1989 to arrive at some assessment of damage to the Gulf region. The public reasoning went like this: if 257,000 barrels of oil were spilled in Alaska and 11 million barrels of oil are spilled into the Gulf, an increase by a factor of 42.8, then this is a self-evident environmental catastrophe. But the conclusion was wrong. First, the initial oil spill estimate of 11 million barrels (462 million gallons) was subsequently reduced to the now accepted standard of between 6 to 8 million barrels. Second, at the time it was unclear whether the initial estimates referred to on-shore spills, off-shore spills, or both. Third, and most important, an oil spill event is not equivalent to oil-spill damage. To make or imply a direct comparison between the two environments was inappropriate because the Gulf's capacity to take environmental abuse was much different from that of Prince William Sound. As it turns out, the much smaller Prince William Sound spill resulted in markedly more environmental damage than the Gulf spill.[57]

Regarding shore ecosystems and marine life, initial fears also far overstated the eventually measured effects and need to be seen in the context, at the time, of an annual volume of Gulf oil spills equivalent to at least 250,000 barrels of oil, and possibly of more than 1 million barrels. This is in addition to ongoing habitat destruction of mangroves and reefs on account of commercial development and land reclamation efforts. Early reports on the presumed worldwide catastrophic effects of the smoke plume turned out to be wrong as well (it did not rise high enough to reach the jet stream). Initial global warming predictions due to the oil fires had to be revised downward toward the end of the war year. Of the oil-well fires—fires initially predicted to burn for years to come—the last was capped on 6 November 1991.[58] Chapter 3 summarizes what is now known about the short- and long-run environmental effect of the Persian

Gulf War. With few exceptions it turns out to have had relatively benign environmental effects.

One scholar complains about a "lack of scientific interest" in the war-related environmental plight of developing countries.[59] News agencies' vested interest lies in reporting on what is of likely importance to the home market. Thus, Agent Orange defoliation of Vietnamese forests received more attention than the probably more damaging bulldozing and bombing of the forests. Atmospheric nuclear tests received much more attention due to the global fallout implications than did underground testing. The smoke plume over Kuwait and Saudi Arabia received more attention than the desert flora and fauna. The gorillas of western Rwanda received more attention than the far more adversely affected Akagera National Park in the east of the country. War-related environmental effects of civil war are rarely even mentioned in media or policy circles. The resulting public, media, and funding bias impedes ecology-wide studies on the effect of war on nature. Recent improvements on these failings, and suggestions for further improvement, are discussed in chapter 5.

ASSESSMENT: ANECDOTAL, MEDIATED, AND BIASED. Assessment is frequently anecdotal and fragmented. Much consists of hearsay, single-instance events, scattered reports in the news media, reports by advocacy groups whose standards of evidence may fall short of those required by scholars and scientists, and of undocumented assertions (especially in popular books). Consider some examples. It has been asserted that South Vietnam's "lobster industry was wrecked by over-production to provide this delicacy for American soldiers . . . [and that] . . . the tiger population was similarly decimated for the souvenir trade." No sources are given to document the assertions made, and verification of the claims has not proved possible. To the contrary, regarding the tiger population there are several documented reports of increased populations (due to increased feeding opportunities). And what exactly does it mean to say that the lobster industry and the tiger population were "wrecked"? Or take this passage: "The Laysan rail and Laysan finch were confirmed completely wiped out during World War II as a result of a rat infestation brought by the troops and destruction of habitat. . . . [Other] species to suffer this end include the Wake Island rail, the Marianas mallard, the Marianas megapode, and the brown booby." No evidence or source is given. A search for possible source material suggests that the original source for these claims appears to have been Arthur H. Westing. He, in turn, took information regarding the Laysan rail and Laysan finch from Fisher and Baldwin, for the Wake Island rail from Fisher and Baldwin, Greenway, and Peterson, for the Marianas mallard from Baker and Greenway, for the Marianas megapode from Greenway, and for the brown booby from Fisher and Baldwin. But unlike the author of the quoted passage, for whom all of these birds became extinct as a result of the Second World War (other "species to suffer this end," namely extinction), Westing correctly makes this claim only for the Laysan rail and the Wake Island rail. The case of the Laysan finch is referred to by Westing as "probable extinction," that of the Marianas mallard as in "danger of complete extinction," that of the Marianas megapode as "seriously endangered," and that of the brown booby as "extirpated from" Guam, but it "still appears to be quite plentiful on a number of other Pacific islands." A fact check reveals that the Laysan finch is not extinct. Neither is the Marianas megapode. The brown booby is widespread. The Marianas mallard has not been sighted since 1979 and is now believed to be extinct but not, or not solely, because of World War II. Westing himself cites Ngan and Curry-Lindahl as writing that the Vietnamese kouprey (*Bos sauveli*) is "on the verge of being extirpated" and that "the fear of some Indochinese zoologists [is] that the Second Indochina War may have provided the *coup de grâce* to the already highly endangered kouprey." Yet the IUCN Red List lists the kouprey as nonextinct (although critically endangered).[60] For other species Westing refers to, a search reveals that the *Ursus thibetanus* is listed by IUCN as "vulnerable," as is the tapir (*Tapirus indicus*). The pheasant *Lophura imperialis* was recorded in 2000 in Vietnam, but current knowledge of it is scant.[61]

1.5 The Environment in International Law of War

Discussion of the environment in international law of war claims a history that reaches far into the past. Its modern treatment, however, derives from the Environmental Modification Convention (ENMOD) of 1976, which places limits on the modification of the natural environment for use as a weapon of war, and from the Protocol Additional I of 1977 (additional to the four Geneva Conventions of 1949), which includes articles that prohibit acts of war injurious to the natural environment.

Neither document applies to conflict within states, which of course make up the vast majority of violent conflicts today. The 1977 Protocol Additional II (to the 1949 Geneva Conventions) does apply to such conflict, but with significantly weaker legal language. One possible reason is that states party to international treaties do not wish to undermine their own legal standing by seeming to condone insurgencies.[62] As to states, whereas ENMOD prohibits actions that cause "widespread, long-lasting or severe" environmental effects, Protocol Additional I prohibits weapons uses that cause "widespread, long-term and severe" environmental effects. To the layperson this seems straightforward enough. Yet there are problems. For example, one document uses the disjunctive "or," the other uses the conjunctive "and"—a more stringent requirement. Neither document offers a definition of what is widespread, or long-lasting, or severe. Regarding the Persian Gulf War, for example, Iraq did not ratify either treaty and was not found liable for environmental damage imposed on Kuwait on account of these treaties.[63] The United States has not ratified Protocol Additional I either. Indeed, it declared an exception for damage resulting from the use of nuclear weapons. Likewise, countries such as Italy, Germany, and the United Kingdom submitted various statements of interpretation. Regarding ENMOD, the United States, along with Russia and the United Kingdom, ratified it, but France and China are not parties to that treaty. And here again, a number of countries have submitted interpretative statements that would limit liability under the treaty (e.g., Turkey).[64]

Be this as it may, the premise of this book is that legal wrangling necessitates first and foremost a scientific understanding of damage done, if any. If there is no damage, there can be no economic or legal claim for compensation and restitution. Thus, the remaining chapters of this book center on what scientific claims can in fact be made about nature in war.

Appendix: Why Nuclear Weapons?

Despite the grave potential, and potentially multiplied, environmental and ecological effects of nuclear war and nuclear weapons testing, it cannot logically be concluded that there exist no reasons to possess atomic weapons in the first place. This is so for at least two related points. The first has to do with escalation from small size, the second with arms race ratchet effects. As to the first, physics, economics, and the logic of weapons use impose an upper limit on their size. Physics poses an efficiency limit on the relation between bomb weight (i.e., its mass) and bomb yield so that ever larger yields can be obtained only by ever larger bomb mass. But ever more massive bombs are militarily and economically impractical because bombs must, after all, be constructed, mounted, lofted, aimed, directed, and delivered, and their effects be contained to the intended area. Military forces thus both need and prefer arsenals of many smaller bombs of varying sizes and varying yields to an arsenal consisting of a single big "super" bomb. Variety is valued because variety generates options. It is this "chunking" of available total yield into parcels that leads to the danger of escalation in warfare. But escalation is optional, not certain. (In fact, the major purpose of nuclear weapons testing is to discover their optional qualities.) Thus one cannot reason backward from the totality of the ill effects of a full-scale nuclear war to the irrationality of possessing nuclear weapons. Instead, one must reason forward from a single bomb and the option to escalate.[65]

Second, escalation requires a stockpile from which to escalate. To construct it, an accumulation (an "arms race") must have taken place. If party A has one nuclear weapon and party B has none, B is a nuclear hostage to A. Once more, the key is that one must not imagine an encompassing global nuclear catastrophe with the effects described in section 1.2. Instead, one must imagine, as for Japan in 1945, a severe but nonetheless localized effect stemming from a "one-off" event. To counter the actual or implied threat, B thus faces a strong incentive also to acquire at least one weapon. To regain the advantage, A increases its force by another weapon, and so on. As each party adds weapons, an internal proliferation takes place as well whereby many different weapons of many different types are constructed and deployed within each state. This generates and preserves options for their use.

Overall, a ratchet effect takes hold because, metaphorically speaking, parties A and B have entered a room through a one-way gate. Once in, exit is difficult because sequential de-escalation at some point would reach the zero-one state of affairs whereby one party has an advantage over the other. Whoever disarms first becomes vulnerable first. This is why disarmament is so difficult; the parties remain locked in their room. In mathematics-based arms race models, it can be shown that, under certain conditions, falling below a distinct disarmament threshold the danger of nuclear-weapons use increases. Simultaneous disarmament is difficult, too, because it relies on difficult-to-arrange verification and subsequent monitoring.

Despite the inherent danger of unleashing a global catastrophe, these two reasons—the arms race logic with its one-way gate feature and the "chunking" to create an option to escalate from small size—combine to account for the arsenals some states have and that others seek. Ultimately, successful disarmament relies on reduced threat perceptions and mutual credibility and trust: in other words, reduction in weapons demand rather than supply.[66]

Notes

1. As measured by the Stockholm International Peace Research Institute (SIPRI), average military expenditure out of countries' GDP for 1999–2003, for example,

was 2.5 percent for low-income countries, 1.9 percent for middle-income countries, and 2.0 percent for high-income countries. See SIPRI (2007). World military expenditure as a percentage of world GDP in 2007 was 2.5 percentage (SIPRI, 2008). Because of the generally good economic times during the 1990s and early to mid-2000s, GDP levels were high. Fairly substantial amounts of military expenditure can thus appear "hidden" by high GDP.

2. In the United States, for instance, military expenditure is often reported as being equivalent to the outlays of the Department of Defense. But numerous military-related expenditures are placed in other budget categories. Military-nuclear expenses, for example, fall within the Department of Energy budget, Iraq reconstruction costs have appeared in several different budget categories, and many of war's legacy costs, such as for environmental remediation and veterans' care, likewise are spread out across federal government agencies. Although incomplete, an economically more appropriate accounting is done by the U.S. Department of Commerce's Bureau of Economic Analysis. See Brauer (2007). In this regard, it must be said that no one knows the exact size of annual world income either. It is well-known that GDP, as conventionally measured, understates the monetary value of economic activity. As one example, illegal activity generates plenty of income but, for obvious reasons, is not reported to government authorities for inclusion in their GDP calculations.

3. Nonmilitary state armed forces include for instance paramilitary troops, border and coast guards, customs and secret service agents, wildlife rangers and anti-poaching patrols, and police forces. Nonstate armed forces include revolutionaries, rebels, warlords, insurgents, terrorists, members of organized crime groups, and others such as private military and private security companies. For an example of resources used by a nonstate group see the story in *The Economist* on the Sri Lankan army uncovering sophisticated supply depots of the Liberation Tigers of Tamil Eelam in the north of the country (19 February 2009). These apparently include boat yards, submarines, fast-attack craft, underwater fuel tanks, and much more, all of which require natural resources for their production, maintenance, and use. Likewise, the former Blackwater USA, a military contractor rebranded as Xe in February 2009, sports formidable training facilities and a considerable weapons arsenal.

4. Some information is available for NATO countries. For example, because its armed forces are so capital-intensive, the United States allocated only 34.8 percent of its 2005 military expenditure toward personnel, the second-lowest percentage among all NATO countries. The highest such percentage was 77.1 percent, for Italy. See table 5 of "Defence Expenditures of NATO Countries (1985–2008)," available at http://www.nato.int/docu/pr/2009/p09-009.pdf [accessed 22 February 2009].

5. Data taken from the International Energy Agency's *Key World Energy Statistics 2007*. Updated versions are available at www.iea.org [accessed 22 February 2009].

6. In the same year, Latin American and African military expenditure came to a combined total of $48 billion, or 4.3 percent, of $1,113 billion worldwide (SIPRI, 2008, p. 208, measured in constant 2005 U.S. dollar prices and exchange rates). Their combined MTOE share was 9.6 percent (1,105/11,468).

7. See p. 5 of the President's Council of Advisors on Science and Technology's November 2006 report entitled "The Energy Imperative: Technology and the Role of Emerging Companies," available at http://www.ostp.gov/galleries/PCAST/pcast_energyimperative_final.pdf [accessed 22 February 2009].

8. Durant (2007, p. 2).

9. Durant (2007, p. 11). As Durant acknowledges, the military's own and its cooperative efforts are not to be dismissed. See, for example, the website of the United States Army Environmental Command (USAEC) at http://aec.army.mil/usaec and Bentley, Ripley, and Powledge (2008) who have produced a guide to conserving biodiversity on military lands; see http://www.dodbiodiversity.org/introduction/index.html [both accessed 22 February 2009].

10. Balkans: To quote a key sentence from the document: "Economic decline and the UN sanctions against the FRY have in general led to reduced pollution of air and water." UNEP (1999, p. 23). Fall in economic activity: The Stern Review on the economics of climate change reports estimates according to which a one percentage point change in GDP is associated with a 0.9 percentage point change in carbon emissions (see p. 179 of http://www.hm-treasury.gov.uk/stern_review_report.htm [accessed 24 February 2009]). War preparation: Postwar replenishment of stocks of weapons and ammunition also absorb natural resources. It is correct to treat this as a war-induced environmental effect of war. But in the absence of war, civilian consumption implies replenishment of civilian consumables, which absorbs natural resources as well. So long as substitution effects hold—more guns, less butter, or fewer guns, more butter—resource requirements and waste generation are not necessarily reduced from one case to the other. What reduces resource requirements from nature's point of view are resource-use efficiencies regardless of whether they are gained in the military or nonmilitary sector.

11. See the Scientific Committee on Problems of the Environment of the International Council of Scientific Unions (ICSU-SCOPE) at http://www.icsu-scope.org/ [accessed 25 February 2008], where volumes 1 and 2 of report 28 on "The Environmental Consequences of Nuclear War" may be downloaded. Volume 2 was published prior to volume 1. In the list of references, the volumes are listed as Harwell and Hutchinson (1985) and Pittock, et al. (1986). In 1998, ICSU was renamed the International Council for Science. A classic reference on environment and nuclear war is Glasstone and Dolan (1977).

12. A technical definition of an airburst is "[t]he explosion of a nuclear weapon at such a height that the expanding fireball does not touch the earth's surface prior to the time the fireball reaches its maximum luminosity" (U.S. Department of Energy, 2000, p. 157).

13. "Any consideration of a post-nuclear-war world would have to consider the consequences of the *totality* of physical effects. The biological effects then follow" (Pittock, et al., 1986, p. xxvi). Unless Earth itself were split and its parts flung into different heliocentric orbits, an environment (physical and chemical habitat) will remain to sustain life. Certain underground and oceanic bacterial chemotrophs, for example, derive energy by oxydizing inorganic compounds, but Earth's ecosystem as we now know it would be changed irrevocably.

14. From the described dire global effects of a major nuclear war one cannot, however, logically conclude that there exists no reason for nuclear weapons possession in the first place. See the appendix to chapter 1 for a brief explanation.

15. Use-risk: In economic studies of crime behavior, a connection is made between the probability of apprehension and the probability of conviction. A high probability of conviction is not a binding constraint on behavior if the probability of being caught is low. Conversely, even if the probability of being caught is high, if it is followed by a low probability of conviction (or of serving time) then behavior again is unlikely to be much influenced. This reasoning may be applied to war, including nuclear war, namely as the probability of war initiation times the probability of the scale of its environmental effects. The high likelihood of a global catastrophe resulting from global nuclear war probably contributed to restrain the parties during the Cold War and helped keep the likelihood of nuclear war initiation low. But the likelihood of war initiation might be driven up if it were thought that the adverse environmental effects of regional-scale nuclear wars would be relatively small. Precisely because the likely effects may be thought not to be global, the risk of usage is enhanced.

16. Information and quotes from Toon, et al. (2007). Their report picks up on the SCOPE studies.

17. "A test is defined in the Threshold Test Ban Treaty as either a single underground nuclear explosion (detonation) conducted at a test site, or two or more underground nuclear explosions (detonations) conducted within an area delineated by a circle having a diameter of two kilometers and conducted within a total period of time not to exceed 0.1 second. Sixty-three of the 1,054 nuclear tests conducted by the United States consisted of more than one underground nuclear explosion (detonation)" (U.S. Department of Energy, 2000, p. xv).

18. Simon, Bouville, and Land (2006, p. 50) and similar accounts elsewhere. Also see Johnson and Barker (2008) and U.S. Senate (2005). A large number of documents on the human toll regarding medical experimentation, forced relocation, property and land use losses, compensation claims, and so on, are readily found on the Internet. See Republic of the Marshall Islands Nuclear Claims Tribunal and U.S. congressional documents related to compensation legislation. Also see IAEA (1998b). Whereas the United States has long accepted legal responsibility for its conduct in the Marshall Islands, the French followed suit regarding its French Polynesian tests by introducing a compensation law into the French national legislature only in late 2008.

19. Simon, Bouville, and Land (2006, p. 55). The article provides additional U.S. estimates for leukemia and other cancers, as well as for the Marshall Islands, and emphasizes that fallout-related cancers are long-term consequences of nuclear testing. It does not address effects on nonhuman organisms.

20. For documentation, see the reports of the two independent commissions, Brown (1998) and IAEA (1998a). Quotes from Brown (1998).

21. Quote from IAEA (summary: 1998a). The IAEA study involved fifty-five scientists from thirty countries. The International Geomechanical Commission study (i.e., Brown, 1998) consisted of seven international scientists, including two Australians and a U.S. American Commission Chair. On French tests in Algeria, not reviewed here, see IAEA (2005).

22. Test number: see U.S. Department of Energy (2000). Human effects: see especially U.S. Senate (2005) and Johnson and Barker (2008).

23. Bikini Atoll lies in the northwest corner of the Marshall Islands. Winds generally come from the northeast; currents from the southeast. The atoll consists of twenty-three islands and islets, the largest of which is Bikini. The information in the text is taken from Richards, et al. (2008). Nuclear testing on Bikini ended in 1958; the new coral survey was taken in 2002 and published in 2008, hence the "five decades" in the title of this publication. Also see the IAEA study on Bikini (IAEA 1998b).

24. Muller and Vander Velde (1999, p. 19).

25. The literature on this topic is now vast. For an example see Homer-Dixon (1994); for an early critique, see Gleditsch (1998); for a recent critique, see Theisen (2008).

26. For primatology, see, for instance, de Waal, Aureli, and Judge (2000); for migration, see, for instance, Ferguson (1989) and Uvin (1996).

27. Crises related to freshwater: Pryor (2007, p. 11), citing Wolf (1997). For examples of intrastate and interstate water-related conflict, see, for instance, the articles in *The Economics of Peace and Security Journal*, Vol. 2, No. 2 (2007). On institutional water conflict and cooperation in the United States, see, for instance, Scholz and Stiftel (2005). On water and cities, see the special section articles in *Science*, Vol. 319 (8 February 2008).

28. Fischer and Huber-Lee (2005, p. xiv); emphasis omitted.

29. Philips (2007, p. 22).

30. Michael Klare, in particular, has explored the topic of "resource wars." See Klare (2001; 2004; 2008).

31. See, for instance, BMU (2002) and very many other sources.

32. Income transfer: Schelling (2006a, p. 58); quote: Schelling (2006b, pp. 34–35).

33. On the relation between and among security, economic development, and environmental sustainability, see Brauer (2008) and literature cited therein.

34. Collier (2004). Ross: http://www.unepfi.org/fileadmin/documents/conflict/ross_2003.pdf [accessed 5 March 2008]. Also see the papers in the August 2005 special issue of the *Journal of Conflict Resolution* on natural resources and war and the scholarly literature cited there. Also see Collier (2007).

35. Ross: http://www.unepfi.org/fileadmin/documents/conflict/ross_2003. pdf [accessed 5 March 2008].

36. As regards country appellations, the preference is to refer to Burma rather than to Myanmar. The latter term, now common in international political and media circles, was introduced in 1989 by Burmese leaders of a military coup d'état but never ratified by any legislature. As to "the Congo," the Democratic Republic of the Congo (DRC) is meant, unless explicit reference to the Republic of the Congo (or Congo-Brazzaville) is made.

37. Brashares, et al. (2004). Even longer-term consequences of overfishing are discussed in Jackson, et al. (2001).

38. Blaustein and Johnson (2003).

39. Lanier-Graham (1993, pp. 11–12). Westing (1993, p. 948) adds another category, "intentionally amplified environmental damage," to refer to environmental modification as a means of war. U.S. attempts during the Vietnam War to induce local climate change by cloud seeding so as to cause heavy rains and subsequent topsoil erosion would be an example.

40. Classification: Dahl (1992, pp. 113–115). Dahl ignores the possibility that nature might have existence value—value for its own sake. That humans might act as guardians of nonhuman life and represent nature's legal interests the way parents represent the legal interests of their children is a relatively new concept that has yet to find its way into international law of war and international environmental law. A huge literature on legal aspects of war-related environmental effects has sprung up. A useful early bibliography is provided by the Environmental Law Institute (1998).

41. Scientific classification: Levy, Shahi, and Lee (1997, p. 52). The physical environment includes subject matter such as weather and climate, soil condition, vegetation, and water sources as well as human infrastructure such as water supply and sanitation, and transportation and communication networks. The chemical environment refers to factors affecting air, land, and water quality, and the biological environment to effects on micro- and macro-organisms and their ecological interaction in and over time and space. Figure 1.1: Alsdirawi (1994, pp. 120–121). Alsdirawi also traces possible pathways by which the use of war machinery may have affected Kuwait (1994, pp. 120–121). Ecology-wide assessment: An exception is Stoddart, who in an early paper on the effects of military activity on coral atoll ecosystems argues that "the character of human use of several atolls has so changed in tempo and in mode as to amount to ecosystem replacement rather than change" (1968, p. 25).

42. Satellite images: El-Baz, et al. (1994). Standards: An acceptable example is given by Westing (1980, p. 52) who writes that forests covered about 11 million hectares (or 20 percent) of the French land area before World War I. The war was estimated to have involved about 600,000 hectares of forest (5.5 percent of the total), about 200,000 of which (1.8 percent) were so damaged as "to require artificial reforestation." One gains a sense of relative magnitude.

43. Disturbance and recolonization: Begon, Harper, and Townsend (1996, p. 958). A compressed classification, and without reference to war, is given in Begon, Harper, and Townsend (1996, pp. 922–923) which lists, in order of severity, habitat disturbance, degradation, and destruction.

44. UNEP (2003a). Also see UNEP (2001, 2002), with similar findings. This differs dramatically from the findings regarding radiation effects due to atmospheric nuclear testing and nuclear war discussed in section 1.2.

45. The following facetious analogy highlights the use of the terms. Combing one's hair amounts to an environmental *difference*. No damage is done. In contrast, there are various degrees of *disruption*. First, an ordinary haircut is a *disturbance* in the topography and morphology of the hair. Full recovery is expected. Second, if the hairstyle—cut or otherwise—rattles the norms of the socially acceptable, it might be viewed as a *degradation*, but a comparable richness will still emerge. Third, a *depleting* haircut results in baldness. Recovery is prevented by design. Although not everyone might view this as an impoverishment, from the hair's "point of view" it is. And fourth, environmental *destruction* is equivalent to scalping, the removal of the head's skin. In that case recovery is impossible.

46. German occupation: Lanier-Graham (1993, p. 23). Regrowth: by the 1990s, only a single herd of wild reindeer of 15,000 members was left in Norway, but there were some 200,000 domesticated reindeer. See http://www.norsk.net/e_98-17.htm by University of Oslo biology professor Leif Ryvarden [accessed 17 February 2009].

47. Example from Lanier-Graham (1993, p. 24). Dutch use of deliberate flooding to impede advancing enemy troops goes back at least to the siege of Leiden in 1574. Construction of sluices, to control the extent of flooding, started in 1629 under Prince Frederick Henry of Orange Nassau. The line, in modernized form, found use into World War II. A modern-day example of self-damage is that of the Second Sino-Japanese War (1937–1945). In June 1938, writes Westing (1993, p. 950), China intentionally "dynamited the Huayuankow dike of the Huang He (Yellow River) near Chengchow," drowning not only "several thousand Japanese soldiers," stopping their advance, but also drowning "at least several hundred thousand Chinese." In the process, millions of square kilometers of farmland, crops, and topsoil were damaged.

48. Green Cross International (1998). The environmental risk assessment model is described on pp. 91–97 of that publication.

49. Scientists usually do provide a ratio of affected to nonaffected individuals; but others mostly repeat only the numerator of the ratio. Incidentally, bird stocks in the Gulf did recover (see chapter 3).

50. Guatemala: Gardner, Garb, and Williams (1990, p. 2). El Salvador: Hall and Faber (1989, p. 9); Bruch (1998, p. 11). Africa: see chapter 4; Vietnam: see chapter 2; Kuwait: see chapter 3.

51. Deliberate: the case of Vietnam, reported in Bruch (1998, p. 11). This story is unconfirmed, and one manuscript reader rightly questioned why Vietnam would be interested in tampering with samples that probably would only have helped it to make its case. Inadvertent: Arkin, Durrant, and Cherni (1991) for a Greenpeace Persian Gulf War mission. Quote: Canby (1991, p. 16); similarly in Bloom, et al. (1994, p. 133). Research vessel: Mathews, et al. (1993, p. 253). Personal account: Al-Hassan (1992, pp. 17–18).

52. This shortcoming was partially rectified with a 2003 UNEP desk study. See UNEP (2003c).

53. J. Perry Robinson writes with respect to chemical warfare in World War I and in Vietnam: "These two cases suggest much but in fact demonstrate little. In order to show that chemical warfare may cause grave indirect damage to human populations—environmentally mediated damage—one needs 'before' and 'after' data of great specificity. For the World War I case we have little of either. For the Vietnam case we have some of the latter and could no doubt get a good deal more; but the problem of baseline data would remain. And on top of all this there are the fundamental methodological problems stemming from our as-yet slight understanding of all mechanisms of ecosystem function" (1981, pp. 80–81).

54. In many cases one can collect nothing more than news reports. For example, "War tears apart Uganda's parks," *Oryx*, Vol. 20, No. 4, 1986, pp. 255–256. While indicative, this does not amount to usable data.

55. Comparable habitats quote: Westing (1983, p. 379). On gorillas, a note in chapter 4 explains at an appropriate place the current classification of gorilla species and subspecies.

56. Greenpeace (1992, p. 34). Bruch (1998, pp. 8, 10). On Kuwait, see chapter 3 for details.

57. Perry Robinson quote: Perry Robinson (1981, p. 81). Barnaby: Barnaby (1991). Barnaby was a former director of the Stockholm International Peace Research Institute. Little of what he predicted actually did occur (see chapter 3). Likewise, Nobel Peace Prize laureate Jody Williams wrote a piece entitled "Land Mines: Dealing with the Environmental Impact" (1997) that is devoid of information on the environmental impact of land mines. A more apt title would have been "Land Mines: Dealing with the Humanitarian Impact"—a compelling subject that does not need masquerading as an environmental issue. Even Arthur Westing, usually a meticulous researcher and careful writer, penned a piece entitled "The Environmental Aftermath of Warfare in Viet Nam" (1983) that deals almost exclusively either with the human impact of that war or with its impact on cultivated, that is human-shaped, environments and with environmental effects as transmitted to humans. A similar story unfolded with an oil release off the Galápagos Islands early in 2001. Almost instantly, news media corralled highly visible scientists to deliver on-the-spot assessments that turned out to be inflated. A simple check with the website of the Darwin research station would have provided much more accurate, and much less catastrophic-sounding, information. *Exxon Valdez*: Arkin, Durrant, and Cherni (1991). The size of the *Exxon Valdez* spill of 24 March 1989 was 10.8 million gallons or, at forty-two gallons per barrel, 257,000 barrels. Initial Gulf War spill estimates: Arkin, Durrant, and Cherni (1991, p. 63). Regarding destruction of on-shore well-heads, a Greenpeace team reports that by June 1991 hardly any scientific data had been released and much of what was available were speculations of various sorts. See Arkin, Durrant, and Cherni (1991, p. 68).

58. Warning: Bruch (1998, p. 10). Fires: Earle (1992, p. 134).

59. Biswas (2000, p. 314).

60. The IUCN's nomenclature has changed over the years: "IUCN was founded in October 1948 as the International Union for the Protection of Nature (or IUPN) following an international conference in Fontainebleau, France. The organization changed its name to the International Union for Conservation of Nature and Natural Resources in 1956 with the acronym IUCN (or UICN in French and Spanish). This remains our full legal name to this day. Use of the name 'World Conservation Union,' in conjunction with IUCN, began in 1990. From March 2008 this name [i.e., World Conservation Union] is no longer commonly used." See http://www.iucn.org/about/ [accessed 18 February 2009]. The remainder of the text generally uses the designation IUCN.

61. South Vietnam: Thomas (1995, p. 113). Contrary evidence: for example, Constable (1981–1982, p. 250). Island birds claim: Lanier-Graham (1993, p. 28). Island birds evidence: Westing (1980, p. 138); Peterson (1942–1943); Baker (1946); Fisher and Baldwin (1946); Greenway (1967). Fact check: Laysan finch: http://hbs. bishopmuseum.org/endangered/laysfinch.html. Mariana megapode: listed as alive at several websites, for instance, http://www.fws.gov/pacificislands/wesa/mega-podeindex.html and http://www.worldwildlife.org/wildworld/profiles/terrestrial/oc/oc0203_full.html, as is the brown booby: http://www.mbr-pwrc.usgs.gov/id/framlst/i1150id.html and http://www.fws.gov/midway/wildlife/brbo.html. Regarding the Marianas mallard, the U.S. Fish and Wildlife Service reports the last confirmed sighting in the wild in 1979; a captive-breeding program failed, and what is believed to have been the endling (the last surviving member of a species) died in San Diego in 1981 (see http://www.fws.gov/pacificislands/wesa/mal-lardmariaindex.html) [all sites accessed on 28 January 2008]. Kouprey: Westing (1976, p. 72); Ngan (1968); Curry-Lindahl (1972). IUCN Redlist: http://www.iucnredlist.org/search/search-basic [accessed 28 January 2008]. Pheasant: http://www.orientalbirdimages.org/search.php?action=searchresult&Bird_ID=94&Bird_Image_ID=1113&Bird_Family_ID=&p=3 [accessed 28 January 2008].

62. Weaker legal language: Bruch (1998, p. 6). Seeming to condone: Westing (2000, p. 180).

63. Schmitt (2000, p. 89). To be liable, four conditions need to be met. First, a duty to act in a certain way must exist; second, there must be breach of that duty; third, there must be injury; and fourth, there must be injury due to breach of duty. The duty derives from treaties to which a state is party. Since Iraq was not party to ENMOD or Additional Protocol I, there was no legal liability. Instead, Iraq was held liable by the United Nations Security Council under U.N. Charter Article 2(4)—wrongful occupation of Kuwait (Schmitt, 2000, p. 89). See U.N. Security Council Resolution 687, paragraph 16: the Council "[r]eaffirms that Iraq . . . is liable under international law for any direct loss, damage, including environmental damage and the depletion of natural resources, or injury to foreign Governments, nationals and corporations, as a result of Iraq's unlawful invasion and occupation of Kuwait." The specific international law that might establish such liability is not mentioned. In paragraph 18, the Security Council then creates a United Nations

Compensation Commission (see http://www.uncc.ch/; accessed 18 February 2009) to handle claims arising from the invasion and occupation, including those for environmental damage and natural resource depletion. These include claims for damage caused by allied forces on the reasoning that such damage would not have occurred in the absence of Iraq's aggression (see http://www.uncc.ch/decision/dec_07r.pdf) [accessed 18 February 2009]. Note that even though Iraq did not ratify ENMOD, it signed it and, in at least one scholar's view, it is thereby "obligated to do nothing inconsistent with the terms of the convention until [it has] expressed an intent not to ratify it" (Schmitt, 2000, p. 94).

64. Nuclear weapons: Falk (2000, p. 147). Italy, Germany, United Kingdom: Roberts (2000, p. 63, text and note 41). France and China: Schmitt (2000, p. 94). Turkey: see Schmitt (2000, p. 108, note 72). These details can be verified via the www.icrc.org/ihl website, maintained by the International Committee of the Red Cross (ICRC) [accessed 18 February 2009]. The site contains the full text of treaties, lists signatories and ratification by state and date, and also includes the full text of any state's reservations.

65. Major purpose: U.S. Department of Energy (2000, pp. viii, xvi, 159). This U.S. Department of Energy document reports on all U.S. nuclear weapons tests conducted by the United States between 16 July 1945, and 23 September 1992. Of 1,149 tests, the purpose of one hundred of them is classified as "weapons effects," and another 891 are classified as "weapons related" (p. viii). Weapons effects are defined as "[a] nuclear test to evaluate the civil or military effects of a nuclear detonation on various targets, such as military hardware." "Weapons related" is defined as "[a] nuclear detonation conducted for the purpose of testing a nuclear device intended for a specific type of weapon system." (The remaining tests related to safety, to storage and transportation, and to other concerns.) Thus, at least 86 percent of the tests were directly related to the weapons' optional qualities for military purposes. While the explosive testing of nuclear weapons has been halted by states party to the Comprehensive Nuclear Test Ban Treaty, computer-based testing continues. The United States also maintains an underground test readiness program. So, presumably, do other states.

66. This discussion is obviously a synopsis. The upshot is that a compelling logic exists that makes credible arming easy and credible disarming hard (for all weapons systems, not just atomic arms). In logic, nuclear weapons differ from non-nuclear weapons only in degree, not in kind, which infuses the potential environmental consequences of nuclear arms use with a particularly unsettling edge. For a fuller discussion on arms rivalry and arms race models see, for instance, Anderton and Carter (2009) and the literature cited therein. In addition, a powerful economic reason for nuclear forces exists: they are far more efficient militarily than costly manpower (see, for instance, chapter 7 in Brauer and van Tuyll, 2008).

The Vietnam War   2

From 1884, Vietnam was a French colony. After World War II, an anticolonial war of independence led by Ho Chi Minh concluded with the French defeat at Dien Bien Phu in May 1954. This was formalized at a conference held in Geneva in July 1954, and Vietnam became an independent state. The first Indochina (or Vietnam) war thus is usually dated 1946–1954. The second Indochina war was a direct continuation of the first, lasting until 1975. Especially in the United States, however, the second war tends to be dated from March 1965 when, in addition to military supplies and thousands of military advisers that the United States already provided, President Johnson ordered the introduction of U.S. combat troops into the conflict as well.

The second Indochina war is an example of a long, major, international war. The literature on its environmental effects is, to a large extent, written or mediated by a single, formidable researcher, Arthur H. Westing. Although he has published on Cambodia, on Laos, on environmental aspects of international law of war, and on related topics, his voluminous writings center on Vietnam. A forester by training, Westing may well be regarded as the father of the modern, continuous interest in the environmental effects of war. While there is much in his body of work that is admirable, there is also much that is written in the form of news reports, that is, without source attribution, so that it can be difficult to find and inspect original sources and form one's own judgment. In addition, Westing's oeuvre includes advocacy pieces and reprinting under various titles that makes it tedious to identify and sort out original contributions and data. His 1976 book on Vietnam is, however, an essential reference item, as is his 1980 book on the environmental consequences of wars other than Vietnam.[1]

During the Vietnam War, the United States engaged in "massive rural area bombing, extensive chemical and mechanical forest destruction, large-scale chemical and mechanical crop destruction, wide-ranging chemical anti-personnel harassment and area denial, and enormous forced population displacements." In what follows, section 2.1 (nonherbicidal destruction such as bombing and bulldozing) relies on Westing's 1976 book and on as many other scientific sources as it has been possible to find. With respect to the use of herbicides (section 2.2), reliance is placed on Westing's 1989 summary, supplemented by the work of other scholars published in Westing's 1984 edited book and in other sources. In particular, an effort has been made to go back to studies conducted in the late 1960s and early 1970s under the auspices of the American Association for the Advancement of Science (AAAS) and the National Academy of Sciences (NAS). These studies were widely, and heatedly, debated at the time. Efforts have also been undertaken to locate studies from the 1980s, 1990s, and 2000s to gauge long-term environmental effects of the war.[2]

The literature on the environmental effects of the Vietnam War is dominated by attention to U.S. spraying of defoliants over Vietnam's landscape. Particular concern was expressed over the short- and long-term effects on humans (Vietnamese and foreigners) of dioxins usage, a prominent class of chemicals used in one of the defoliants. This use spawned a vast literature. It does not diminish the importance of the impact on human beings when emphasis is placed in this chapter on the war's effects on nonhuman nature. But the chapter begins with nonherbicidal destruction.

2.1 Bombing, Bulldozing, and Other Nonherbicidal Destruction

2.1.1 Bombing

Westing estimates that the United States released more than 14 million tons of explosives during its portion of the war in Indochina. These were delivered from the air, ground, and sea. More than 10 million tons affected South Vietnam; the remainder were discharged on North Vietnam, Cambodia, and Laos. As in other wars, many explosives did not detonate, and remain dangerous remnants of war. For comparison, the tonnage dropped in World War II on Germany, comparable in land area to Vietnam, amounted to 1.4 million tons.[3]

In terms of immediate effects, exploded munitions create a shock wave, obliterate nearby flora and fauna, injure plants and animals farther away, and damage soil by producing impact craters. Westing estimates the South Vietnamese surface area of craters at 1,470 km² and the area affected by shrapnel at an additional 87,970 km² for a total of nearly 90,000 km² (or 9 million hectares). As the entire land area of South Vietnam is only 173,260 km² this might seem an unduly high estimate. Indeed, Westing clarifies that there may have been significant overlap of one bomb's effects with another bomb's effects. There are no data on the amount of overlap. Allowing for a 25 percent overlap for shrapnel and 5 percent for bomb craters, one would still arrive at roughly 67,500 km², or nearly 40 percent of the land area. Since peak bombing, when about one-third of all explosives were released, occurred in just two years, 1968 and 1969, the environmental effects would have had to be fairly concentrated.[4]

If one assumes that vegetation, especially trees, once covered the areas now occupied by craters, and if one further assumes an average of 10 trees per hectare, one arrives at an estimate of nearly 1.5 million trees killed in South Vietnam and a further 700,000 trees killed in North Vietnam, Cambodia, and Laos. But this would account only for the immediately lethal part of the shock wave of the munitions, on average only less than 10 meters in diameter. Beyond this area, blast overpressure would inflict a gradient of injury. One must presume that shock wave injury would result in eventual deaths in large numbers because, unlike humans, injured animals and plants cannot go and seek medical assistance. Actual fatality data, of course, are not available. Death and injury would also result from metal fragments of the explosives, that is, shrapnel. The area affected by shrapnel in South Vietnam was estimated at nearly 88,000 km². Again assume 10 trees per hectare: this brings the total number of trees to 88 million. Assume a one-third direct or indirect kill rate, and one arrives at about 30 million trees killed in South Vietnam alone (or more than 45 million in all of Indochina).[5] Finally, because of crater, blast, and shrapnel overlap, reduce this number by 25 percent to arrive at an estimate of about 20 to 25 million killed trees in South Vietnam on 40 percent of its land area, surely no insignificant effect and death rate.

There are further effects: loss of vegetation means loss of evapotranspiration, the water table will rise, not only affecting the remainder of the local ecosystem, but affecting downstream ecosystems through increased water flow, possibly resulting in soil erosion (especially of loose, cratered soil), nutrient loss, and flooding. Cratering also implies soil compaction. Compaction can last for decades and limits vegetative regrowth. Many craters filled with water, resulting in an increasing number of inland fish ponds. However, still water attracts mosquitoes and other disease carriers.

Westing estimates that 21 million bombs and 229 million shells were exploded throughout Indochina and that a comparable number of small and large craters were created. In fact, Westing and Pfeiffer report that between 1965 and 1971, 26 million bomb craters were created in Indochina, affecting an area of 1,710 km² and involving an earth movement of some 2.6 billion square meters.[6] In three visits to South Vietnam to personally inspect ecological damage and talk with farmers, loggers, and plantation owners, Westing and Pfeiffer observed drastically altered landscape and vegetation surrounding the cratered areas. Rice paddies were disrupted (craters are too deep for rice growing) and grasses invaded the cratered terrain, precluding regrowth of hardwood forests.

2.1.2 Bulldozing

In addition to direct bombing and shelling, the United States also disturbed the countryside by the bulldozing of habitat, using 20-ton tractors made by Caterpillar Company and plows manufactured by Rome Plow Company (of Cedartown, Georgia), hence the designation Rome plows, or Rome plowing. These plows were ruthlessly effective, literally scraping vegetation off the earth and exposing the subsoil—rather like stripping off one's skin to expose subcutaneous tissue—and totally eliminating all vegetation over 3,250 km² (about 2 percent of South Vietnam's land area). Initially, the plows were used to clear strips 100 to 300 meters wide along each side of major roads. By 1968, however, plows were organized into companies to systematically eradicate hundreds of square kilometers of contiguous forest. The military purpose was ambush prevention and area denial.

Apart from death of trees and vegetation and complete habitat destruction for animals, the subsoil is exposed to erosion and, likely, to nutrient dumping and water runoff. Replacement vegetation that eventually grows will establish a completely different ecosystem (primary stage) so that those animals that were able to flee the destruction still are unlikely to be able to return. Soil scraping also is likely to change the microclimate, the interchange between atmosphere and geosphere. For instance, exposed soil is subject to "elevated insolation [exposure to the sun], raised temperatures, increased wind velocities, decreased humidity and reduced levels of carbon dioxide."[7]

Unfortunately, no studies appear to exist that confirm the presence and magnitude of these presumed effects.

2.1.3 Other Nonherbicidal Destruction:
Blast Munitions, Antipersonnel Chemicals,
Weather Manipulation, Flooding, and Fire

In addition to crater-forming bombs, from 1967 the United States experimented with concussion bombs designed to create instant helicopter landing pads. This necessitated total vegetational and animal clearing with a single blast. The affected area of total obliteration is estimated at 1.3 hectares per bomb. The casualty range extends up to 49 hectares. It is not clear how many such bombs were applied in Indochina. A second noncratering type of bomb used was the fuel-air bomb, also introduced in 1967. This bomb annihilated virtually all life within an area one hectare in size and caused injury, and likely subsequent wildlife death, over an area exceeding 10 hectares, depending on the size of the bomb. Antipersonnel gas (CS gas) was acquired by the U.S. Department of Defense in substantial quantities, enough to apply to between 10,000 and 90,000 km^2. However, warfare usage of the gas is not publicly known. The gas produces tears, incites sneezing, and irritates the upper respiratory tract in humans. According to Westing, direct ecological damage is not reported in the literature of the time, but effects are likely to have occurred as experiments on terrestrial and aquatic plant and animal life report various sensitivities, both less so and more so than for humans.[8]

The United States also undertook extensive efforts between 1966 and 1972 to manipulate weather patterns, especially an attempt to induce increased rainfall in the border regions of Laos and South Vietnam. It is not clear that these efforts succeeded. Further, the United States attacked "dams, dikes and sea-walls . . . especially in North Viet Nam," threatening flooding, drowning of flora and fauna, soil erosion, and/or soil degradation when saltwater flooding is involved. However, again no studies appear to exist that document such damage. Finally, on several occasions the United States deliberately set fire to forests in South Vietnam. On the whole, these appear to have been militarily ineffective, in large part due to the fairly high degree of rainfall and humidity of the areas.[9]

2.2 Herbicide Attacks

2.2.1 Background

In addition to the activities mentioned in the preceding subsection, the Vietnam War is famous for the U.S. use of herbicides as an agent of war.

These were applied for two distinct purposes, defoliation to deny tree cover and crop destruction to deny food. Under the code-name Operation Ranch Hand, herbicide spraying took place from 1962 to 1971. The herbicides, which at the time were in common agriculture use in the United States, were named for the color-coded drums in which they were stored and shipped: Agent Orange, Agent White, and Agent Blue.[10]

Agent Orange was a 50/50 mixture of 2,4,5-trichlorophenoxyacetic acid (abbreviated as 2,4,5-T) and 2,4-dichlorophenoxyacetic acid (2,4-D). By-products of the manufacture of 2,4,5-T are trace levels of the dioxin TCDD (2,3,7,8-tetrachlorodibenzo-para-dioxin).[11] One of the manufacturers, Dow Chemical, reportedly listed TCDD concentrations of between less than 0.05 to about 50 milligrams per liter (mg/l).[12] A report in *Scientific American* states that concentrations were "generally from two to 10 times as high as for civilian purposes." In addition, spray application—liter per hectare—was "far greater" than would ordinarily be used in normal forestry operations. In a word, there was a twofold concentration: more milligrams per liter, and more liters per hectare. Very few Agent Orange production lots have been recovered for content analyses. These suggest that, in all, perhaps 170 kg of dioxin may have been released over South Vietnam. In much more recent work, a set of researchers provide a far more detailed and disconcerting account according to which contamination varied considerably but cannot be fully reconstructed anymore. It is not unlikely, however, that the total amount of dioxin released over Vietnam may be twice or more than previously believed.[13]

The active ingredients in Agent White were an 80/20 mixture of 2,4-D and 4-amino-3,5,6-trichloropicolinic acid (picloram). Less volatile and less subject to drift but equally effective and more persistent, it was not used as widely, apparently because of its expense. Agent Blue consisted of cacodylic acid, mostly used in crop destruction. The active ingredients in Orange and White are growth regulators that "cause destructive proliferation of tissues in plants," whereas the organic arsenic in Blue "killed crops by causing them to dry out."[14]

Information on the chemical agents and the amounts used, the location and extent of the areas sprayed, the number of repeat applications, and the years during which the spraying occurred all can be gleaned in much detail from Westing and other sources. To this day, however, that information is still subject to change.[15] Here is a synopsis of Westing's account. Of the total South Vietnamese land area of 173,260 km², about 60 percent (104,000 km²) was covered by woody vegetation, namely dense primary and secondary inland forest (58,000 km²), open forest (20,000 km²), bamboo areas (8,000 km²), true and rear mangrove areas (3,000 and 2,000 km², respectively), rubber plantations (1,000 km²), pine forest (1,000 km²), and miscellaneous forest (11,000 km²). Agricultural (17 percent) and miscellaneous cover (23 percent) accounted for the remaining 40 percent of land. Westing estimates that some 72.4 million liters of herbicides were sprayed from 1962 to 1971 onto 16,700 km², or 9.6 percent of the total South Vietnamese land area: 60.6 million liters on forests, 10.2 million liters on crops, and 1.6 million liters of miscellaneous other vegetation. About 75 percent of the spraying was concentrated in the years 1967 to 1969, especially in Military Region III, an area of roughly 30,000 km² lying predominantly to the north, east, and west of what was then Saigon (now Ho Chi Minh City). This area received nearly a third of all sprayings.

Until recently Westing's estimate of the amount of spray would have been thought remarkably accurate. Young's calculations confirm Westing's estimates (see table 2.1). But Young reports single or multiple herbicide applications to a smaller area, only 13,100 km² (about 11,000 km² of inland forest, 1,278 km² of mangrove forest, and 1,053 km² of cropland). If Young is correct, the spray concentration (liter per hectare) would have been correspondingly higher.[16]

A U.S. National Academy of Sciences (NAS) report of 1974 relied on wartime military logs that NAS collated in the so-called HERBS computer tapes. This includes U.S. flown missions but excludes Vietnamese use of herbicides as well as military base perimeter and other ground-based spraying. In 1985, the U.S. Army and the Joint Services Environmental Support Group corrected coding errors in the HERBS files and constructed an additional database, called Services HERBS. This effort resulted in an increase in identified spray missions flown to 8,930 and herbicides sprayed

Table 2.1.   Herbicide Use in South Vietnam, 1962 to 1971

Code Name	Herbicide	Quantity (in liters)	Period of Use
Orange	2,4-D; 2,4,5-T	44,953,560	1965–1970
White	2,4-D; picloram	20,616,860	1965–1970
Blue	Cacodylic acid	4,712,920	1965–1970
Purple	2,4-D; 2,4,5-T	)	1962–1965
Pink	2,4,5-T	) 117,600	1962–1965
Green	2,4,5-T	)	1962–1965
Unknown*		2,339,460	
Total		72,740,400	

Source: Young (1988, pp. 12–13)
* Mission records do not identify the herbicide used.

from 67 million to 72.7 million liters, hence Westing's apparent accuracy. Much more recently, all files were recoded again (by Stellman, et al.), eliminating additional coding errors and entering new, previously unrecorded information. This further increased the number of known missions flown and resulted in a spray volume increase by 9,440,028 liters. This work also estimated a much larger sprayed area, namely 26,313 square kilometers.[17]

Recall from the previous section that the bulldozing, bombing, and shrapnel-affected areas amounted to about 70,750 km^2 (67,500 km^2 for bombing and shrapnel and 3,250 km^2 for bulldozing). Compared to Westing's estimate of the sprayed area of 16,700 km^2, this is larger by a factor of 4.2. Compared to Young's estimate of 13,100 km^2, which is based on the HERBS files only, this is larger by a factor of 5.4. And even compared to the Stellman, et al. estimate of 26,313 km^2, the areas affected by bombing, shrapnel, and bulldozing would have been larger by a factor of 2.7. Yet the bombing and bulldozing effects received far less scientific attention than did the herbicide spraying.

2.2.2 Inland Forests: Terrestrial Plant Ecology and Forestry

Following Rachel Carson's 1962 best-selling book *Silent Spring*, serious questions about the effects of herbicide spraying were first raised in U.S. newspaper accounts carried in the *St. Louis Post-Dispatch* on 6 February 1963, and later in the *Washington Post* on 27 May 1964. On a variety of grounds, some scientific, some not, the Federation of American Scientists in 1964, the National Academy of Sciences (NAS) in 1966, and—at the instigation of E. W. Pfeiffer, and not without considerable internal disagreement— the American Association for the Advancement of Science (AAAS) in 1967 expressed various degrees of concern and opposition to herbicide spraying in the Vietnam War. In 1969, AAAS created the Herbicide Assessment Commission (HAC). HAC, in turn, sent a team to Vietnam in August and September 1970. It consisted of Matthew Meselson, Arthur Westing, John Constable, and Robert Cook. They report that with few exceptions they were given every assistance by U.S. forces in the region, including the use of helicopters for overflight and aerial inspections, but ground-level inspection rarely was possible, nor were databases available for quantitative assessments to be carried out. In the spring of 1966, the U.S. government had sent a forestry team to Vietnam, in recognition of the commercial importance of the forests for charcoal and fuel wood production as well as for timber production and exports. At the instigation of U.S. government foresters working in South Vietnam, the U.S. mission in Vietnam itself then decided in late 1967 to form the Mission Herbicide Review Commission to undertake a complete review of its herbicide spraying policy. This took place during 1968. At the urging of this commission, the U.S. Department of State sent a U.S. Department of Agriculture researcher, Fred Tschirley, on a one-month mission in March and April 1968 to undertake an ecological assessment of defoliation.[18]

Regarding upland forests, Constable and Meselson remark on the destruction of large trees and their replacement with dense underbrush, bamboo, and grasses, especially *Imperata cylindrica.* No information with respect to fauna could be obtained but populations "must certainly have been severely changed." Crop destruction was carried out primarily in South Vietnamese mountainous areas. "A total of about 530,000 acres [~2,150 km^2] has been sprayed through 1969, destroying enough rice to feed an estimated 600,000 people for a year." As might be expected from an assessment mission, members bemoan the lack of actual scientific studies but overall are doubtful about chances for ecological recovery. The estimate of about 2,150 km^2 of cropland spraying is more than double Young's later calculation.[19]

According to Westing's later writing, of the 58,000 km^2 of dense primary and secondary inland forest, an area of 10,770 km^2 (19 percent) was sprayed at least once. This is about 65 percent of the total sprayed area of 16,700 km^2. Whereas the 5,000 km^2 of mangrove stands were very sensitive to herbicide spraying and often succumbed to a single application, the roughly 11,000 km^2 of sprayed dense inland forests—this estimate is in agreement with Young's—showed some resilience, depending on tree species, and repeated herbicide applications were needed to cause complete defoliation in upper- and lower-story trees. Defoliation would occur for the season, and the extent of refoliation would depend on species. However, perhaps 10 percent of the inland forest trees "were killed outright by a single military spraying." Survivors sustained various injuries, in some instances surely resulting in delayed mortality although the extent of that is not known. In addition, once upper-story trees are killed, lower-story trees are exposed to harsher environmental conditions and consequently may die. The extent of such secondary effects is also unknown. When trees received multiple sprayings, mortality increased roughly exponentially, more so the shorter the spray intervals. Nonetheless, Westing himself refers to the "modest degree of kill" among inland trees, at least relative to the kill among mangrove trees.[20]

In all, Westing estimated a loss of merchantable timber on the order of 47 million m^3. His estimate, based on a visit in August 1970, is close to that arrived at by foresters Flamm and Cravens, who estimated a loss of 47.25 million m³. Their work was based on in-country experience in 1967 and 1968, but the basis of their loss estimate is not explained. Both reports, it must be stressed, emphasize the loss of forests as commercial propositions rather than as ecologically important areas. As Flamm and Cravens describe it, even the scientists only gradually became aware of the ecological importance of Vietnam's forests. Indeed, this is why Tschirley was invited to carry out an ecological assessment. In his report, he concludes that "defoliation in Vietnam has no significant measurable effect on atmospheric moisture and thus would have no effect on precipitation" (p. 780)[21]; that he did not detect evidence of soil erosion due to defoliation (p. 781); that he did not think that the herbicides would significantly affect soil microorganisms (p. 781); that although he did not think that a single spraying would do much harm to inland forests, moderate concern about multiple spraying when it combines with invasion by hardy bamboo species is warranted (p. 785); and that for utter lack of data he did not wish to express an opinion with regard to animal life (p. 785). In sum, Tschirley writes that "the defoliation program has caused ecological changes. I do not feel the changes are irreversible, but complete recovery may take a long time" (p. 786), for mangroves perhaps twenty years, and an unknown time for semi-deciduous forest. Tschirley repeatedly stresses lack of prewar data and, to find reference points, frequently refers to findings outside of Vietnam, such as the Philippines and Puerto Rico.[22]

These estimates and reports, together with a 1970 report of zoologists Orians and Pfeiffer that emanated from the AAAS, caused considerable unease in the United States. In 1971, the U.S. Congress then mandated that the U.S. Department of Defense contract with the National Academy of Sciences (NAS) to study the effects of the military use of herbicides in Vietnam. The NAS study, or rather the set of studies, was published in 1974. With one clear exception, they appeared to exonerate studies the Department of Defense had commissioned to be conducted by the Midwest Research Institute in 1967 in that relatively few adverse effects of herbicide spraying on Vietnam's forests were found.[23] According to the NAS studies, the crux of the matter of the estimate of commercial timber losses lay in that Westing, and Flamm and Cravens, based their loss calculations on the assumption of average merchantable timber stands of 100 m³/ha,[24] even as available prewar forest inventories and density estimates suggested that Vietnam's forests were in poor condition from slash-and-burn agriculture and commercial timbering. In addition, and in contrast to these researchers, the NAS team had access to reams of prewar aerial photography at various resolutions, requested and received special aerial photography from the Department of Defense, and received access to the "flight path locations, number of aircraft employed, quantity of herbicide delivered and date of flight for each mission flown." From all this, they calculated an average tree density of only 7.8 m³/ha.[25] Using two independent models, the calculations resulted in an estimated range of merchantable timber losses of 0.5 to 2 million m³, about 95 percent less than Westing's estimate. The NAS estimate conforms to that of the South Vietnam Forest Service and, it turns out, when Westing's, and Flamm and Cravens' estimates are adjusted for the 100 m³/ha timber assumption by substituting the observed timber density of 7.8 m³/ha derived from the aerial photography and ground inspection, their estimates would have fallen at or only slightly above the upper end of the NAS estimated range.[26] Indeed, some 92 percent of the difference to the Flamm/Cravens and Westing estimates is due solely to the pre-spray tree density estimate.[27]

What is clear from the prewar literature is that Vietnam's forests were already substantially depleted by traditional slash-and-burn agriculture and commercial timber harvesting. All agree that Vietnam's forests were far from pristine. A good portion might instead be described as cultured, hence the initial emphasis on merchantable timber rather than on ecological effects. Swanson adds that prior to World War II, Vietnam's forests "had already become impoverished by an improvident [French] colonial administration which granted many agricultural concessions on land better adapted to forests. Many observers believe that this cause of forest destruction is greater than any other, including devastation by war." War certainly did not assist the forests. During the world war years, Japanese occupiers and the Viet Minh resistance both helped themselves freely to the forest. This destruction continued during the first Indochina war, so that by the time of the second war, U.S. defoliation, "although it killed trees, did a bare minimum of actual deforestation." By the late 1960s, then, NAS tree counts resulted in the aforementioned average of 7.8 m³/ha commercial timber tree density. Thus the NAS study arrives at relatively modest conclusions regarding the effect of herbicide spraying on Vietnam's forests.[28]

The NAS assessment was subject to "considerable debate." This occurred because a dissenting member of the NAS leaked selective portions of a prepublication version of the official report to the press, resulting in much public debate based on incomplete and inaccurate reporting. The New York Times was eventually reprimanded for its part of the ensuing scandal, and the NAS president tendered a written apology to the NAS study team. In the opinion of the team, "the most important causes of [the war's effects on forests] were not herbicides but were fire, bombing, shelling, and military harvesting," and the committee members regretted that the public controversy over herbicide use obscured the nonherbicidal effect which "was by a wide margin the most important and long lasting effect of war upon the inland forests." Westing agreed with that assessment.[29]

As noted, it was generally accepted that Vietnam's forests were not pristine before U.S. herbicide spraying began. They had already been "disturbed by shifting slash-and-burn agriculture, logging, fuel gathering, or other means," write Galston and Richards in a contribution to a book edited by Westing. Most of the forest consisted of secondary stands interrupted by bamboo thickets, cultivated plots, and swamp areas. Specifics about succession in severely damaged tropical forests were not well known, but it appears that in South Vietnam three general types of recovery took place: replacement, reforestation, and natural recovery. First, in some affected areas, replacement vegetation took the form of invasion by grasses and bamboo and thus prevented forest regrowth, especially if the grasses were repeatedly burnt. Second, in areas "degraded by soil erosion," recovery calls for artificial reforestation, a complex, costly, and time-consuming intervention strategy as bare land must first be planted with leguminous plant cover to restore nitrogen to the depleted soil, and then be replanted with successive species of plants to arrive ultimately at something resembling the original forest. For a country as poor as Vietnam this might be difficult to achieve. Swanson reports that reforestation needs amounted to about 20,000 km^2 and that U.S. and Vietnamese efforts resulted in reforestation of 12 km^2 in 1972, 60 km^2 in 1973, and 150 km^2 in 1974. Interestingly, the major emphasis was placed on planting nonnative teak, an especially valuable commercial hardwood timber. One difficulty involved "serious competition for forest land with other government agencies, particularly in relation to the resettlement of war refugees in rural areas." In the event, after the fall of Saigon, reforestation efforts stalled and were not renewed until 1995 (see table 2.2).[30]

Natural recovery is the third recovery possibility, but this appears to have occurred very slowly. In January 1983, Galston and Richards were able to visit Ma Da forest reserve, and they noted natural regrowth in about 20 percent of the sprayed area. "It is evident," they conclude, "that it will be many years before these forests will again approximate anything close to their original level of productivity by means of natural processes alone. It was further clear that the more severely damaged parts of the forest had been invaded [by undesirable species] and were liable to be burned during the dry season, a process that serves to perpetuate their presence." They further believe "that if there is to be substantial inland forest recovery within decades rather than centuries, fires must be controlled and silvicultural techniques must be applied to accelerate the natural regeneration process."[31] It is not entirely unreasonable to base such general conclusions on two brief visits (they also visited in 1971) at a single forest reserve, but one would have more confidence if more extensive field research had been carried out. Another visitor writes:

> Since the last spraying (14 years ago) the forest has not returned. Most of the land is covered with imperata grass. This grass dries out in the dry season, and it is either set on fire by Vietnamese hoping to use the land for agriculture, or it suffers from spontaneous combustion from electric storms. The repeated burnings prevent saplings from forming.[32]

Galston and Richards, as well as Carlton, were attending a scientific conference on the ecological and human effects of the U.S.-Vietnam War, held in Hanoi 13-20 January 1983. Also in attendance, Hiêp reports on the actual damage in Ma Da (table 2.2). Evidently, about 150 km² of rich and 470 km² of medium and poor inland forest were destroyed between 1965 and 1973. Examination of a 1981 satellite image and on-site inspection in 1982 "revealed almost no natural regeneration of forest trees," except in scattered areas along the forest margin. Another researcher, Peter Ashton, made two one-day visits to Ma Da, on sprayed and unsprayed areas, also in January 1983, in addition to examining aerial photographs from 1965, 1969, and 1972. The photographs and on-site inspection revealed that forest damage followed primarily the north-south spray pattern, that the opened-up areas were colonized by *Imperata cylindrica* and *Pennisetum polystachyon* grasses and, along the waterways, bamboo brakes. The on-site

Table 2.2.   Changes in Ma Da Forest Cover, 1965 to 1973 (in hectares)

	Pre-1965	1973
Inland forest	114,470	52,540
Rich	14,770	0
Medium plus poor	99,700	52,540
Treeless land	37,460	98,970
Cultivated land	16,500	16,920
Total	168,430	168,430

Source: Hiêp, 1984a, p. 32, table 2.B.1.

inspection showed recent burning. Importantly, Ashton noted "an abundance of bovine and cervid hoofprints as well as some elephant dung," and he adds that "it appears that ungulates are prospering on the young grass shoots that follow from burning." Also important is that comparison of the sprayed and unsprayed sites both showed similar soil and "abundant" tree flowering but "poor" fruit production. Thus, it appears that recurrent fire is the major culprit in preventing forest regrowth.[33]

In this regard, Phung Tuu Boi recently published the data displayed in table 2.3.[34] The original source for the table, which apparently refers to North and South Vietnam combined, is listed as the Vietnamese Ministry of Agriculture and Rural Development with the note that there are no accurate data available for the time period between 1943 and 1976. But the text accompanying the table states, as does Westing, that during the war *South* Vietnam alone had forests of 10,400 km². That does not appear to go well with the numbers provided in the table. Be that as it may, from 1976 to 1999 natural forest cover of about 1.5 million hectares was lost, which is approximately the cover gained by plantations. Overall forest cover appears to have been remarkably constant since 1976 but this is so only because of a remarkable trend reversal occurring between 1995 and 1999. In the twenty postwar years prior to 1995, Vietnam apparently lost as much natural forest cover as in the thirty-three years before 1976—which included the years of the Japanese occupation and the first and second Indochina wars.

There is little information as to the quality of Vietnam's natural forests today. Clearly, the war was not benign but neither, it appears, was the pre-1940 or post-1975 peace, at least not until 1995 when a deliberate reversal was sought, financed, and implemented. In light of the information assembled here, the scale of disruption might be ranked, using the gradation provided in table 1.2, as ranging between disturbance (transitory damage) and degradation (only partial recovery of the original ecosystem is expected but an ecosystem of comparable richness will emerge). It has not been possible to identify current information regarding the bulldozed and cratered areas.

2.2.3 Forest Fauna: Animal Ecology

Diminished forest cover and food resources, particularly for species depending on the more heavily affected upper tree story, led, Westing suggests, to depletion of invertebrate and vertebrate animal species. However, he does not report any data, nor does he refer to any studies from which

Table 2.3. Changes in Vietnamese Forest Cover, 1943 to 1999

	1943	1976	1980	1985	1990	1995	1999
			(in thousands of hectares)				
Natural forest	14,000	11,077	10,486	9,308	8,430	8,252	9,444
Plantation	0	92	422	584	745	1,050	1,471
Total	14,000	11,169	10,908	9,892	9,175	9,302	10,915
Percent of total land area	43.0	33.8	32.1	30.0	27.2	28.1	33.2

Source: Phung Tuu Boi (2002, p. 7, in Westing, et al., 2002).

one might learn any details. During a two-week visit to Hanoi and Ho Chi Minh City, Constable took a single 200 km countryside trip from Hanoi to the Chinese border. He also interviewed Vietnamese scientists and officials. According to these, "larger wildlife has been essentially eliminated," apparently referring to the Mekong Delta. This is attributed not to the war but to forest conversion to cultivation under the French colonial regime. Constable notes continued forest cutting as a wildlife threat generally and hunting for primates specifically. Because he was part of the 1970s AAAS HAC team, it is surprising that Constable writes with respect to the herbicide effect:

> The toxic effects of the arsenical Agent Blue, used patchily for crop destruction, is not long-lasting and was not used extensively enough to have much effect on the wildlife. Agent Orange, however, the defoliant that in fact killed so much of the forest and mangrove, remains an open question as much for its effects on wildlife as on man. The mangroves are re-vegetating, but the most desirable species have to be hand-planted. The inland forests, some of which lost as many as three-quarters of their older trees, seem to have retained seedlings capable of regenerating as long as the clearing, originally the result of herbicide destruction, is not maintained by cultivation. For some species the destruction of the large trees and consequent increase in undergrowth has probably been beneficial, and even in the most extensively defoliated areas there were usually skip zones that could serve as refuges for the larger or more wide-ranging species.[35]

Constable continues with some remarks regarding elephants, koupreys, birds, and primates. All together, these are important observations and comments, at a time when "biodiversity" had yet to become a common term, but nonetheless they amount to anecdotes. Tellingly, Mark Leighton opens his article on terrestrial animal ecology in Vietnam with this statement: "Perhaps in no other aspect of the long-term consequences of chemical warfare in Viet Nam are we as ignorant as in the effects on the animal component of the inland forest." The reason for this is that there are no baseline faunal data for the time periods before, during, and after the Vietnam War. This absence of baseline data does not mean that we cannot learn about the effect of war on animal life. For instance, population densities can be compared between sprayed and unsprayed areas. But the "daunting list" of biotic and abiotic factors that "define the niche of each tropical forest animal" and the lack of knowledge about "the causes of local site-to-site variation in animal abundance" make it "difficult to maintain that specific population densities after the fact are the result of chemical applications *per se*, rather than from the habitat transformations that have occurred following attack by herbicides."[36]

As for the case of inland plant ecology, it is not unreasonable to stipulate that herbicide attacks led to direct vertebrate and invertebrate animal fatalities and to migration to unsprayed areas where carrying capacity might have been strained, possibly leading to additional deaths. Indeed, field trials with Agent Orange on various animal taxa indicated toxicity for individual animals. But the death of individuals does not imply the death of a species. One can surmise environmental disruption, but because it is of unknown extent one cannot infer degradation, depletion, or destruction.

On the argument that floral habitat destruction will induce changes in faunal composition, a stronger case can be made from the theory of ecology. Some sprayed inland forest areas were permanently invaded by new plant species, providing shelter and livelihood to new animal species. This of course is a process not uniquely attributable to war. At any rate, mammalian and avian studies conducted in A Lưới Valley, west of Danang, near Vietnam's border with Laos, show a reduced vertebrate species count in sprayed as contrasted to comparable unsprayed areas. Data on invertebrates are not reported. Of all woody vegetation, the dense inland forests were and are the most species rich; they were also subject to the largest expenditure of herbicides. One may infer that a large number of species was affected; conversely, one must then also infer that induced species growth was large in the areas converted by herbicidal attacks to successional forest and open grassland. This does not mean that there are now more species, merely larger populations extending their habitat into the converted areas. But neither do we know that there are fewer species, merely—most likely—smaller populations, in the attacked areas. To show how complicated the situation is, consider a mammalian census carried out in 1981 and 1982 on geographically comparable sprayed and unsprayed habitat sites in A Lưới Valley. Of twenty-seven species, twenty-five were present prior to spraying. After spraying, twenty-four were still present, although in reduced, at times much reduced, numbers (rodents, though, increased). But on the unsprayed control site only eight species are listed as present! (Oddly, the authors do not comment on the status of the other nineteen species in the unsprayed area.)[37]

The urgent need to establish baseline data becomes abundantly clear. Environmentalists and conservationists worldwide must agree on a strategy to collect and to continuously update baseline data (land, air, and still and flowing waters, including the oceans) and for representative samples to be drawn from all biomes. It is also important to settle on a sensible, operational definition of biodiversity and on a scale by which environmental disruptions may be graded. There is no question that large numbers of individual plants died in Vietnam as a consequence of herbicidal attack, and that associated floral and faunal species were adversely affected. But this opened up space for colonization by other floral and faunal species. There is no evidence of species extinction, only evidence of changes in species frequency and composition. What is and remains unclear is the overall ecological effect of the war.

2.2.4 Herbicide Persistence, Mobility, and Soil Ecology

Massive herbicide-induced leaf abscission (defoliation), it was thought, causes leaf falling, leaf decomposition, nutrient loss to, and accelerated soil erosion of, the local ecosystem. These effects are sustained until refoliation or replacement vegetation emerges in the subsequent growing season. The direct effects depend upon the applied herbicide amounts, the density of the vegetative cover, the duration of herbicide storage in the soil, the nature of herbicide decomposition (whose elements may be more toxic than the parent compound), and on the eventual transport either from soil to micro- and macroflora or, via water infiltration, runoff, and evaporation, out of the affected area.[38] Zinke reports on dioxin persistence and finds dioxin traces in soil and sediment samples, cultured vegetation (oats and soybeans), and aquatic life (fish and shrimp) but, beyond detection, does not report damage or threshold levels.

Nutrients, especially nitrogen, potassium, as well as phosphorus, are stored in vegetation. Massive defoliation without vegetative regrowth is likely to lead to nutrient losses through water runoff, erosion, or leaching. Zinke reports on several studies that found reduced nutrient counts, especially among steeply banked forested areas and among mangrove stands, and increased counts in downstream or depressed shallows which essentially served as nutrient catchment areas. However, he does not say what one may conclude from this information, only that "many questions remain" and that "it is essential that these be answered because of the utility of herbicide use in tropical agriculture and forestry. To deny such use because of lack of answers, or because of the emotions attached to the wartime use of herbicides, would be unfortunate."[39]

In an earlier study Zinke is more explicit: "Opinions and conclusions concerning effects of any disturbances (such as defoliation) of the forest soil fertility, unless based upon adequate numbers of samples taken in a random (unbiased) manner, are to be considered as doubtful conclusions subject to the biases of the observer. This pertains to the results of this study as well" (which ended with an inadequate number of samples). Still, comparing defoliated with nondefoliated sites seven years after herbicide application, Zinke found "significant changes," namely a one-third reduction in phosphorus and a one-tenth reduction in nitrogen in the defoliated areas. Soil acidity also increased (i.e., lower pH levels). A paper by Huay and Cu is more detailed. They sampled soils from five sprayed and unsprayed but otherwise comparable sites: (1) alluvium on level forested mountain valleys; (2) brown soil overlying alluvium on level forested plateaus; (3) red ferralite overlying sandstone on steep, forested mountain slopes; (4) red ferralite overlying granite on steep, forested mountain slopes; and (5) saline muck on level, forested mangrove sites. For each, they measured total organic matter, total nitrogen, total and available phosphorus, exchangeable calcium, exchangeable magnesium, mobile iron, mobile aluminum, and active exchange and hydrolytic acidity. The results are interesting, even if not well interpreted. For example, total organic matter decreased on the sloped sites (soil erosion) and increased on the level sites (soil accumulation): soil washed down mountain slopes into valley catchment areas. Total nitrogen increased on two of the five sites (both level). Phosphorus, calcium, magnesium, and mobile aluminum appeared to follow no particular pattern. Mobile iron was reduced on all sprayed sites. Soil acidity appeared relatively unaffected in inland forest and mangrove forests.[40]

Persistence and mobility are determinants of long-term environmental effects of herbicide spraying. The former refers to herbicide effectiveness over time, that is, retention, natural decay, leaching, and the like. Retention, for example, depends on soil type. Mobility can have two effects. One is thinning, as herbicide dispersion takes place over space and time; the other is thickening, or ecological amplification through food web accumulation. Dioxin is generally not downwardly mobile; lateral movement does occur, primarily by water and wind transport.[41] The herbicides consisted of differently proportioned mixtures of base chemicals, plus various inert materials and contaminants such as the dioxin in Agent Orange. In tested plant species, the chemical 2,4-D, contained in 48 percent of the total spray, reaches environmental insignificance within about one month. For 2,4,5-T, used in 44 percent of the total spray, this takes about five months. Eighteen months to environmental insignificance is the number for picloram, about 2 percent of total spray, and for dimethyl arsinic acid, the remaining 6 percent, it is about one week. Trace elements can be found for longer time periods but would not obviously affect the plants' health.

Agent Orange field trials conducted in South Vietnam showed that plant survival and growth ceased to be affected after four weeks for planted corn, 10 weeks for upland rice and peanuts, and 18 weeks for beans. Trials for Agent White resulted in insignificant damage after 10 weeks for corn and upland rice, 31 weeks for beans, and 24 weeks for peanuts. All are cultivated species. Blackman and co-authors conducted field trials in Vietnam and the Philippines and searched the literature for other countries. They found that:

- Herbicide effects are comparable across countries.
- Detection one and one-half years after application is possible only in cases where the most heavy applications took place.
- In mangrove areas "the levels were such that the likelihood of damage to crops that could be grown under these conditions can be discounted."
- There were no herbicidal effects on mangrove seedlings.
- No "phytotoxic residues could in general be detected" in areas sampled one and one-half years after application.
- A variety of crops could safely be grown on affected soils within about six months.

They conclude: "Claims that the herbicides as they were used during the war have rendered the soil 'sterile,' permanently or at least for prolonged periods, are without any foundation."[42]

Similar trials for mangroves resulted in similar findings. Moreover, seedlings transplanted into treated soil forty days after spraying showed survival rates similar to those transplanted to untreated soil. Herbicide persistence apparently did not pose a problem. Agent Orange contained dioxin, which possesses an environmental half-life of about three and a half years. Still, assuming for the sake of an exercise that of the estimated 170 kg of dioxin used all was released in 1968 and that half degenerated nearly immediately through photodecomposition, then "perhaps 8 kg remained present in 1980, 3 kg in 1985, and 1 kg will presumably be present in 1990." By this calculation, residual dioxin should be reduced to about 0.02 kg by the year 2010 (figure 2.1), but scattered by natural transport (wind, water) over a larger surface area than when first released.[43]

2.2.5 Coastal, Marine, and Aquatic Ecology
All contributors agree that mangrove forests were heavily affected by herbicide spraying. Following helicopter overflights and brief ground surveys

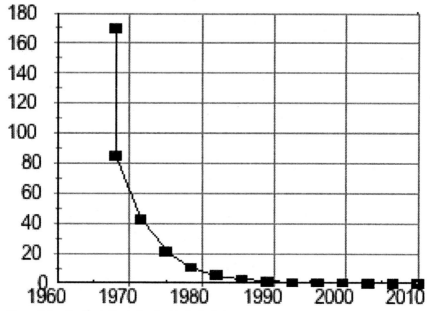

Figure 2.1.   Residual dioxin (vertical axis: kg/ha).

in August and September 1970, while the war was ongoing, Constable and Meselson write with regard to the mangrove stands around and south of Saigon that "we are deeply impressed by the total destruction of *all* vegetation even by a single spraying and by the absence of any mangrove seedlings or other evidence of forest regeneration." This was three years after the spraying. They continue: "In these devastated areas most of the animals and birds must have been driven out or perished as a result of being cut off from a new habitat by excessive distance or waterways." E. W. Pfeiffer, who visited Vietnam in March 1969 (with ornithologist Orians) and in the summer of 1971 (with forester Westing), provides a good description of growth patterns and ecological function of mangroves. In an account published in 1990, he suggests that "natural regeneration is occurring at a very slow rate—and not necessarily because of the residual effect of herbicides" but because of huge numbers of herbivorous crabs that in the absence of mangrove leaves feed on mangrove seedlings, inhibiting natural regrowth. In addition, in the follow-on effects of the large-scale herbicidal mangrove destruction, soil became subject to erosion both by flooding into the Mekong Delta and by wake action from ships going to Saigon. Furthermore, people began to move into the denuded areas, and they harvested dead wood for fuel and began human encroachment on the mangrove swamps.[44]

Of the 5,000 km² of mangrove stands in South Vietnam, about 3,000 km² were so-called true swamp mangroves, and the remainder were rear mangroves. The former received heavy spraying, 41 percent or 1,240 km², the latter about 13 percent or 270 km². Mangroves were highly sensitive to the applied herbicide and usually died with a single spraying. Salvage of dead limbs and trees (e.g., for fuel wood) further depleted the ecosystem and contributed to significant soil erosion. "Little if any immediate recolonization occurred" on the affected areas. Food and cover was correspondingly affected, probably leading to the reduction in observed bird numbers, especially insectivorous and frugivorous birds. But the number of observed fish-eating birds were not as reduced as had been expected. Hiêp studied one mangrove site on Ca Mau peninsula for 1965 and 1973 and found a 62 percent reduction in *Rhizophora*, the most important mangrove genus, or from 533 to 201 km² of the 649 km² site. Treeless land increased accordingly from 71 to 364 km² and cultivated land from 0 to 21 km². A field visit in 1980 showed minimal *Rhizophora* regeneration.[45]

Westing describes how the aquatic fauna in mangrove stands could be and has been affected and writes that, consequently, there were "indications of post-war declines in . . . offshore fishery . . . attributed to the wartime spraying." But he later writes that "whether this phenomenon finds its roots in the wartime herbicidal attacks . . . has not been demonstrated." In fact, other data by Westing (reported below) suggest that the herbicides used in the war may not have persisted sufficiently long to affect postwar fishery. In the four years between the end of herbicide spraying (1971) and the end of the war (1975) the herbicides would have degraded to negligible amounts. Regarding inland fisheries, one study suggests that long-lasting herbicidal effects on algae and aquatic invertebrate production subsequently reduced food availability for vertebrate fish and thereby reduced catches.[46]

As in the case of inland forests, Westing suggests possible effects on coastal, marine, and aquatic flora and fauna. From the known general ecological relation between habitat type and size and number and density of species, he suggests that a 10 percent reduction in mangrove habitat might lead over time to a 3 to 4 percent "loss in the indigenous plant and animal species." This is not unreasonable but conjectural. Snedaker puts the matter forcefully: "For these aquatic and semi-aquatic ecosystems, the full range of potential acute effects are matters of speculation, as are the longer-term chronic effects, including the important question of the rate at which the affected ecosystems will recover." In what is becoming a refrain, Snedaker concentrates his writing on the mangrove ecosystem because "little is known about the basic ecology of Viet Nam's aquatic freshwater ecosystems," and he laments "the relative paucity of information and data that can be interpreted in a rigorous manner."[47]

Even with regard to estuarine and marine areas affected by spray or spray drift, Snedaker writes that "there are essentially no data available upon which estimates can be developed for determining the impact on these water areas." The only definitive conclusion that one may draw is that one specific species of mangrove tree, *Rhizophora apiculata*—the predominant species—was directly affected by herbicide spraying. Its mortality followed the spray path. By 1981, 220 km² had been replanted. Some sprayed mangrove areas were subsequently colonized by palms, preventing recolonization by true mangroves. By the early 1980s, it was unclear whether these invading species should be controlled and *Rhizophora apiculata* replanting continued. Barren areas in the Rung Sat mangrove forest covered about 2 or 3 percent prior to the war and 35 percent thereafter. These areas were already marginal, vulnerable, and located around the fringes of Rung Sat. It appears that "the herbicidal destruction of these marginal areas magnified and accelerated the natural geomorphic process," as a result of which no mangrove regeneration is expected. Good evidence exists on abnormally high estuarine turbidity within and around mangrove areas. Although the ultimate source of that turbidity is unknown, it is associated with detrimental effects on "primary (green-plant) productivity and on the estuarine and near-shore filter feeders." In addition, turbidity can affect water drainage and circulation, thereby changing water salinity gradients. However, these points of general knowledge have not been studied for Vietnam. They remain hypotheses. Moreover, "there is no evidence to confirm the presence of toxic materials in the areas of accretion, nor is there confirmatory evidence that any of the various colonizing forms are inhibited or affected by toxic materials."[48]

As before, hypotheses of likely effects of herbicide spraying on estuarine and marine environments can be developed from general knowledge of ecology. For example, "there exists a strong correlation between tropical estuarine environments dominated by mangrove vegetation and the commercial yields of penaeid shrimp." But there are no "useful comparative data available that indicate the fishery yields obtained for a given level of fishing effort." To the contrary, there is "a paucity of direct evidence on the probable effect of herbicides on the estuarine and marine biota." Without disputing that offshore fishery catches declined, Snedaker observes that after the war, many Vietnamese emigrated using fishing vessels as their means of escape. With an estimated decline of 60 to 70 percent in fishing vessels, one would expect to find declines in total fish catch as well, Snedaker argues. This would be compounded by poorly maintained vessels and fishing gear. Thus, it is not clear whether declines in fish yield are attributable to herbicides or infrastructure failings. Other scholars also were "unable to relate the observed [estuarine] effects directly to chemical toxicity of the herbicides" and "unable to state whether or not the reported changes [in fishery yields] were due to herbicides and their indirect effects or to the overall effects of the war on the fishing 'effort' required to maintain a sustained annual harvest."[49]

With respect to freshwater streams and lakes, "there is essentially no valid information available on Viet Nam that would permit specific conclusions on the long-term consequences to aquatic ecosystems of the wartime use of herbicides." Two studies carried out in A Lưới Valley found an absolute drop in species count and algae deformation (morphological aberration). While Snedaker does not find it possible to attribute these findings to herbicide use, it is clear that he attributes this to the war and its various forms of damage-inflicting means other than herbicide use. Yen and Quynh sampled two sites, a river and a lake, in 1981 and 1982 in the South Vietnamese A Lưới Valley. Regrettably, the results are not clearly reported ("a total of 24 species were recorded, substantially less than would be found in a comparable unsprayed location"), but at least some species were recognized as colonizers from North Vietnam. Locals reported reduced catch (reduced biomass) as well. Many aquatic plants expected to be found were absent, as were plant-feeding fish. Aquatic invertebrates were reduced in numbers (shrimp, crab, snails, mussels, water fleas) or altogether missing (certain worms, larval two-winged flies, mountain crabs). Conversely, certain insects with aquatic larvae had increased in number, as did fish feeding on them.[50]

Regarding herbicide persistence and bioaccumulation, Snedaker writes unequivocally that "the very limited laboratory analyses of residual herbicides and their breakdown products in aquatic or marine sediments indicate that most do not persist at concentrations that warrant concern." He continues: "The meagre data do not suggest that these materials are biologically accumulated or magnified to a significant degree . . . [but] . . . there are no corresponding data for the Viet Nam situation, thus making it difficult to arrive at a viable conclusion." This is not to say that there have not been or are no short- or long-term deleterious effects, only that there are no studies upon which to base conclusions. This was true in 1984. As the next subsection details, additional scientific information has since then become available that qualifies Snedaker's writings somewhat.[51]

2.2.6 Long-Term Effects

Long-term effects on Vietnam's inland forests depend on a large variety of factors such as "pre-spray conditions of the stand; frequency and season of original spraying; species composition; steepness and other features of the terrain; local climate; areal extent of damage; availability of a seed source; and subsequent fire history." For areas sprayed once or twice, poor recovery might be expected in three or four decades (that is, by between 2000 and 2010), and full recovery might take eighty to one hundred years. For areas sprayed more than twice, the stands were usually so damaged (nutrient loss, soil depletion, and subsequent soil erosion) that replacement vegetation encroached, usually grassy cover. The areas were subsequently invaded by humans who repeatedly burned the grass cover, thereby preventing forest regrowth. Encroachment expanded into forest fringes, exacerbating the original area of forest damage. A comparison of two unsprayed forest areas with a sprayed, and subsequently burned, area revealed 145 and 170 bird species, respectively, in the unsprayed areas and only twenty-four in the sprayed and burned area. For mammals, the numbers were thirty and fifty-five as against five. This does not mean that the species became extinct or even locally extirpated, only that their habitat shrank. Non-avian and non-mammalian species counts in the grassland (sprayed and burned) area are not reported. The area may be equally, but differently, biodiverse.[52]

Regarding the 1,240 km^2 of destroyed true mangroves, De Sylva and Michel write that "it may be concluded that defoliation of the mangrove area of the Rung-Sat Special Zone probably did not have a permanently damaging effect on the estuarine ecology of SVN [South Vietnam]. Biological productivity appears to be sufficiently high, although far from optimum, to permit the survival and feeding of a variety of organisms living in the estuary." The major problem De Sylva and Michel note is siltation and the possibility of follow-on problems not then studied. Westing undertook a "rough field survey" in 1980 and found the following resettlement pattern: about 5 to 10 percent barren patches; only 1 percent natural mangrove regeneration; 10 percent artificial mangrove regeneration (plantings); 5 to 6 percent conversion to rice and other crops; and 75 percent natural regeneration with less desirable species (ferns, palm, poorer-quality mangroves). Where true mangrove stands did regenerate (naturally or by planting), closed canopy might be expected within one or two decades (say, during the 1990s) and a "harvestable crop of wood (small timbers and firewood) in perhaps four or five decades." An early study by Davis found essentially no adverse permanent effect on various species of mollusks in the Rung Sat mangrove area. But another study found that deforested mangrove areas were being populated by disease-carrying mosquitoes and rats at rates much higher than in unaffected mangrove areas.[53]

Concern lingered, of course, particularly about the long-term effects on humans. In this regard, a useful, more recent set of papers comes from a U.S. National Institutes of Health cosponsored U.S.-Vietnamese scientific conference held in Hanoi, 3-6 March 2002, on the long-run effects of dioxin. The conference contained relatively few papers dealing specifically with Vietnam.[54] The approach frequently taken is that of studying comparable organisms in comparable habitats to arrive at conclusions by inference. In this vein, Giesy reports, with regard to fish and fish reproduction in the North American Great Lakes, that "currently it is felt that PCDD and PCDF and some of the non- and mono-ortho-substitute PCBs are responsible for blue-sac disease and impaired reproductive performance of lake trout in the lower Great Lakes" and that measures of TCDD dioxin toxic equivalents (TEQ) are "near the threshold for mortality in lake trout fry." However, recent discoveries have shown that "some of the effects that have been attributed to OCs [organohalogen compounds] might be due to thiamine (vitamin B1) deficiency" and other causes. Moreover, Cohen and Nacci report the discovery that populations of *Fundulus heteroclitus*, a common estuarine prey fish, sampled from contaminated and uncontaminated areas along the U.S. Atlantic coast "inherited tolerance to the toxic effects of local chemicals," especially PCBs. This is an example of "chemically adapted populations" in which dioxin-like compounds act as "selective agents." In particular, "some percentage of the population will have antigen-binding receptors . . . that will be able to recognize that pathogen and prevent disease from developing. . . . These results suggest that exposures to persistent, bioaccumulative and toxic contaminants may be producing evolutionary effects on a geographic scale larger than previously considered." This is an important finding since it would suggest why fish-eating humans in particular continue to show elevated TCDD levels (see summary of findings below).[55]

Embryo deformities and lethality among fish-eating birds in the Great Lakes region show a correlation to uptake of PCDD, PCDF, and PCBs at population levels but are due "to the toxic effects of multiple compounds." Among fish-eating mammals—otters, mink—researchers also find susceptibility to the toxins, especially among mink (*Mustela vison*), which "are one of the most sensitive organisms to the effects of dioxin equivalents."[56]

Globally, van den Berg, et al., however, find evidence of a declining organohalogen compound threat to fish-eating wildlife as OCs disperse over space and degrade over time. On Midway Island in the Pacific Ocean two species of albatross (the black-footed albatross, *Diomedea nigriceps*, and the Laysan albatross, *Diomedea immutabilis*) were observed. Adverse population-level reproductive effects on account of OCs were 2 to 3 percent for the black-footed albatross (and not stated but implied as zero for the Laysan albatross). In contrast, reproductive success was impeded by fishery by-kill: "Adult loss and widowing was estimated to result in a decrease in reproduction of 17.6 percent for the Laysan Albatross and 27.2 percent for the black-footed Albatross." Regarding the common tern (*Sterna hirundo*) and great cormorant (*Phalacrocorax carbo*) in western Europe, studies showed differences in hatching and breeding success in line with contamination levels at breeding sites for the latter but "no overt effects on growth and development." In the Great Lakes region in the United States, populations of herring gull (*Larus argentatus*), double-crested cormorant (*Phalacrocorax auritus*), common tern and Forster's tern (*Sterna forsteri*), and bald eagle (*Haliaeetus leucocephalus*) decreased through dioxin-like contamination. But "concomitant with the observed declines of the concentrations of first DDT and later dioxin-like compounds, populations of several avian species have been restored." Finally, studies on marine mammals also point to strong correlation between exposure to dioxin-like compounds and lack of reproductive success but "one should consider this generalization with caution," particularly for seals, as declines in pollution are associated with declines in reproductive impairment. "This may suggest that the majority of seal populations and communities are still affected by chronic and insidious, rather than acute OC-induced impacts on reproduction and population health." In terms of the classification offered in table 1.2, these effects would be environmental disturbances since full recovery of the population is expected were it not for the presence of pollutants from ongoing anthropogenic causes other than war.[57]

Bioaccumulation, chemical adaptation and selection, and degrading[58] of dioxin-like compounds emerge as the primary issues. This appears to be borne out, specifically for human populations in Vietnam (and, to a smaller extent, in Cambodia and Laos), by an examination of 64 peer-reviewed studies. The upshot is a strong, continuing correlation (but declining in strength over time) between dioxin-spraying and dioxin uptake in breast milk and blood lipid samples in fish-eating South Vietnamese populations living in or near sprayed areas. For humans, "elevated" exposure levels are those greater than 5 parts per trillion (>5 ppt) TCDD. There is an unmistakable gradation in exposure levels among North, Central, and South Vietnamese populations. People moving south from other areas of the country are shown to have experienced toxin accumulation after moving. Sediment and fish and shrimp samples show elevated levels. However, TEQs were high, in part "due to contributions from other dioxins not characteristic of Agent Orange," and sediment sample pollution in South Vietnam is not dissimilar to sediment pollution in the North American Great Lakes and in Alpine lakes. Food samples collected in South Vietnam differ noticeably from those sampled from North Vietnam and from the Netherlands. Samples of turtle ovaries showed 250 ppt TCDD, of turtle liver 88 ppt, gall bladder 39 ppt, and snake muscle 11.6 ppt, but no comparative information is given for turtles and snakes in unsprayed areas nor whether these levels are of any significance to turtles and snakes. The review states that "to date, no elevations of TCDD in humans or in environmental samples have been found in Cambodia or Laos."[59]

Of particular relevance, if not surprising, is that two studies now appear to confirm that heavy perimeter spraying and/or spills at and near former U.S. military bases in Vietnam are strongly associated with elevated TCDD levels of nearby Vietnamese populations by the mid- to late 1990s. Measured concentrations in samples taper off the farther away is the population from the base. Elevated contamination levels are, however, not (yet) indisputably linked to particular diseases. The first study took samples in 1999 of soil, sediment, and human blood from around Bien Hoa, home to a former U.S. military base 35 km north of Saigon (Ho Chi Minh City). The second study was conducted between 1996 and 1999 in A Lưới Valley in Central Vietnam, with samples collected from the village of A So, a U.S. military base between 1963 and 1966. Samples were drawn from soil, fish fat, duck fat, pooled human blood, and human breast milk. It now seems a settled issue among scientists that the chain of transmission goes from dioxin contamination of Agent Orange to soil and sediment contamination to uptake by aquatic life to uptake by humans. To find answers to questions about soil and sediment disturbance and transport becomes urgent. Importantly, however, the second study found essentially no contamination of vegetable matter. Contamination of humans through bioaccumulation and biomagnification thus appears to take place via aquatic life that grazes on and ingests sediment particles. Obviously, soil, sediment, and aquatic life near other former military bases should be tested. It also would be of interest to repeat the Cohen and Nacci study on chemical adaptation for pond-fish in Vietnam.[60]

2.3 In Sum

Military use of herbicides in Vietnam preceded its use by the United States. Herbicide use for large-area defoliation was tested at Camp Drum,

New York, and at Camp (then Fort) Detrick, Maryland, before making the chemicals available to South Vietnam, at the latter's urging. South Vietnam was particularly interested in crop destruction to deny food to the Vietcong. From 1961 until 1964 crop destruction spraying was carried out by South Vietnamese personnel using their own equipment. From the start of Operation Ranch Hand in November 1961 until October 1962 all spray missions conducted by U.S. personnel needed special Oval Office approval. Thereafter, decision-making authorization was delegated to the U.S. ambassador and to the U.S. military commander in South Vietnam. As the United States became more deeply involved in the war, so did its direct use of herbicides. Spraying peaked in 1967 at "1.7 million acres [6,883 km^2], 85 percent for defoliation and 15 percent for crop destruction."[61]

Agent Orange was in widespread private use in the United States. Between 1966 and 1969, about 32,400 km^2 in the United States were sprayed with 2,4,5-T, the ingredient containing the TCDD dioxin. According to the estimates by Stellman, et al., this compares to 16,797 km^2 sprayed in Vietnam from 1962 to 1971 with 2,4,5-T containing herbicides (of 26,313 km^2 overall).[62] Herbicide use within the United States had been deemed safe, just as use of the pesticide DDT had been deemed safe, but application on the scale employed in Vietnam, especially for areas receiving repeated spray applications and in large amounts per capita, raised safety questions.[63] Moreover, during the mid- to late 1960s, reports emerged of possible teratogenic effects (birth defects). Military use of Agent Orange was suspended in 1969. Domestic use in the United States was effectively banned in April 1970, leading to production stoppage. In Vietnam, the U.S. military continued to spray its existing stock. The last defoliation mission was flown on 9 May 1970, the last crop destruction mission on 7 January 1971.[64]

Beyond herbicides, a debate took place, among other places in the pages of *Science* and *Nature* in the late 1960s and early 1970s of asking how the United States would have fought the war without herbicides. The official U.S. assessment of the military use of herbicides was generally rather more favorable. To achieve similar military effects, either more bombing and more bulldozing would have been necessary; in light of the (scant) evidence presented in this chapter, this would likely have caused more harm to the environment than the herbicides did. Alternatively, more U.S. soldiers (and Vietnamese) would have had to fight and die.[65]

How shall one assess, in sum, the environmental evidence on Vietnam? Bombing affected about 40 percent of South Vietnam's land area, bulldozing another 2 percent, and herbicide applications about 10 percent. One can safely say that approximately half of South Vietnam was environmentally affected. Certainly, the effects were widespread. They were also severe and, in at least in one sense, long-lasting. They were severe for example in the millions of trees and other vegetation that undoubtably were injured and killed. Removal of vegetation deprives animals of food and shelter. Ecological succession takes decades, hence the effects were (and are) long-lasting. But every affected area is recolonized by plants and animals, and comparative studies of biological diversity are few. It is troubling that so much of this conclusion—widespread, severe, and long-lasting environmental effects—relies on ecological theory, even if well established, rather than on actual studies in Vietnam. In biology, theory predicts ex ante not as much as it explains ex post. And what studies have been done tend to tilt firm conclusions toward the cautionary side.

How does one assess the degree of disruption caused? For bomb cratering and vegetative recolonization with grass species, one may hazard to speak of environmental depletion (whereby an ecosystem of comparable richness may not reemerge); this would need empirical confirmation. In other cases, the less severe grade of degradation (partial recovery, whereby an altered ecosystem will emerge but with eventually comparable richness) may be the proper assessment, and in still other cases, the grade of disturbance (transitory damage and full recovery) appears warranted. Although it might have taken place, in no case do we know of environmental destruction (species extinction). The environmental disruption imposed by the United States on Vietnam was severe in some areas, was widespread in some areas, and was long-lasting in some areas, but we do not know for sure. Arthur Westing, that great contributor to the literature, himself repeatedly makes statements of this sort. For example, with respect to soil damage, he writes: "But to quantify this damage or otherwise suggest its level of importance appears not to be possible." With respect to nutrient cycling, he writes: "The overall level of this form of damage seems even more difficult to quantify than that attributable to the soil erosion." With respect to vegetation, he writes: "Whereas at least a rough estimate can be made for the trees, it is not feasible to attempt this for the remaining flora." With respect to fauna, he writes: "The fauna of Indochina underwent severe disturbance . . . most of it probably from habitat disruption. . . . How one evaluates the significance of such perturbations is hard to say."[66]

Notes

1. Non-Vietnam writings: Cambodia: 1972; Laos: 1981a; environmental aspects of international law of war: 1993. Also see Westing (1985) on unexploded

ordnance. Without source attribution: for example, Westing (1981b). Repetition/ reprinting: for example, Westing (1989) is a somewhat abridged but otherwise almost verbatim reprint of Westing (1984) which, in turn, is largely a summary of Westing (1976). Compared to the 1984 piece, the 1989 leaves out the effects on humans. I heartily thank Professor Westing for his thorough reading of and commenting on the penultimate version of this book's entire manuscript. As well as helping me find my way through his work, this helped eliminate some errors of fact and some, no doubt, of judgment.

2. Quoted passage from Westing (1989, p. 337).

3. 14 million tons: Westing (1976, p. 13, table 2.1). Westing refers to the period of active U.S. assistance with advisers, supplies, and combat troops, 1961–1973. Bombing distribution: Westing (1976, p. 14, table 2.2). Germany: this is the combined tonnage dropped by Britain's Royal Air Force and the U.S. Army Air Forces, The United States Strategic Bombing Survey (USSBS), September 30, 1945, p. 1; also see Brauer and van Tuyll, 2008, chapter 6). A further 1.3 million tons were expended in non-German European theaters of war, for instance in German-occupied territories such as France. (East and West) Germany's land area is about 350,000 km^2, (North and South) Vietnam's is 325,000 km^2. Portions of Cambodia and Laos were bombed as well, mostly along their respective borders with Vietnam, so that the land area of Germany and that of Vietnam and the bombed border areas is quite comparable.

4. Land area: Westing (1976, p. 19, table 2.5, note e). One km^2 equals 100 hectares (abbreviated ha). To find the corresponding number in hectares, add two zeroes to every number given in km^2.

5. Westing (1976, p. 20).

6. Westing and Pfeiffer (1972, p. 24).

7. Westing (1976, p. 48).

8. Westing (1976, pp. 53–55).

9. Quote: Westing (1976, p. 57). Effectiveness: Westing (1976, p. 59).

10. Herbicides as agents of war: An extensive annotated bibliography of materials published up to the mid-1980s is in Harnly (1988). Major research efforts revolved around three sets of studies: (1) those conducted by the Midwest Research Institute as commissioned by the U.S. Department of Defense and reported on in December 1967 (see Boffey, 1968); (2) those made by the American Association for the Advancement of Science's Herbicide Assessment Commission, reported on in late 1970 and early 1971; and (3) those conducted by the National Academy of Sciences, also commissioned by the Department of Defense, as mandated by the U.S. Congress, and reported on in 1974. Long-term studies are sparse and are discussed later in the main text. Operation Ranch Hand: see Buckingham (1982, 1983); Cecil (1986); Stellman, et al. (2003). Common agricultural use: see, for instance, Young (1988, p. 9).

11. TCDD is one of many dioxins, a family of structurally similar chemical compounds that permit chlorine atoms to occupy a number of positions in

the structure. There are some seventy-five possible structures (compounds) in polychlorinated dibenzo-dioxins (PCDDs) and another 135 compounds in the related polychlorinated dibenzo-furans (PCDFs). Dioxins and furans consist of a three-ring structure. Two paired, multiply chlorinated benzene rings are joined by a third ring which, in dioxins, contains two oxygen atoms and, in furans, one oxygen atom. Between one and eight chlorine atoms can be bound to the benzene rings in various combinations, for a total of 210 compounds, which collectively are referred to as dioxins. The most toxic is the PCDD with chlorine substitution in the 2, 3, 7, and 8 positions in the molecule, hence the moniker "2, 3, 7, 8-tetrachlorodibenzo-p-dioxin" (TCDD). Only seventeen other dioxins have an associated toxicity. To relate the toxicity of these dioxins to TCDD, it is common practice to use International Toxicity Equivalent Factors to calculate the total dioxin concentrations in terms of their equivalent toxicity (TEQ). Dosage information needs to be separated out from dose-response relations that, in turn, need to be separated from threshold levels per organism.

12. Dow Chemical: Dwernychuk, et al. (2002, p. 118). Young (1988, p. 11) shows that Agents Purple, Pink, and Green, precursors to Orange, contained dioxin content 16 times as high as that of Orange. These precursors were used from January 1962 to June 1965, Orange from July 1965.

13. *Scientific American* quote: *Scientific American* (1974, p. 49). Spray concentrations: Flamm and Cravens (1971, p. 786); Bethel, et al. (1975a, p. 30). In normal forestry operations, spray concentration would be commensurate to the species targeted. Bethel, et al. (1975a/b) have a useful background discussion. Content analysis and total release volume: see Rappe (1984, p. 179, and literature cited therein). Others claim up to 500 kg; see the report by Carlson (1983, p. 507). Recent work: Stellman, et al. (2003, pp. 682–684).

14. Drift: Orians, Pfeiffer, and Leuba (1969, p. 442). Expense: Constable and Meselson (1971, p. 6). Agent Blue: Constable and Meselson (1971, p. 6); Young (1988, p. 11). Quote: Buckingham (1983, p. 43).

15. Westing and other sources: Westing (1976, 1984, 1989); Young (1988). Dispute and change: see, for instance, Stellman, et al. (2003).

16. Young (1988, p. 14).

17. Services HERBS: Young (1988, pp. 12–13). Recoding: J. M. Stellman, et al. (2002; 2003); spray volume increase: 2003, p. 682; spray area increase: 2003, p. 685.

18. Newspapers: Buckingham (1983, pp. 44–45). AAAS HAC team: see Boffey (1971); Constable and Meselson (1971); Westing (1971). U.S. government forestry team: Flamm and Cravens (1971, p. 785). Mission Herbicide Review Commission: Flamm and Cravens (1971, pp. 788–789). U.S. Department of Agriculture: Tschirley (1969).

19. Quotes: Constable and Meselson (1971, p. 8). The authors were able to inspect one recently sprayed site in the Song Re Valley in Quang Ngai Province, as well as a refugee camp of Montagnard people. The authors note that "every

indicator of enemy presence relied upon by the chemical staff proved mistaken," so that crop destruction, at a minimum, was unnecessary (Constable and Meselson, 1971, p. 8). Doubtful: "At the scene of Waterloo or Gettysburg almost no trace of the battle remains, and even the scars of Verdun or Guadalcanal are hard to find; Vietnam's defoliated forests may be a more permanent memorial" (Constable and Meselson, 1971, p. 9). Young: Young (1988, p. 14).

20. Repeated herbicide applications: two herbicidal attacks resulted in an "estimated average mortality rate of 25 per cent"; three attacks in 50 percent; and four or more attacks in 85 to 100 percent (Westing, 1976, p. 31). Quotes: Westing (1989, p. 346); Westing (1989, p. 348).

21. All page references are to Tschirley (1969).

22. Merchantable timber losses: Westing (1971, p. 782); Flamm and Cravens (1971, p. 789, table 2). Ecological importance: Flamm and Cravens (1971, p. 788).

23. The exception concerned mangrove forest that "would not return to its natural state for perhaps a century without extensive reseeding" (Buckingham, 1983, p. 49; so, too, Norman, 1974, p. 186; Swanson, 1975, p. 368; and other sources).

24. Bethel, et al. (1975a, p. 56). Westing explicitly acknowledges that his calculations are based on assumed, not observed, tree densities of 100 m³/ha. He refers for that estimate to personal communication with Flamm in June 1970 (Westing, 1971, p. 781). Also see note 27 below. One can infer Flamm and Cravens' assumption from the numbers reported in their table 2 (1971, p. 789). They estimate a 10 percent to 20 percent tree kill on 900,000 ha, and 50 percent to 100 percent on a further 450,000 ha. For the first they estimate 13.50 million m³ loss, and for the second 33.75 million m³, for a total timber loss of 47.25 million m³/ha. Take a 15 percent average kill for the first area (0.15 x 900,000 = 135,000 ha) and a 75 percent average kill for the second (0.75 x 450,000 = 337,500) to arrive at a 100 percent equivalent kill for 472,500 ha. Thus, estimated timber losses of 47.25 million m³ divided into 472,500 ha, yield exactly 100 m³/ha. There is no reference to prewar forest density data.

25. Quote: Bethel, et al. (1975a, p. 56). Ground observations were also carried out, but in limited fashion as the war was ongoing at the time (Bethel, et al., 1975b, p. 229). Average density: Bethel, et al. (1975a, p. 59).

26. Nonmerchantable timber losses were estimated by the NAS as between 5.6 and 11.9 million m³, somewhat higher than the South Vietnam Forest Service estimate.

27. In addition to information gleaned from Barry Flamm (see note 24 above), Westing made the 100 m³/ha assumption based on his own observations, from helicopter overflights and some ground inspections, and based on discussions with South Vietnamese foresters. The estimate also matched Westing's Cambodian and North Vietnamese experiences. A debate on this took place in the pages of the *Journal of Forestry*: see Westing (1974; 1975) and Bethel, et al. (1975a; 1975b). The

latter group argues that prewar vegetation estimates would have been available to Westing (1975b, p. 233). Westing still believes that the NAS value is far off the mark (Westing, personal communication to the author, 31 May 2008).

28. Substantial prewar depletion: see Bethel, et al. (1975a; 1975b) and literature cited therein; Flamm and Cravens (1971); Westing (1971, p. 781). Both quotes: Swanson (1975, p. 368).

29. Considerable debate: Norman (1974, p. 187). Reprimanded: Bethel, et al. (1975a, p. 60). Quotes: Bethel, et al. (1975a, pp. 61, 58). The NAS report noted that nonherbicidal destruction, bulldozing, and bombing, "had had a worse effect on inland forests than had the herbicides" (Buckingham, 1983, p. 49). Agreed: Westing (1971, p. 782). Those interested in the internal squabble at the NAS may wish to read the account by Shapley (1974).

30. Quotes: Galston and Richards (1984, pp. 39, 41). Reforestation: Swanson (1975, p. 368, table 1); quote: p. 370.

31. Galston and Richards (1984, pp. 41, 42). Silviculture: regulating the establishment, growth, composition, health, and quality of forests.

32. Carlson (1983, p. 509).

33. Quotes: Hiêp (1984a, p. 32); Ashton (1984, pp. 35, 36).

34. Phung Tuu Boi (in Westing, et al., 2002).

35. Quotes: Constable (1981–1982, pp. 250, 252). Constable, however, was a plastic surgeon and had neither trained nor professional experiences in botany, zoology, forestry, or ecology.

36. All quotes: Leighton (1984, p. 53).

37. Avian: Leighton (1984, p. 55). Mammalian: Huynh, et al. (1984).

38. Zinke (1984, pp. 75-77).

39. Quotes from Zinke (1984, p. 80).

40. Quotes from Zinke (1974, p. 38). Huay and Cu (1984, p. 72).

41. Retention: see reference 2 in S.D. Stellman, et al. (2002, p. 1). Mobility: Olie (1984, p. 175).

42. Field trials: information from Westing (1989, pp. 349–350). Blackman, et al. (1974, pp. 56–58); quotes from pp. 57, 58.

43. Dioxin half-life: Olie (1984, p. 175) computes five years; Westing (1978, p. 290) computes 1.3 years. The half-life depends on a variety of environmental factors. Quote: Westing (1989, p. 351). Westing (1978) does not find reports on dioxin-related effects on flora, but faunal and human effects are reported based on four dioxin-release episodes (in South Vietnam, in northwest Florida, in eastern Missouri, and in northern Italy). At average concentrations of 46 to almost 1.4 million times as high as those in South Vietnam, these can result in immediate injury and rapid death mediated by skin uptake, through direct ingestion of plant matter, or indirect uptake via bioaccumulation in the food web. For further discussion of dioxin, see section 2.2.6.

44. Quotes: Constable and Meselson (1971, pp. 6, 7); Pfeiffer (1990, p. 40).

45. Quote: Westing (1989, p. 348). Birds: Orians and Pfeiffer (1970, p. 548). Ca Mau: Hiêp (1984b).

46. Offshore fisheries: Westing (1989); quotes pp. 348, 353–354. First quote based on Westing (1983, pp. 377–380). Inland fisheries: as reported in Westing (1989, p. 354).

47. Quote: Westing (1989, p. 349); based on findings reported in Westing and Westing (1981). Based on "comparable habitats" in the East Indies and Galápagos, Westing (1983, p. 379) suggests that a 10 percent mangrove habitat loss in Vietnam may lead to a 3 and 4 percent species reduction, respectively, in plants and birds in the affected mangrove habitat. Snedaker (1984): quotes pp. 94, 95. The relation between habitat loss and species loss — the so-called species-area relationship, or SAR — is conjecturally straightforward but the theoretical and empirical details are not. Species require a minimum range. If this is cut to below the requisite minimum, species can become locally extinct. However, much depends on species distribution and abundance levels within the range and on the precise way in which habitat is lost and whether or not the loss involves habitat fragmentation. A foundational work is MacArthur and Wilson (1967). A recent piece qualifying some of the early thoughts and findings reported in the literature is, for instance, Ney-Nifle and Mangel (2000, especially figure 3 on p. 897). In some instances, actual species losses are far higher than those predicted under older theoretical assumptions; in others, they are lower.

48. Snedaker (1984). Quotes from pp. 96, 100, 101, 104.

49. Fishing vessels: Snedaker (1984, p. 105). Quotes: Snedaker (1984, pp. 98–99), and summarizing De Sylva and Michel (1974, p. 119).

50. Quote: Snedaker (1984, pp. 100). War, not herbicides: Snedaker (1984: pp. 104–105). Quote: Yen and Quynh (1984, p. 92).

51. Quotes: Snedaker (1984, p. 101).

52. Quote: Westing (1989, p. 352). Numbers: Westing (1989, p. 353).

53. Quotes and materials from De Sylva and Michel (1974, p. 117); Westing (1989, p. 353); Davis (1974, pp. 23–26); Lesowitz, et al. (1974, pp. 46, 51).

54. Most of the papers authored by Vietnamese scientists were not available online as of 7 March 2008, even though *Nature* reported that they were supposed to be translated into English; see *Nature*, vol. 416, no. 6878 (21 March 2002), p. 252.

55. Comparable habitats: Westing (1983, p. 379). Great Lakes: Giesy (2002, pp. 1, 2). Atlantic Coast: Cohen and Nacci (2002; pp. 1, 2, 4).

56. Giesy (2002). Quotes p. 3.

57. Van den Berg, et al. (2002). Quotes pp. 2, 3, and 4.

58. Bunge, et al. (2003, abstract) find the presence of dioxin-eating bacteria: "*Dehalococcoides* species in four dioxin-dechlorinating enrichment cultures from a freshwater sediment highly contaminated with PCDDs and PCDFs. We also show that the previously described chlorobenzene-dehalorespiring bacterium *Dehalococcoides* sp. strain CBDB1 . . . is able to reductively dechlorinate selected dioxin congeners. Reductive dechlorination of 1, 2, 3, 7, 8-pentachlorodibenzo-p-dioxin (PeCDD) demonstrates that environmentally significant dioxins are attacked by this bacterium." It would be useful to search Vietnamese soil samples for the presence of these or similar bacteria.

59. Schecter, et al. (2002). Quotes pp. 2, 6. Sediment sample pollution: table 3, p. 4.

60. Two studies: Schecter, et al. (2001); Dwernychuk, et al. (2002). Cohen and Nacci (2002). On human effects in South Vietnam, also see Westing (1978, pp. 290–291).

61. Herbicide usage by Vietnam prior to use by U.S.: for instance, Buckingham (1983); Stellman, et al. (2003). Quote: Buckingham (1983, p. 44).

62. Stellman, et al. (2003, p. 685). Buckingham says that 6 million acres were sprayed in Vietnam. This would convert to about 24,300 km^2, a figure substantially higher than Westing's 16,700 km^2 but remarkably close to the Stellman, et al. (2003) estimate of 26,313 km^2.

63. Westing (1976, table 3.5, p. 29). Buckingham raises an interesting point. Studying disease and fatalities among Operation Ranch Hand soldiers—and they were studied extensively—would not necessarily reveal significant differences relative to the U.S. population at large since nearly every U.S. citizen would have received some dioxin contamination from the widespread private and commercial use of Agent Orange in the country. It is also useful to remember that marine biologist Rachel Carson's (1907–1964) famous book, *Silent Spring*, had been published only in 1962. In it she demonstrated the link between the pesticide DDT and death among birds (through eggshell thinning and reproductive failure). The book sparked a worldwide debate that changed public perception of industrial and agricultural chemistry. Instead of viewing chemistry as contributing to better life, many people began to take an antagonistic view toward chemical products.

64. Military use suspended: Constable and Meselson (1971, p. 6). Last missions flown: Buckingham (1983, p. 48); Young (1988, p. 12) gives slightly different dates: 6 June 1970, for Orange and 9 January 1971, for White and Blue.

65. Buckingham (1983, p. 52).

66. Westing (1976). Quotes pp. 66, 68-69, 69, 73.

The Persian Gulf War   3

To assess the effect of war on nature, one overriding fact makes the Persian Gulf War of 1991 a case study par excellence: we actually possess a relatively good set of pre- and postwar data as well as studies that use nonpolluted sites as controls. On 2 August 1990, Iraqi troops invaded Kuwait. Allied air forces entered the war on 16 January 1991; ground forces joined on 23 February. Following a cease-fire order issued by President George H. W. Bush, the war effectively ended on 28 February 1991. On 3 March, Iraqi authorities formally accepted cease-fire terms.[1]

With the start of the air war, Iraq began firing Kuwaiti wells at Wahfra oil field on 16 January 1991. Three days later, on 19 January 1991, Sea Island oil terminal storage tanks were opened to release oil into the Persian Gulf. The oil flow stopped on 26 January. The oil reached its southernmost contamination point on 21 February 1991, at Abu Ali Island, about halfway down the Saudi Arabian coast. Estimates of oil releases range from 0.5 to 12 million barrels in all. Even though the exact amount cannot be determined, the most frequently cited estimate is a range of 6 to 8 million barrels (at 42 gallons each).

The firing of oil wells peaked on 22 February. The U.S. General Accounting Office (now called the Government Accountability Office) cites the National Oceanic and Atmospheric Administration (NOAA) finding that of a total of 904 oil wells, 611 were set on fire, 79 were gushing, 108 damaged, and 106 remained intact, before Iraqi troops started withdrawal on 23 February 1991. When the last oil well was capped, on 6 November 1991, in addition to the sea spillage, a total of perhaps 25–30 million barrels of oil had been spilled on land. The equivalent of a further estimated 4.6 million barrels of oil and natural gas were burning per day, and 12,000 tons of particles poured into the atmosphere daily. These numbers need to be seen in the context of an average annual volume of Gulf oil spills estimated at between 250,000 barrels, equal to the 1989 spill at Prince William Sound in Alaska, to more than one million barrels of oil per year. In addition, regularly occurring habitat destruction, such as of mangrove areas and coral reefs, on account of commercial development and land reclamation efforts had been commonplace.[2]

Information on damages suffered on Iraqi territory is scant.[3] While one must therefore focus on Kuwait and Saudi Arabia, it should at least be considered that the environmental, let alone human, impact of the war on Iraq was possibly worse than that on Kuwait and Saudi Arabia. Bombing of Iraqi weapons production and storage sites, destruction of industrial production facilities, and of water and sanitation infrastructure surely spewed some quantity of hazardous materials into the environment while limiting Iraq's ability to respond. Furthermore, the intense bombing and ground force movements that took place in the Iraqi desert and marsh areas will have led to some environmental disturbances. Unlike for Kuwait and Saudi Arabia, the international community did not (or could not) provide postwar environmental monitoring and remediation assistance to Iraq.

Section 3.1 details the scientific missions and data collection efforts undertaken in the wake of the war (3.1.1) and describes the geography and oceanography of the western Persian Gulf (3.1.2). Then follows an examination of the war's effects on the marine environments in section 3.2: the western Gulf's coast, supratidal, and intertidal areas (3.2.1); subtidal areas, benthic communities, bivalves, fish, shrimp, coral reefs, and islands (3.2.2); and marine mammals and turtles (3.2.3). As bird life in the Gulf revolves around marine resources, this is examined in section 3.3. Section 3.4 concludes. Close to twenty years have passed since the war. Long-term effects, where known, are discussed within each section. The bibliographic note in section 3.5 attends to effects on air pollution and the terrestrial environment, a full discussion of which could not be accommodated within the space constraints of the main text.

3.1 The Persian Gulf

3.1.1 Scientific Missions and Data Gathering
Unique among wars, the Persian Gulf War elicited a huge amount of scientific interest and political and financial support for damage assessment,

containment, restoration, and associated scientific study. For example, in Saudi Arabia the Meteorology and Environmental Protection Agency (MEPA), the Royal Commission for Jubail and Yanbu (RCJY), the National Commission for Wildlife Conservation and Development (NC-WCD), the King Fahd University of Petroleum and Minerals (KFUPM), and the petroleum giant Saudi ARAMCO cooperated with a large number and variety of international teams in oil containment and recovery, rescue operations, and restorative activities. In Kuwait, the Kuwait Institute for Scientific Research (KISR) was the main cooperative agency. The Regional Organization for the Protection for the Marine Environment (ROPME) supported many scholars. International assistance came from nongovernmental organizations such as the World Wide Fund for Nature and IUCN, the governments of the United States, Japan, and those of members of the European Union, as well as from international organizations such as the World Maritime Organization and others.

In addition, health complaints by U.S. soldiers following the war (Gulf War syndrome) eventually led to substantial legislative and executive U.S. government efforts that, in turn, required an underlying effort to pull together all known data about oil releases, oil burning, and other pertinent facts. The U.S. Department of Defense, for example, maintains the GulfLink website that serves as a collection point for a variety of reports on environmental and occupational exposure relating to oil well fires and particulate matter emissions, water use, pesticides and paints, equipment reshipment to the United States, and depleted-uranium munitions use.[4] With respect to air pollution, for instance, the U.S. Interagency Air Quality Assessment Team (USIAAT), the U.S. Army Environmental Hygiene Agency (USAEHA), and the World Meteorological Organization, a U.N. body, all undertook a variety of air sampling missions in 1991. The World Meteorological Organization, in turn, drew on assistance from the following countries and agencies:

1. The U.S. National Oceanic and Atmospheric Administration
2. The Kuwait Environmental Protection Department
3. Air pollution measurements by a French team (AIRPARIF)
4. Air pollution measurements by the Norwegian Institute for Air Research
5. The British Meteorological Office
6. The U.S. Department of Commerce's National Institute of Standards and Technology
7. The National Toxics Campaign Fund in the U.S. (an advocacy group)

8. The U.S. National Science Foundation
9. The U.S. Environmental Protection Agency
10. The U.S. National Aeronautics and Space Administration
11. The U.S. Department of Energy
12. Das Bundesamt für Umweltschutz (German Ministry for Environmental Protection)
13. The Japan Environment Agency

These efforts resulted in a large number of reports. In addition, at the request of a skeptical U.S. congressman, Representative John Conyers, Jr. (D-MI), the General Accounting Office reviewed an interagency interim report issued by the U.S. Environmental Protection Agency, audited numerous records in conjunction with that report, interviewed team members involved in its production, obtained independent outside scientific information, and even consulted with advocacy groups—the National Toxics Campaign Fund, Greenpeace, and Friends of the Earth—none of which would be expected to play the government's hand.[5]

Other scientific missions pertaining to bird and marine life included the following:

1. Three missions conducted by the International Council for Bird Preservation, now known as BirdLife International, and headquartered in Cambridge, U.K. The missions were conducted in March 1991, April to May 1991, and November to December 1991.
2. A mission by Greenpeace was carried out onboard the *MS Greenpeace*, sailing the Persian Gulf from 8 August to 1 October 1991. To permit data comparison, the mission resampled prewar sites.
3. The U.S. National Oceanic and Atmospheric Administration (NOAA) undertook a 100-day scientific mission in six legs, conducted aboard the research vessel *Mt. Mitchell* between 21 February and 20 June 1992. Sylvia Earle, NOAA chief scientist from 1990 to 1992, co-led the expedition. The mission involved more than 140 marine scientists from fifteen nations. Where possible, comparisons with prewar data were made. A special 380-page issue of the *Marine Pollution Bulletin* reports findings.
4. IUCN carried out three missions, in August of 1991, 1992, and 1993, and compared data to same-site data collected in 1986.

5. An EU-sponsored set of research handled via the Senckenberg Research Institute of Frankfurt-am-Main, Germany, and the Saudi Arabian National Commission for Wildlife Conservation and Development produced two volumes of research findings. This was based on two missions lasting from October 1991 to June 1995 and involved about forty scientists from six EU countries and thirty scientists from Kuwait and Saudi Arabia.

6. Two missions by the Japanese research vessel *Umitaka Maru* in the periods 15–16 December 1993, and 25–27 December 1994.

7. Further, there is a volume by Bloom, et al. that contains an extensive set of interviews with some of the scientists who conducted the postwar work.

8. Green Cross International produced a useful postwar summary report.[6]

Findings published in international, peer-reviewed scientific journals are easily accessible. Others are part of the gray literature, generally not available in or through public libraries. These have to be collected one by one on the Internet or by writing to the issuing agency or the person or persons involved in the report production. Then there are studies and reports that simply cannot be traced. For example, although allusions to a study by the British Meteorological Office are made in the literature, a citation that would have allowed tracking it has not been found. However, all twelve coauthors of a study published in *Nature* are identified as associated with the office.[7] Nonetheless, the available material is massive enough and sufficiently varied. Moreover, the materials cross-reference and tend to confirm each other, regardless of whether they are produced by U.S. agencies, other government agencies, international organizations, or advocacy groups in the United States or abroad. One may therefore be confident that virtually all relevant studies have been identified. In all, they tell a surprisingly consistent story.

3.1.2 Geography and Oceanography of the Western Persian Gulf

At roughly 1,000 km in length and 200–300 km in width, the Persian Gulf covers an area of about 240,000 km². During the late Pleistocene era (1.8 million to 10,000 years ago) the Gulf was dry land. Water from the Indian Ocean reentered the current Gulf area about 17,000 years

BCE, and present water levels were achieved only about 7,000 years ago. Therefore few endemic species are found in Gulf waters, and little speciation is observed. Today, the Gulf is a relatively shallow plain with an average depth of only about 35 meters, easily accessible to research divers. Maximum depth does not exceed 120 meters. Air temperatures reach 50°C in summer, contributing to high evaporation and salinity (40 to 70 ppt). Water surface temperatures vary greatly from about 11°C in winter to almost 40°C in summer. Freshwater influx is limited to a few Iranian rivers off the Zagros mountains in the east, and decreasing amounts from the Shatt-al-Arab in the north on account of the upstream drainage of the Iraqi marshlands.[8] Evaporation far exceeds influx. Combined, these factors make for difficult living conditions for the Gulf's marine life.

The Gulf lies on a northwest-to-southeast axis. The Gulf's currents run in a roughly counterclockwise direction. Combined with prevailing winds from north-northwest, it follows that the marine oil release and the smoke from the oil fires therefore affected mainly the northern Saudi Arabian coast of the Gulf. From time to time, occasional southwest winds refloated beached oil, which was then redeposited farther south due to current direction and prevailing winds. The major oil impact area in Saudi Arabia reached from Ras Al Khafji in the very north of the Saudi shoreline to Abu Ali Island, about halfway down the Saudi Gulf coast toward Bahrain and Qatar. In all, about 700 linear km of shoreline were affected to various degrees. Abu Ali Island sticks out into the Gulf like a thumb and effectively served as an oil catchment area into its adjacent bays. No adverse effects of Gulf War oiling were reported south of Abu Ali. The northern Gulf, including the Kuwaiti shoreline, was affected only to a small extent. As will be seen, with the exception of two islands off Jubail, neither were any of the Gulf islands affected.[9]

3.2 Marine Environments

Gulf "baseline surveys and environmental monitoring programs have not been maintained historically, so comparison between pre- and postwar levels of contaminants in the marine environment is not possible."[10] The bulk of this section concerns Saudi Arabia. The sparse information on Kuwait, Bahrain, the United Arab Emirates, and other countries in the region has also been collected and is interspersed in the text or collected in the chapter notes.[11]

3.2.1 Supratidal and Intertidal Areas

PHYSIOGRAPHY, EXTENT OF OILING, AND OIL DEGRADATION. The oil spills covered just over 1,500 km² of the Gulf surface and affected about half of the Saudi Gulf coastline, essentially the entire stretch between Khafji and Abu Ali Island. This included about 100 km² of crucially important intertidal habitat, especially the major embayments at Ras Tanaqib and the Dawhat ad-Dafi and Dawhat al-Musallamiya embayments west of Abu Ali.[12]

Degradation of oil depends on whether the oil is in the water column or beached. In the water column, evaporation of volatile compounds degrades the oil's toxicity quickly. Physical wave and wind action and biological action (bacteria in the water) further weather and degrade it. In addition, thinning through current and wind action disperses the oil. Of the six to eight million barrels of oil released into the Gulf (the most common range of estimates), one estimate is that perhaps 40 percent of the oil evaporated, 10 percent dissolved, and the remaining half floated. Of that remaining half, 22 percent was recovered, 50 percent beached (that is, 25 percent of the original total or 1.5 to 2 million barrels), and much or most of the remainder (15 percent of the total) probably sunk. These numbers are disputed. Rather than 25 percent of the total, one author claims that perhaps 45 percent of the total spilled oil beached along the northern Saudi Gulf coast, that is, 2.7 to 3.6 million barrels, nearly twice the first estimate. Regarding sunken oil, some authors dispute that any sank at all, and various marine researchers indeed failed to find any evidence of sunken oil.[13]

Degradation of stranded oil depends on the nature of the beach. Rocky beach (high-energy sites) is subject to physical wave action that breaks up, degrades, and disperses the oil. In contrast, shallow mud flats (low-energy sites) allow the undisturbed deposition and accumulation of oil that then is baked into tar mats of asphalt by the sun's heat and is much more slowly degraded by pioneer colonization of bacteria. At sites unfavorable to physical break-up of the oil, "very active" oil-degrading bacteria were found in sediment and sea water. Still, no change was found in hydrocarbon concentrations at low-energy sites even twenty-seven months after first sampling. In another study, no cyanobacteria were found at monitored sites in June 1991, but cyanobacterial mats were found in 1992, 1993, and 1994 at the same sites. These initiated bioremediation processes in which tar mats covered by a windborne or waterborne layer of sedimentation encourages (re)growth of cyanobacterial mats. When these dry, they shrink and break the underlying tar crust into chunks, exposing trapped bottom sediment. Water current and wind action then remove the tar chunks and further colonizers enter the area, whereupon other species move in. Reductions in hydrocarbon concentrations of intertidal sediment of between 13 and 19 percent were found, depending on clean-up technique. A study of the effect of alternative clean-up methods recommends to let natural recolonization and biological succession processes take their course on rocky shores, where oil weathers fast, but to manually remove tar mats on soft-sediment shores. Beyond a certain point, however, human-assisted tar mat removal can lead to renewed mortalities.[14]

Two important aspects regarding the coast need to be understood. First, even though the entire linear extent of the area between Khafji and Abu Ali was affected, this does not mean that every foot of this length was touched by oil. Because of wind and current directions, beaches facing north and northeast were the most heavily affected; other stretches along the linear extent were completely unaffected. Second, because the oil's effects turn out to have been so varied, it is important to differentiate between inland and tidal areas. The latter are usually further divided into supratidal, intertidal, and subtidal zones, and even finer zonations. Generally, gently sloped intertidal areas allowed oil to sweep inland and back into the Gulf for several kilometers, affecting large areas of saltpans, salt marshes, and mud flats covered with halophyte growth (salt-tolerant plants). Oil percolation into the sediment would depend on sand-grain coarseness, suffocating or oiling burrowing animals such as ghost crabs, bivalves, and polychaete worms. In the shallow sea areas, fish, swimming crabs, even rays and sharks as well as sea grass might be affected.

SEDIMENT POLLUTION. Oil deposited along the fringe littoral of the north and northeast-facing beaches either percolated into the substrate or, due to weathering, was gradually converted into tar mats. This is a common occurrence in the Gulf due to recurring peacetime oil spills and natural oil seepage. Several research missions measured the degree of percolation into the sediment. For example, between Ras as-Saffaniya and Abu Ali, one study reports penetration of between 2 and 50 cm and saturation (oil content of sediment samples) of 5 to 25 percent. (The percentage of surface area oiled was not reported.) The Greenpeace research mission from late August to early October 1991 sampled coastal sites in Kuwait, Saudi Arabia, and Iran. Where possible, sites were sampled for which baseline data existed. The analysis was restricted to measuring oil-content (percentage of total petroleum hydrocarbons, or TPH) in beach sand and sediments. The northern Saudi coast was most affected with high values of up to 7 percent TPH and common values of 1 to 2 percent. For most of the sampled sites, Greenpeace found "no sign of surviving marine life on the shore and the first signs of life start appearing well out below low water . . . forms of life that are present are the more tolerant species (certain bivalves and polychaete worms) . . . often the oil extends well into the halophyte zone, killing many of the plants." Medium- and long-term effects, via the food web, were not known at the time.

The three IUCN missions, in August 1991, 1992, and 1993, examined petroleum hydrocarbons and other contaminants in the coastal ecosystem. Covering areas other than the aforementioned Kuwait Bay satellite study, IUCN found significant increases in algae (and birds and fish) in 1991 as compared to 1986. Oil pollution was much higher in 1991, of course, but by 1993 had been reduced to the 1986 levels. Core sampling of intertidal and shallow subtidal areas, however, showed heavy oil contamination even two years after the war. Yet concentrations of the heavy metals nickel and vanadium, both related to oil, were broadly similar to those measured in the 1980s. On the whole, hydrocarbon contamination was confined to within 400 km of the pollution source and levels were "of the same order as those which have been measured in several coastal areas of the United States and northern Europe; and that outside the immediate area of impact, petroleum hydrocarbon and trace metal levels in sediment and bivalves were generally as low, or lower than, those concentrations measured at the same sites before the war."[15]

Of course, some spots along the Saudi coast were more harshly affected than others. For example, fairly high proportions of trace metals were found around Abu Ali but were within the limits found elsewhere when compared to sites around the world. One pair of researchers concludes that a "comparison with unpolluted sediments throughout the Gulf and world-wide reveals that the effect of anthropogenic enrichment upon the absolute concentration of the [trace] elements is minimal." Apparently, this conclusion obtains because there is "no evidence of large-scale sinking of oil from the spill" in subtidal areas. The oil's volatile compounds evaporated and large amounts of oil were captured and recovered. Oil weathering broke down the remainder. Chemical analysis of oil residues can identify the oil source and its degree of weathering. Samples taken in June 1991 and during the 1992 Mt. Mitchell expedition did connect the oil spill along the northern portions of the Saudi coast to the chemical characteristics of the spilled Kuwaiti oil, but intertidal and subtidal areas around Abu Ali and Dawhat ad-Dafi also revealed oil sources other than that spilled during the Gulf War.[16]

THE TIDAL ZONE. The tidal zone is an area marked by high and low tides. The area above high tide is known as the supratidal, below low tide is the subtidal, and in between is the intertidal zone. Because of the Gulf's extremely shallow geography, averaging a slope of only 35 centimeters per kilometer, in places the intertidal zone is several kilometers wide. Because the oiling visibly affected it the most and because it was already known to be a crucial feeding habitat for migrating birds, the tidal area attracted much study.

Depending on the strength of wave action, beach sand is pushed into a series of berms of various heights running parallel to the water line, the farthest landward extension being the storm berm. Between berms run series of strandlines, usually covered with marine debris, algae, sea grasses, washed-up marine life, waste materials, and the like. This transitional, supratidal edge between marine and terrestrial communities is biologically active and important. Several species that live in the sand assist in the decomposition of the organic deposits (algae, sea grass) and, in turn, serve as a food source for higher trophic levels. Test and control sites were visited in January 1992, May and June 1992, December 1992, January 1993, and again in March and April 1993 in the Abu Ali area. Along the farthest tidal reaches, a "nearly continuous layer of oiled sand and solid tar between 0.5 and 400 m wide" prevents specialized species from gaining access to organic material washed ashore. Researchers found that, on the whole, even two years after the oiling, "there was still no sign of recovery" of characteristic biota. Where the oil or tar is broken up, recolonization does take place and its speed depends on the species' method of dispersal.[17]

Regarding the intertidal, for most study areas examined around Ras Tanaqib and the bay west of Abu Ali one year after the war, "all the halophytes were dead and there was no sign of living epibiota in the mid to upper intertidal areas." But details vary. Extensive damage and recovery studies for invertebrates like crabs, bivalves, and polychaete worms were carried out from November 1991 to November 1992. The researchers established several test and control sites in the embayments west of Abu Ali, the most heavily affected area of all. Already by November 1991 the oil along rocky shore areas had been broken up by physical action and was no longer prevalent. Species diversity and species counts on test and control sites compared favorably. On soft-sediment areas, the verdict (as of November 1992) was more complex, but a marked trend toward recolonization by pioneer and key species was observed. Progress depended on the degree of residual oil pollution and on the precise location (littoral fringe, upper eulittoral, mid-eulittoral, lower-eulittoral, and sublittoral fringe). By 1994, a further study found species diversity "similar to that found on unpolluted shores" on the lower shore and between 50 and 100 percent of control sites on the upper eulittoral. A clear recolonization trend was revealed, reaching from the lower to the upper shore over time: life emerges from the sea. Also, from 1991 high fluctuation of species numbers were observed, which stabilized once the entire ecosystem returned to some semblance of balance by 1994.[18]

Test and control plot studies were carried out between June and November 1992 on species of crabs inhabiting the intertidal mud flats in the Dawaht ad-Dafi and Dawhat al-Musallamiya areas. As in many other cases, little was known about these species' composition, zonation, and ecology. The researcher finds that relative to the nonpolluted control sites, located south of Abu Ali in Tarut Bay (which has a somewhat different ecosystem, perhaps contributing to higher crab population densities there), most crab species were "missing or drastically reduced on the oiled sites." Because the driving factors were not well understood, success for recruitment and recolonization was difficult to predict at the time of the study. This would depend on available larvae and planktonic food material. There is some suggestion that formation of blue-green algae (cyanobacteria) mats on oiled sites prevents crabs, and other burrowing organisms, from settling. A follow-up study, reaching to May 1993, found "good signs" of crab recovery and recolonization in the mid-eulittoral, but less so in the low and upper eulittoral.[19]

Algae appear to play an important role in the tidal area. Satellite images reveal, prior to the oil release, cyanobacterial mats in intertidal zones between Ras Al Saffaniya and Abu Ali. Following the oil release, most mats were severely affected and survived only in the upper intertidal zone. By mid-1992, recovery was apparent, but this depended on the local environment. Areas covered with tar layers and without fresh sedimentation continued to be devoid of cyanobacteria even two years after the oil spill, but where the tar was covered by fresh sediment deposits "extensive growth of blue-green algae [cyanobacteria] occurred in a short time." Some algae mats are of special importance to reestablish the local ecosystem. In particular, in dry conditions, polygonal mats tend to curl up at the edges, breaking away from the underlying substrate, thus lifting the top tar layer. This exposes sediment ready for colonization. But, as noted, the presence of algae mats may also preclude settlement by burrowing species.[20]

Field research in December 1991 and January 1992 studied mangrove stands and salt marshes in embayment areas west of Abu Ali, a study area of 20 km². Test sites were established and measurements taken until 1993. The effect of the oiling depended strongly on the species. Among the marsh species, *Salicornia europaea* is "almost extinct" (99 percent die-off). "Severely damaged" are *Arthrocnemum macrostachyum* (35 percent) and *Halocnemum strobilaceum* (30 percent), and "relatively unaffected" are *Halopeplis perfoliata* and *Limonium axillare* (they "have not been damaged").

The only mangrove species, *Avecennia marina*, is also "severely damaged" (30 percent die-off). But, in all, "more than 50 percent of the intertidal vegetation remained alive and all these plants are flowering and producing fruit." Another researcher clarifies these numbers: of the roughly 20 km² study area, *Salicornia europaea*, for example, is the dominant species on 0.71 km². Of that area, there was a greater than 80 percent destruction on 0.57 km². Likewise, *Arthrocnemum macrostachyum* was dominant on 9.44 km² and a 99 percent destruction occurred on 3.2 km². Similarly, *Halocnemum strobilaceum* was dominant on 11 km², and a 99 percent destruction occurred on 1.1 km². By 1993, of these limited areas, "no evidence of regeneration was found . . . two years later."[21]

Because some areas had been subjected to cleaning during the height of the crisis (e.g., water sprinklers to wash off oil), twelve test plots were studied over time, six in treated (cleaned) areas, six in untreated areas. Table 3.1 shows the results. Plots 3 and 5 in the nontreated areas are those that are naturally protected and were not much affected by the oil. The other plots were badly affected. The cleaned areas show that the treatment helped to prevent die-offs. Further reestablishment is estimated to take "a decade or more." Regarding the salt marsh plant *Salicornia europea*, an annual that dies off in winter, no seeds were observed to germinate after trial planting. In contrast, trial planting of the mangrove *Avecennia marina* into oiled substrate resulted in survival rates of at least two and a half years, the end of the observation period.[22]

Table 3.1.   Mangrove Trees, Abu Ali Embayment, Saudi Arabia

Seeds Quadrant	Seeds Germinated 1991	Seeds Germinated 1992	Living Trees 1992	Living Trees 1993
Treated				
plot 1	22	0	18	16
plot 2	27	0	6	4
plot 3	87	0	8	8
plot 4	35	0	15	15
plot 5	31	0	15	12
plot 6	72	3	12	12
Not treated				
plot 1	0	0	31	31
plot 2	0	0	0	0
plot 3	0	0	18	17
plot 4	0	0	8	7
plot 5	0	0	5	2
plot 6	0	0	0	0

Source: Adapted from Böer (1994, p. 25).

Mangrove areas had already been substantially depleted along the Saudi coast, resulting in only two remaining mangrove hosting areas. The smaller one, comprising about ten hectares, is in Dawhat ad Dafi, the bay west of Abu Ali; the larger one, to the south, and unaffected by the oil spill, consists of eight patches around Tarut Bay. The former contained areas where mangroves were badly affected but also areas where mangroves were almost completely unaffected. Most damage to mangrove stands derives from land reclamation efforts, particularly in Tarut Bay. In sum, regarding the west side of the Abu Ali embayment, "the mid- and upper intertidal zone lost most of its typical plant and animal communities. The lower intertidal was only partly affected and revealed a patchy pattern of oil contamination. . . . Large areas of salt-marshes and mangroves along with their associated fauna were killed." By the same token, recovery was underway within a year or two, and apparently followed a sea-to-land gradient.[23]

3.2.2 Benthic Communities, Fish, Shrimp, Coral Reefs, and Islands

As compared to the 1986–1990 averages for the same months, seawater temperatures dropped significantly from June to September 1991. The only reasonable explanation for this is that the oil-fire smoke plume shaded the sun. Solar radiation measurements in Rahimah, Saudi Arabia, for instance showed a level of 79 percent in 1991 relative to 1990 measurements. Daily seawater temperature measurements have been taken at the Manifa Pier since 1986 at 10-minute intervals. (Manifa, in Saudi Arabia, lies somewhat north of Abu Ali Island.) Because the reproduction cycles of some marine organisms in the Gulf appear to be tied to seawater temperature signals, reproduction may have been disturbed. The mean difference for June 1991 was -2.5°C, for July -4.9°C, for August -4.6°C, and for September -3.5°C. This is somewhat puzzling because the smoke plume traveled along the Saudi coastline and covered only the near-shore waters rather than areas farther out into the Gulf.[24]

BENTHIC COMMUNITIES. One year after the Gulf War, a study around the heavily affected area of Abu Ali concluded that "the levels of oil in subtidal benthic sediments had decreased in most habitats to levels that did not show community stress . . . long term damage to benthic subtidal habitats was limited only to enclosed bays adjacent to the most heavily oiled coastlines." The reference to long-term damage is misplaced (see the later studies cited below). Even if there had been such damage, the finding that it was limited to the "most heavily" affected areas and that there is no "community stress" elsewhere is crucial because benthic communities are not only recyclers of organic materials but are primary producers, vital to hundreds of species of prawn and other invertebrates, fish, and other wildlife. A geographically more extensive study, reaching north and south of Abu Ali, and taking samples from 17 March to 4 April 1992, as part of the second leg of the NOAA mission, concludes that "seagrasses in the northwestern Gulf have not experienced acute or long-term degradation as a direct result of the Gulf War oil spill." Moreover, "composition, distribution and relative abundance of seagrasses and macroalgae . . . were comparable to pre-spill conditions previously described for this region of northeastern Saudi Arabia" and comparable, including in terms of productivity rates, either to the same or ecologically similar species in other regions.[25]

To further study macroalgae and sea grasses, the area between Ras az-Zaur and Abu Ali—much more confined than the study area referred to in the previous paragraph—was monitored over several seasons. Field trips were undertaken 13–28 May 1992, 17 July to 20 August 1992, 30 October to 14 November 1992, and 19 February to 5 March 1993, with an additional trip to Kuran Island in August 1992. Prewar data are scant. In fact, macroalgae and sea grasses had never been intensively studied for this area. The authors observe that both polluted and nonpolluted sites are devoid of algal growth in the salt marshes, mangroves, sandy and muddy coast areas, and rocky substrates so that the oil could not have been responsible for this absence. Instead, the general Gulf climate is held responsible. The researchers note that the subtidal area had not been affected and showed typical vegetation during fieldwork. This is true for both the soft (subtidal sea bottom) and hard (coral) substrates. Moreover, in the authors' assessment, "seaweed and seagrass vegetation of the area between Raz az-Zaur and Abu Ali is very rich." In a follow-on report, the authors note that ninety taxa were recorded, of which forty-two "are new for the Saudi Arabian Gulf coast and fifteen are new for the Arabian Gulf."[26]

To discover whether sea grasses are resistant to oil pollution, researchers also conducted laboratory studies in which sea grass species were experimentally subjected to Kuwaiti oil. Under varying irradiation (light-energy) conditions, no statistically significant differences relative to control groups were noted on the treatment groups' rates of photosynthesis and respiration. This despite the fact that the experiments involved thorough mixing of oil and water whereas the actual spill conditions in the Gulf indicate that little sinking and mixing of oil took place. A zooplankton survey taken a year after the war indicates "that there is no detectable effect of the oil pollution on the Gulf zooplankton abundance and distribution at the population level." The survey covered areas from northern Kuwait to areas just east of Qatar. This is important because zooplankton is an important food source for other marine life.[27]

Sampling in the Dawhat ad-Dafi and Dawhat al-Musallamiya bays in February, May, and June, and October and November 1992 and surveys on benthic communities "revealed the diversity of marine habitats found elsewhere in the northern Arabian Gulf." With the exception of two localized sites, "there was no visual evidence of oil contamination in the subtidal region." Minimal oiling (tar balls) was also found in nonaffected sites. Species richness and composition was in line with a prewar oil-spill study. Whereas the prewar study focused on offshore sites, this focused on inshore sites (that is, inside the bay), confirming that inshore "subtidal benthic areas are also rarely affected by spills with the bulk of the oil being deposited in the intertidal region." Continued studies in May and October 1993 and February, April, and May 1994 confirmed these findings for marine subtidal biotopes such as "coral patch and fringing reefs, seagrass beds, macroalgae-dominated rock outcrops and sand and silt seabeds. . . . These studies failed to suggest any effect of the oil on the subtidal benthic communities." Likewise, benthic macrofauna quantitatively analyzed by another researcher were found in "abundances of individuals and biomass . . . in the range known from other tropical shores. Epibenthic species dominated toward the supralittoral and were the first colonizers of the zones covered with oil."[28]

Because they focus on primary producers, these are very important findings. Even if higher trophic levels had been severely affected by the oil fires and the oil spill, the intact nature of the primary producers would virtually guarantee recolonization by higher levels, assuming that their physical habitat remained intact, as it largely did.[29]

In addition, results have been reported of sediment samples taken from nineteen locations during the Japanese *Umitaka-Maru* cruise on 15–16 December 1993, and further samples from another twenty-four locations during another *Umitaka-Maru* cruise a year later, 25–27 December 1994. The objective was to determine accumulation of the heavy metals lead (Pd), nickel (Ni), and vanadium (V) in sand and mud sediments throughout the Gulf waters and to compare the findings to those obtained from other regions in the world. The researchers found that "the concentrations in the different types of sediments are within the range published in the literature for unpolluted areas. Thus, the effect of anthropogenic enrichment upon the absolute concentration of the tested elements in the sediments analyzed is minimal."[30]

FISH. Early on, "the observed invertebrate mortality (shrimps, crabs, mol-lusks) has been enormous," but "visible fish mortality was more localized," and the "buoyancy of the oil meant that subtidal habitats such as seagrass beds and coral reefs do not seem to have suffered any obvious, short-term, lethal effects." This assessment is echoed by other researchers: "There is no evidence of any large-scale sinking of oil and the damage to subtidal ben-thic habitats was very limited. . . . [While] macroalgal beds, seagrass beds and coral reefs escaped oil contamination . . . fish and shrimp populations obviously were affected."[31] But by how much?

The surface layer of spilled oil in the Gulf substantially degraded within a few months by physical (wave, wind) action and evaporation of volatile compounds. Toxicity tests on marine invertebrate larvae showed that the subsurface water column was not toxic but the sea-surface microlayer was. This is important because this microlayer serves as a spawning ground for many fish, shrimp, and shellfish. A study of fish populations at four coral reef sites, nearshore off Abu Ali and offshore near the islands of Karan, Kurain, and Jana showed that while species counts were low relative to tropical Indo-Pacific regions on account of the special biological status of the Gulf explained earlier, they nonetheless "exceed all previous reports from the area." The researchers continue: "Despite the oil spill, fish popu-lations in the area were in a healthy condition without any visible signs of oil damage. Recruitment by larvae occurred at normal levels. Species diversity and population densities were within the expected range when compared to pre-war data published in the literature."[32]

Another study, referring to studies undertaken between 1992 and 1995, reports that about 280 of the Gulf's approximately 540 fish species had been recorded in the Jubail Marine Wildlife Sanctuary offshore islands, that lowered recruitment rates in 1992 and 1993 "may be attributed to a reduction of planktonic eggs and larvae caused by the oil slick," and that "fish populations had recovered from the oil spill by 1994." The IUCN mission also found abundant fish and large numbers of species around the examined Saudi Arabian coral reefs. At Abu Ali, however, in the winter of 1991–1992, most fish were juvenile, suggesting a mass die-off of adults. All angelfishes and butterflyfishes had disappeared. But by the following summer and fall juveniles were found; in the ensuing winter of 1992–1993, many specimens were found, and by the summer of 1993 larger (adult) specimens were present. From the fish census of species composition and abundance one may conclude that the underlying food web was not ad-versely affected by the Gulf War.[33]

Comparisons with 1985 data for same-site samples provide strong evidence of bioaccumulation of oil-related metals by clams (e.g., cadmium, chromium, cobalt). The higher the concentrations are, the larger the clams are and the closer to the source of the oil spill they are (that is, Kuwait). Another study (for fish and clams) reports similar findings. The highest concentrations were found for samples taken between the heavily oiled areas of Ras Al Khafji to Ras Al Ghar along the northern Saudi coast. Farther south, areas sampled east of the Qatari peninsula were unaffected. There were no statistical differences among samples of benthic and semi-pelagic organisms collected before, during, and after the war. Samples taken from July to September 1991 detected levels of heavy metal concentrations in edible fish that were higher than minimum world ranges but rarely exceeded the maximum world ranges. In a further study, seafood samples bought on Kuwaiti markets contained significant levels of total polycyclic aromatic hydrocarbons (PAHs) but the human daily intake levels "were comparable with those reported for the average American consumer." Immediately following the war, Kuwaiti nearshore sites were inaccessible due to sea mines. Thus, many studies sampled offshore sediment (and found no pollution strictly attributable to the war). But by June 1995, a research team was able to collect nearshore samples from eight sites along most of the Kuwaiti coastline. Samples were analyzed for total petroleum hydrocarbons (TPH) content, total organic carbon (TOC), and the metals lead, nickel, and vanadium (Pd, Ni, V). The findings showed pollution levels determined by distance from nearby known pollution sources such as boat fueling stations and shipping lanes, seaport terminals, power plants, and desalination plants. Only one site, close to the Shuaiba industrial area, showed highly polluted sediment. With that exception, all other sample stations showed "TOC and TPH ranges . . . within the natural baseline data previously reported for the same sites." Metal contamination also is "consistent with levels previously reported." In all, "the pollution of Kuwait's shoreline sediments appears to arise from intermittent discharges of crude oil, fuel oil, ballast water, and land-based wastewaters to the sea; also, the level of contamination is dependent on the distance from the sources of contamination."[34]

SHRIMP. There is consensus that the Saudi Arabian prawn (large shrimp) spawning biomass suffered by about an order of magnitude, and total biomass declined to about 25 percent of prewar levels. This may well have been a direct consequence of the oiling of the Persian Gulf waters, especially because important spawning grounds lie directly in the path of the oil, but the scientific evidence is not clear-cut. For example, researchers Mathews, et al. write:

> The evidence suggests that a manmade recruitment collapse occurred, caused by one or more of the following: reduced spawning success in 1992 and perhaps in 1991, heavy fishing of adults in spring 1991, heavy fishing of recruits in autumn 1991, morbidity of adults due to pollution in 1991, emigration of adults due to pollution in 1991, interference with biological processes and life cycle of *P. semisucaltus*, reducing 1991–92 spawning biomass.[35]

Others express a similar view. Scientists have not been able to sort out war-related possible oil spill effects either from unknown behavior of adults (that is, possible migration to escape oiling) or from the possibility of prior overfishing (shrimp fishing was known to operate near maximum sustainable yields), or other possible causes. Although the timing of the prawn-catch collapse is closely associated with the war, today it remains unclear to what degree the war-related oil spills contributed to the shrimp biomass decline and what the proximate and ultimate causes are. For comparison, the Nowruz oil spill (1983) in the Persian Gulf and the Ixtoc spill (1979–1980) in the Gulf of Mexico did not result in reduced prawn catches, possibly because they were not associated with surface water temperature changes, were of smaller size, were spread out over a longer time period, were diffused over larger bodies of water, and were farther away from spawning grounds, thereby providing more time for the oil to evaporate and disperse. Meanwhile, by 1998 shrimp stocks and shrimp fisheries had recovered to prewar levels.[36]

Regarding Kuwaiti shrimp fishing, it is true that total landings in 1991 dropped sharply, but that was because the fishing industry was largely destroyed. Computed on a c/e (catch/effort) basis, there was no obvious shrimp depletion. For the ten years 1986 to 1995, shrimp catch (in kg/day/boat) was 110, 162, 323, 361, 374, 327, 390, 319, 179, and 276. The depletion followed the war, and the primary reason is postwar fishing liberalization. In addition, attention has been called to gradual reduction in nutrient influx on account of the dessication of the Iraqi marshland.[37]

CORAL REEFS. Like other species, Persian Gulf corals live in a naturally stressed environment of high salinity, turbidity, and comparably cold winter temperatures. Consequently, Gulf corals are not particularly diverse and more vulnerable than are corals in other habitats. This environment could have been stressed further by the war. Toxic components of the spilled oil might have affected coral larvae and slowed reproduction; the oil-fire smoke plume did reduce the already low Gulf winter temperatures and might have been expected to result in a coral die-off. Downing studied Kuwait's offshore islands and coral reefs in July 1991 and found no damage except for the terrestrial environment on Umm Al Maradam Island. Later in 1991, the Greenpeace mission visited previously researched coral reefs in Kuwait, Saudi Arabia, Iran, and Bahrain: "None of the reefs visited showed visible signs of oil or tar coverage. Patches of dead corals were observed on some reefs, but this might not be related to the recent oil spills." Long-term effects are unknown (e.g., if coral larvae, released during spawning, might be killed by residual oil film). Except for Bahrain, all coral reefs have naturally high sea urchin populations (that is, few urchin predators). No visible damage due to the oil spill was noted. Some Iranian reefs were in "poor condition," probably due to bomb damage from the Iran-Iraq War of the 1980s. Bahrainian reefs were completely dead along dredging channels.[38]

In early 1991, divers "didn't see evidence of sunken oil on the . . . main coral areas off Saudi Arabia"; in 1992, NOAA divers did find "a lot of dead coral . . . [but] they don't really know when it died or why." A further study in late 1992 found no impact on Saudi coral reefs and only slight and recovering damage to Kuwati reefs. It surveyed the offshore reefs of Kubbar, Qaru, and Umm Al Maradem 28 November to 1 December 1992, and, on 2 December 1992, the inshore reefs of Qit'at Urayfijan and Getty Reef (Ras Al-Zoor). Also in November, the Saudi Arabian reef islands of Karan, Jana, and Jurayd were surveyed in addition to inshore sites just north of Abu Ali. The Kuwaiti offshore corals were found to be in good health although "limited mortalities of a few species since the 1991 survey" were found on Kubbar and Umm Al Maradem, but not on Qaru. Affected were *Acrophora* n.sp. (on Kubbar) and *Acrophora valida* (on both islands). Regarding Saudi Arabian offshore reefs, only anchor damage from boats was noted at Karan and no damage was noted at Jana. In contrast, Jarayd corals showed heavy damage from anchoring and fishing net entanglement. No oil-related damage was observed at any Saudi reef. In both locales, fish were abundant and the presence of many juveniles is remarked upon.[39]

Inshore, the Getty reef shoreline was affected by oil, with a tar layer still visible when researchers visited. But the underlying corals were healthy, with "no sign of stress in any of the corals and no evidence of recent coral kills." Fish also appeared healthy and plentiful at Getty. The other inshore Kuwaiti reef, Qit'at Urayfijan, lies in shallow water (but is never exposed to air). Oil probably flowed directly over the reef. Corals near the reef crest, that is, near the water surface, were adversely affected, but with new growth visible. Deeper-lying corals were healthy. Sea urchins, often associated with dead corals, were "noticeable by [their] absence." Fish appeared healthy, abundant, and present in many species although baseline comparative data is unavailable for this particular reef. The Saudi inshore reefs near Abu Ali were "evidently healthy, with no sign of bleaching or coral disease," although fish were not abundant.[40]

A study conducted over a one-year period on Saudi reefs established ten research sites in June 1992, three inshore in Dawhat ad-Dafi and seven offshore around Karan, Kurain, and Jana islands. Some sites were revisited in February 1993, others in May and June 1993. The findings are straightforward: "A comparison of the results obtained . . . showed little change in live coral had occurred. During all the periods of fieldwork no abnormal numbers of dead coral were found in any part of the reefs. These findings suggest that no short-term or long-term changes can be attributed to the Gulf War events." In a later publication, the same researcher states the findings more strongly: "Severe reef damage caused mainly by anchoring fishing boats in the reefs surrounding the islands of Juraid, Kurain, Jana and Karan was observed. Considerable numbers of nets and other fishing gear were found littering the reefs."[41]

ISLANDS. Several commentators note that many islands show pollution by debris. One, for example, writes: "All of the islands except Harqus had heavy beach debris loads, particularly on the north and east sides. Most of the debris was milled lumber, with little plastic, metal, or glass (except light bulbs). The plastic debris likely is generated primarily by fishing vessels, and there is a moderate amount of lost net and net fragments on the beaches. The lumber occurs in quantities that interfere with sea turtle nesting," and with hatchlings trying to reach the water.[42]

The thrust of the scientific evidence regarding the war's possible effects on benthic communities, fish, shrimp, coral reefs, and islands in the Gulf could hardly be more unambiguous. The numerous studies summarized here result in a virtually unanimous verdict: the war's effects were minimal, and often nil. In contrast, much concern is raised about the observed effects of nonwar anthropogenic activities.

3.2.3 Marine Mammals and Turtles

Regarding cetaceans in the Dawhat ad-Dafi and Dawhat al-Musallamiya bays, no baseline data were available. One study area was visited in January and February 1992, roughly one year after the oil spill. Traversing the area by helicopter, inflatable boat, and by binocular observations from shore, the researchers counted sightings and identified species. For possible necropsy, they also walked the shoreline to look for skeletal remains washed ashore. Several skeletal parts were found but only one fresh carcass. Examination did not indicate death due to oil-related causes. Four cetacean species were identified: humpback dolphin, bottlenose dolphin, common dolphin, and finless porpoise. Overall counts seemed low, but in the absence of prewar data they cannot be assessed. The researchers cite another authority as having observed dolphins during the first three months of the spill, and only one dolphin is known to have died along the Saudi north coast. The literature suggests that dolphins are able to detect potentially lethal sea conditions and simply choose to relocate themselves.[43]

Open-water mammalian surveys also were conducted by Greenpeace. The mission counted the number of humpback, bottlenose, and common dolphins, and finless porpoises as well as the number of adults and calves of each. The number of observed calves was small relative to the number of observed calves in other marine environments of the world (Gulf of Mexico, California, and South Africa) but we do not know whether these are natural occurrences. In the past, dolphin and dugong die-offs have been associated with oil spills in the western Gulf in 1983 and 1986. But as regards the 1991 war, "although dead dugongs and dolphins have been found from various parts of the Gulf, it is impossible to know if they were killed by the oil." In all, it appears safe to conclude that cetaceans were not adversely affected by the war. Although Greenpeace notes that "there is very little information on the [prewar] distribution and abundance of marine mammals in the Gulf," some baseline data on turtle species, population status, location, and nesting sites is available from studies conducted in the mid-1980s. All seven species of sea turtle are endangered. The green and the hawksbill turtle are important in the Gulf, and the former is more abundant than the latter. Their breeding areas lie, for the most part, outside the oil-affected areas of the Gulf.[44]

The population distribution of dugongs lies largely outside the affected waters. Other studies also state that areas of "superior habitats" for shorebirds (waders), dugongs, and sea turtles along the southern Saudi Arabian coast and the Gulf of Bahrain were "spared." Likewise, "islands, which are important for sea turtle and seabird nesting, were largely spared." Greenpeace could not provide any data except for a single dead turtle found. A necropsy discovered that its liver and stomach were heavily contaminated by oil. Another study recorded three dead green turtles in May 1991 in the

Ras Tanaqib area but did not state the cause of death. Yet another reported four oiled turtles, two of each species, one of which died. (The other three were treated and released.) Green and hawksbill turtles (*Chelonia mydas* and *Eretmochelys imbricata*) were studied on Karan and Jana islands, east and northeast off Abu Ali, during the summer nesting seasons 1991 to 1994. The researchers found that the "morphological [body size and weight] data for adult female turtles were similar to that collected in previous years from the same locality." Unfortunately, the paper does not report prewar data. By the same token, there is nothing in the article that suggests any effect on the turtles or their reproductive success on account of the war. In all, the evidence suggests no adverse effect on turtles from the oil spill.[45]

3.3 Birds

The direct effects of oil on birds are twofold. First, direct oiling reduces the insulating properties of plumage and leads to hypothermia, an effect exacerbated by the relatively cool winter temperatures in the Gulf at the time of the war and the further temperature-reducing effects of oil-smoke cover. February is the coldest month in the Gulf with a mean minimum of 11°C; the smoke plume reduced temperatures a further 5–10°C. Second, oil ingestion through preening and feeding leads to numerous internal dysfunctions, organ damage, and death through poisoning. Moreover, a feedback loop leads oiled birds to preen themselves more frequently, in-gesting more oil in the process. Additional preening also diminishes the birds' energy economy. More time and energy are expended on preening, less time is spent on food search and feeding and thus less energy is received from the food sources (which also may be oiled). In addition, for some birds food availability (invertebrates) was reduced by the oil's coverage of intertidal feeding grounds so that the birds' average search time per unit of food was extended. All this leads to a negative energy budget, depletion of energy reserves, and the possibility of poisoning or starvation. Even if starvation was not the eventual fate of birds, reduced energy stocks (that is, reduced weight) would limit the birds' ability to continue their northward migration to reach Eurasian breeding grounds and would thereby lead to a drop in each affected species' population.[46]

Birds are classified here either as shorebirds, which include waders, or seabirds (pelagic or oceanic birds). For the former, the intertidal areas are crucial feeding grounds. As mentioned, the Kuwaiti coast largely escaped oiling, with the important exception of Sulaibikhat Bay. The Saudi inter-tidal areas are concentrated around four major embayments, containing 95 percent of Saudi intertidal areas, namely (from north to south) (1) Safaniya; (2) Ras Tanaqib/Manifah; (3) the Dawhat al Musallimiyah/Dawhat ad Dafi/Abu Ali area north of Jubail; and (4) Tarut Bay. These areas, largely composed of sand and mud flats, are extremely shallow. Their linear extent between high-tide and low-tide marks ranges up to 5 km, with an average gradient of 35 cm/km, or about 22 inches/mile. They are normally full of invertebrate life, and shorebirds feed on these resources, gaining energy reserves to carry on their spring migrations ranging from South Africa to Siberia along the West Asian Flyway.[47]

The first ornithological survey following the oil releases was conducted from 28 February to 14 March 1991, by Roy Dennis and Burr Heneman for the International Council for Bird Preservation (ICBP), now called BirdLife International. This was followed by a second visit, from 7 April to 28 May 1991, by eight ornithologists and a third visit, in November and December 1991, both also for ICBP. All three visits focused on Saudi Arabia.[48]

3.3.1 Shorebirds

The assessment situation regarding shorebirds (waders) is complex, for two main reasons. First, there exists only a single prewar wader count in the Gulf, and that was conducted in winter, namely in January and February 1986. This is important because the oil slick reached its southernmost extent on 21 February 1991, when it beached on Abu Ali's northern shores. By 7 April, 100 percent of the tidal areas had been affected one or more times by oil (due to tidal reflotation and redeposition). Thus, the oil's predominant impact occurred in the spring (March to May), a time for which no previous census data were available at all. Second, exceedingly few dead waders, on the order of 0.1 percent of all dead birds, have ever been found in other major oil-spill instances, such as the *Exxon Valdez* case off the coast of Alaska. Indeed, shorebirds, even if oiled, are known to fly hundreds of miles to alternative habitats so that their ultimate fate is not known. "It is incredibly difficult to know the actual direct mortality from the oil," says one researcher. Nonetheless, it has been speculated that "the likelihood of the waders successfully establishing themselves in equally good feeding areas elsewhere is considered low, due to the predicted occurrence of overcrowding effects." This seemed a reasonable hypothesis but was thoroughly challenged a mere year later (see below).[49]

Taken together, these points raise difficult questions of assessing how many waders there might have been in the impact areas in the spring of

1991 and of determining where the presumably missing birds may have gone. Migrants work on well-established time frames and tend to revisit the same feeding grounds year after year, and ornithological observations of migrant populations still residing south of Abu Ali as well as around the Black Sea and Kazakhstan suggested that the shorebirds of the impact zone did not migrate south or north (respectively, few and no oiled birds were observed there). Moreover, it was known that birds generally do not instantly recognize and avoid oil slicks and so the presumption was that the birds in the impact zone simply died. But where were the corpses? Along a 4 km stretch at Ras Tanaqib, only eight out of 207 dead oiled birds were waders even while 2,000 living oiled waders were observed. Most likely, it was thought, the living oiled waders scrambled and flew as long as their energy reserves would permit, sought shelter and food in unusual habitats, died, and were then scavenged, for instance by red foxes.[50]

Based on the previous winter counts (taken in 1986), it was estimated that perhaps 130,000 waders may have been present before the war in the major oiled intertidal areas along the Saudi coast.[51] Of those, perhaps 4,000 or less remained after the oil affected the areas. If so, that would be a reduction of 97 percent of the migrating population. But as few wader corpses were found, it is impossible to know what actually happened to the waders. Given that their food supplies were destroyed, did they simply move elsewhere? If they stayed, were they oiled? If so, were they partially oiled and continued to migrate, or were they heavily oiled and died in situ? If so, again, where were the corpses? The only answer to these questions is that we do not know enough to provide definitive answers. We do know from surveys of the few waders remaining in the impact zone, that 50 to 75 percent of the birds were oiled. And we do know that in the next winter season, January to February 1992, about 100,000 migrating waders showed up along the entire Saudi coast, when perhaps a 250,000 were expected on the basis of the 1986 counts. Thus it would appear that "a real and major reduction in the wader carrying capacity of the Saudi Arabian intertidal zone appears to have occurred. What exactly happened to the large number of waders which disappeared from the oiled coast in February is not known."[52]

But a year later, researchers report that "birds initially color-marked at Sabkhat al-Fasl while they were heavily oil-fouled in November–December 1991, have been re-sighted totally clean the following winter (1992–93), indicating that at least a portion of the oil-fouled waders survived." Moreover, intense observation of feeding areas showed feeding densities consistent with recovery of 70 to 76 percent of the prewar wader populations, as estimated by the 1986 winter counts. If wader populations were in fact drastically reduced by the fouling of their feeding habitats in the spring of 1991, two years later their population had substantially recovered.[53]

3.3.2 Seabirds

Seabirds are divided into wintering and breeding seabirds. Obtaining food by diving through the water surface, they become heavily oiled by surface penetration. Breeding seabirds (four species of terns) on six Persian Gulf islands off Abu Ali were studied from June to August 1991. The authors conclude that "the massive oil and smoke pollution of the marine environment during the 1991 Gulf War did not have any major impact on overall breeding success."[54] The most likely reason, the authors suggest, was that most of the pollution dissipated by the time the terns arrived at their breeding grounds and that, by then, the oil slicks had been driven onto the Saudi coastline rather than into the Gulf itself.

Comparisons of this study with a 1986 census turned out favorably. Two species' populations declined, and the other two species' populations increased. Overall, the population for all four species increased from 47,830 to 66,660 breeding pairs between 1986 and 1991, an increase of 39 percent. Less than 1 percent of the adult population showed moderate to heavy oiling and only one-tenth of 1 percent of adult terns were found dead from oil-related causes. Even though the incidence of oiling among lesser-crested and white-cheeked tern chicks was high, very few dead chicks were found. Overall hatching and fledgling success among all four species of tern chicks was very high. A follow-up study a year later showed that the number of nests had increased further, to over 78,000. The proportion of moderately or heavily oiled birds had increased to 1.1 and 1.4 percent but those lightly oiled decreased from 3.8 to only 0.6 percent.[55]

In an interview Burr Heneman suggested that pit-digging on Gulf islands to pump in and recover oil assisted lesser-crested terns' reproductive success in that the digging cleared off vegetation and enlarged the areas available for breeding. Breeding and breeding success are different things. A follow-up study through four successive summers (1991–1994) noted significantly lower breeding success in 1992 and 1993, probably due to food shortages "as a direct result of the impact of the oil spill on fish eggs and larvae." But by 1994 food sources recovered, and so did tern breeding success, so that there has been "no long-term impact of the oil spill." The authors also note a new oil spill affecting the breeding colony on Karan Island in 1994.[56]

Carcasses of wintering seabirds were surveyed between February and April 1991. A total of 10,243 dead birds were found along the northern

Saudi Gulf Coast, 97 percent of which belonged to two species of cormorants and two species of grebes. The survey consisted of physically walking 197 km of coastline, counting and identifying dead birds. Because the entire affected coastline was estimated at 560 km, the authors arrive at a total estimate of 23,644 dead birds (weighted by exposed and sheltered coastlines). In addition to dead seabirds washed ashore, a number of birds are sure to have died at sea, so the total number of dead seabirds cannot be determined. Prewar population studies on these species are not available, and the authors note that the high number of dead grebes came as a shock as it was not known that such high numbers even existed. To estimate what the prewar populations might have been, the authors arrive at a minimum of 3,500 great-crested and 5,000 black-necked grebes based on site surveys stretched along the northern and southern Saudi Gulf Coast conducted two years after the war, in the winter season 1992–1993. If one now assumes, as the authors do, the existence of similar numbers off Qatar and the United Arab Emirates and further assumes that these represent prewar figures, then the grebe die-off would have been in the neighborhood of around two-thirds of its prewar population (estimated grebe deaths of 11,195 as a percentage of 2 times 8,500 equals 65.9).[57]

Using the same method, the wintering population of great cormorants was estimated at 15,000 individuals in 1991–1992 and 12,000 in 1992–1993, with large concentrations seen around Abu Ali Island and Tarut Bay. Again assuming that the Saudi great cormorant population is half of the total western Gulf cormorant population, for a total of 24,000 to 30,000 birds, and that this represents prewar totals, the Gulf War oil spills would then be estimated to have killed about 18 to 23 percent of the prewar great cormorant population (5,417 estimated deaths as a percentage of 24,000 to 30,000).

The socotra cormorant (*Phalacrocorax nigrogularis*) is endemic to the Gulf. Mortality at its northern breeding colonies has been estimated at 17 to 20 percent. But in a follow-up study, the three breeding colonies in Saudi Arabia tripled from 10,000 pairs in 1991–1992 to 30,000 pairs in 1994–1995; this would still represent a 40 percent decline as compared to a population estimate made in 1981. The authors add that they doubt the entire reduction was due to the oil spill in 1991 and conclude that their "study clearly illustrated that the oil pollution had no long-term effects which could threaten the continued existence of this endemic species in the northern Arabian Gulf." An earlier study concludes that "although the estimated mortality of grebes and cormorants was very high, the Gulf War oil spills did not diminish any of these populations to a level from which full recovery is impossible." In terms of table 1.2, these species were degraded but neither depleted nor destroyed.[58]

Depending on the birds' migration and feeding habits, the effects of the war-related oil spills were different. A set of prominent researchers concludes that "no bird species has had its world population reduced to such an extent that recovery is impossible . . . but four seabird [species] suffered severe mortality (22–50+ percent)" and that the oiling of the Saudi Arabian intertidal flats drastically reduced available feeding grounds of migratory wader populations. Among shorebirds, three species were heavily affected; the terek sandpiper in particular lost perhaps 10 to 15 percent of its worldwide population. Tern colonies were unaffected. Wintering grebes suffered a mortality rate of perhaps as high as 65 percent of the resident population, and cormorants one-sixth to one-fourth of their population. The endemic socotra cormorant lost perhaps 1 percent of its worldwide population. Even though data were arrived at by a good bit of extrapolation, it seems clear that wader species suffered the most. But only two years after the oil spill, in the mid-November 1992 to mid-January 1993 season, about three-fourths of the prewar wader populations appeared to have been reestablished, and this corresponds well with observed recovery rates in the United Kingdom and Mexico, following similar disasters.[59]

All sources agree that bird habitats south of Abu Ali Island and the Gulf of Bahrain were unaffected, that none of the Gulf islands were affected to any appreciable extent, and that only one small area in Kuwait was affected. Furthermore, none of the bird populations suffered irreversible population declines, and several populations increased in size. The Greenpeace mission report merely repeats reports of an estimated 15,000 to 30,000 pelagic seabirds being killed and of destroyed feeding grounds for 100,000 or more shorebirds.[60] Another, and telling, finding of the various ICBP studies concerns the nonwar impact on bird habitats in Saudi Arabia:

Landfilling since 1973 has eliminated large areas of shallow intertidal and subtidal habitat in the region of Jubayl-Abu Ali, Tarut Bay and Damman to Aziziyah. . . . Material for landfill of intertidal areas often comes from suction-dredging of nearby subtidal areas associated with the creation of shipping lanes, harbours and marinas. When mangroves, intertidal flats, saltmarshes and seagrass beds are dredged and/or covered with landfill, they are destroyed and lost forever to the marine ecosystem . . . the process is irreversible . . . more than 100 km² of coastal habitat has been buried and destroyed under landfill in the last 20 years along the Saudi Arabian Gulf shore. A much larger area of surrounding habitat has been affected by changes in water quality and shifting substrates due to landfill. This habitat destruction and degradation is more serious, in the long term, than that wreaked by the Gulf War oil spills, because it is permanent; the oiled and polluted coastline between Khafji and Abu Ali will recover its former value as a natural, life-sustaining resource, given enough time (perhaps ten years minimum), but no amount of time will ever bring back land-filled habitat.[61]

The preservation and protection of bird habitat is obviously crucial. In this regard, surveys carried out between May 1992 and May 1995 in the newly established Jubail Marine Wildlife Sanctuary show 275 bird species, "representing more than 75% of all bird species ever recorded in the Eastern Province of Saudi Arabia," including a number of globally endangered species.[62]

3.4 In Sum

The scientists' reports certainly suggest a fair amount of environmental disruption, even damage, some perhaps long-lived. But it is remarkable that a large part, perhaps even the larger part, of these damages are attributable to pre- and postwar peacetime commerce rather than to the war of 1991. By their nature, long-term environmental effects are unknown and could yet subtly affect environmental outcomes in years and decades to come. Just because damage has not been scientifically demonstrated does not imply that such damage may not be present. Still, years after the war, the evidence of environmental damage directly due to the Persian Gulf War of 1991 is remarkably slim. Regarding air quality, research has not found it possible to separate pre- and postwar industrial and natural background effects from those of the war itself. Fire-related chemicals in the smoke plume were generally below applicable (and generally more stringent) U.S. environmental or occupational exposure levels. There is concern but no evidence that smoke and soot particulates trapped in soil may eventually break loose through soil erosion and dust storms. The impact on the terrestrial environment is more ambiguous, but the major concern is with actual or potential groundwater contamination. As of 1998, grasslands appeared to have recovered quite well; native perennials were not fully reestablished. Because some oil fires were fought with saltwater pumped from the Gulf, salination occurred in those areas, thus changing the environment for prewar vegetation and creating competition with salt-tolerant plant species. This affects an area of less than the 49 km² of oil lakes (out of nearly 18,000 km² total Kuwaiti land area). However, one such area is located in an important freshwater aquifer that supplied about 40 percent of Kuwait's freshwater needs, mostly for farming. The aquifer was closed for human consumption. In contrast, brackish groundwater, used for livestock, was found free of contamination.[63]

Regarding the marine environment, the Green Cross International report on the medium to long-term environmental effects of the war comes to a remarkable conclusion: "Seven years after the war, the impacts of oil contamination due to the war on the marine ecosystems and living species such as fish and shrimp are difficult to distinguish from the impacts of chronic pollution from the oil industry and coastal development. Currently, the coral reefs appear healthy and the quantity of shrimp harvested each year are similar to the ones recorded before the war." It should be noted that Saudi Arabia did not have even one marine protected area until after the Gulf War.[64] The Green Cross conclusion is supported by others:

> Two years after the war, it is obvious that there are no long-term effects of the oil spill on subtidal ecosystems, such as macroalgal beds, seagrass beds and coral reefs. Fish populations, turtles and marine mammals are in a healthy condition. . . . The lower eulittoral and the subtidal fringe are still covered by an almost continuous band of oil and tar [in 1993]. While limited recolonization by the original plant and animal communities occurs on high-energy sandy beaches and rocky shores . . . mudflats and salt-marshes in sheltered bays show almost no sign of recovery. Population densities on the impacted shores remain much lower than on unaffected control sites, but in general there is a trend towards recovery with species diversity and population densities increasing.[65]

Similarly, researchers surveyed 35 sampling sites in Saudi Arabia in August 1991 and August 1992 and compared the results to those obtained at the same sites in 1986. Based on results obtained only less than a year after the last oil fire was put out, they write:

> The observed ecosystem abundance patterns may be attributed as much to seasonal variability, "background" human impacts, and the semi-quantitative nature of the survey [a rapid survey technique] as to war-related environmental incursions. Nevertheless, the apparent increase in certain faunal and floral elements clearly indicates that the Gulf conflict had not caused a complete environmental collapse. The surveys also revealed that other pollutants (e.g. plastics, metals) and coastal infilling, in particular, remain a major environmental problem.[66]

As a rule, air pollution effects disperse quickly and widely by wind. Water pollution effects disperse somewhat less quickly and less widely by wind and current. In contrast, soil effects disperse slowly and not widely. Soil stays put, mostly, and so does any harm done to soil. Just how substantial the war's effects on Kuwait's soil and terrestrial water sources were, we cannot say as the available information is too limited to allow us to draw reasonably solid conclusions. The soft conclusion is that the effect was probably substantial but not irreversible. There is nothing in the literature that suggests altogether altered ecosystems. The terrestrial effects of the war on Saudi Arabia were minimal.[67]

3.5 Bibliographic Note

In addition to the sources listed in section 3.1.1, hereunder is an alphabetical listing of additional literature pertaining to air, soil, floral, and faunal studies for Kuwait and Saudi Arabia: Abdali and Yakoob (1994); Abo El-Nil (1996); Al-Ajmi (1994); Al-Ajmi and Marmoush (1996); Al-Ajmi and Misak (1995); Al-Awadhi (1996); Al-Awadhi, Balba, and Kamizawa (1996); Al-Daher, Al-Awadhi, and El-Nawawy (1998); Al-Gounaim, et al. (1995); Al-Hassan (1994); Al-Houty, Abdal, and Zaman (1993); Ali (1994); Al-Muzaini and Jacob (1996a, 1996b); Alsdirawi (1994); Al-Senafy, et al. (1997); Bader and Clarkson (1995); Bakan, et al. (1991); Balba, et al. (1996); Balba, et al. (1998); Barth and Niestlé (1994); Bloom, et al. (1994); Böer and Warnken (1996); Bouhamra, BuHamra, and Thomson (1997); Bou-Rabee, Bakir, and Bem (1995); Browning, et al. (1991); Canby (1991); Earle (1992); El-Baz (1994); Goudie (2000); Green Cross International (1998); Greenpeace (1992); Hamzah (1996); Hobbs and Radke (1992); Kock and Nader (1996); Kwarteng (1998); Malallah, et al. (1997); Martens (1996); Obuekwe and Al-Zarban (1998); Omar, et al. (2000); Omar, Misak, and Shahid (2001); Pearce (1995); Pilcher and Sexton (1993); Radwan, et al. (1996); Radwan, Sorkhoh, and El-Nemr (1995); Salam (1996); Spektor (1998); UNEP-Partow (2001); United States General Accounting Office (1992); Westing (2003); and Yateem, et al. (1998).

Notes

1. Elsewhere, the Persian Gulf is also referred to as the Arabian Gulf. For consistency, the former is used throughout, except when quoting or using source materials that use the latter term in the original. Dates are in U.S. time; that is, depending on the time of day, 16 January U.S. time may be 17 January Kuwaiti time.

2. Number of wells: US GAO (1992, p. 10). Pilcher and Sexton (1993, p. 8), based on a September 1991 paper by F. Al-Jassim, report a total of 1,073 oil wells,

of which 613 were fired, 76 gushed, and 99 damaged. Elsewhere in the literature one finds different estimates. Last oil well capped: for instance, Earle (1992,
p. 134). Spillage: Bader and Clarkson (1995, p. 1046) double this to 60 million
barrels. Burning: Hobbs and Radke (1992, p. 987); also Al-Ajmi and Marmoush
(1996, p. 280). Background spills/Prince William Sound: Earle (1992, p. 133); also
Abdulraheem (2000, p. 341) and Michel, Gundlach, and Hayes (1986), cited in
Abuzinada and Krupp (1994, p. 7). Peacetime destruction: for instance, Abuzinada
and Krupp (1994).

3. But see UNEP (2003c).

4. Available via http://www.gulflink.osd.mil/ [accessed 25 March 2009].

5. See US GAO (1992).

6. Resulting reports are in Dennis (1991); Heneman (1991); Evans (1992);
Harbard and Wolstencroft (1992); Evans and Keijl (1993b); Greenpeace (1992);
Bloom, et al. (1994); Price and Robinson (1993); Price, et al. (1994); Abuzinada
and Krupp (1994); Krupp, Abuzinada, and Nader (1996); Krupp and Khushaim
(1996); Green Cross International (1998).

7. See Browning, et al. (1991).

8. Following the overthrow of Saddam Hussein in the 2003 Iraq war, a UNEP
project to assist with marshland restoration called the Iraqi Marshland Observation
System (IMOS) was introduced (see http://imos.grid.unep.ch/) [accessed 15 February 2009]. Compared to the predrainage marshland extent, averaged for 1973 to
1976, the recovery rate reached 58 percent by 15 December 2006.

9. Marshland: UNEP and Partow (2001). Northern Gulf: Sen Gupta, Fondekar, and Alagarsamy (1993, p. 90); Pilcher and Sexton (1993). Information in
this and the preceding paragraph based on Abuzinada and Krupp (1994) and
Abdulraheem (2000).

10. Abdulraheem (2000, p. 345). This is not quite correct. For specific instances, prewar data are available. Abdulraheem himself notes that the former
Kuwait Environment Protection Department had baseline data for 1986 on petroleum hydrocarbons (PHCs) that could be, and were, compared to levels in 1991
and in 1995. (A fivefold increase between 1986 and 1991; then a drop by 50 percent by 1995; see Abdulraheem, 2000, p. 346). But even where there are baseline
data, it is not always clear how much of any given increase from some prewar year
to 1991 might have been due to the war or to nonwar anthropogenic input.

11. Even though Kuwaiti oil was the source of the fires and spills, its marine
environment was little affected; see Pilcher and Sexton (1993). The releases generated by Iraqi occupying troops from oil tankers and from the tanker terminal at
Mina Al-Ahmadi were floated offshore by strong northwest winds and eventually
beached on Saudi Arabia's northern Gulf Coast. Much the same happened to oil
terminal releases from Mina Al-Bakr in the northeast of Kuwait. Ninety-five percent
of Kuwait's coastline remained unaffected. One patch, Sulaibikhat Bay, an important waterfowl habitat due west of Kuwait City, was affected by pollution, but it is
unclear to what ecological extent. The prevailing Gulf winds early in the year are

from north-northwest. Had the winds been from the north or northeast, the oil would have struck the southern Kuwaiti coast. Instead, the northwest winds basically pushed the oil slick south along the southern Kuwaiti coast. When the winds turned north, they pushed the oil onto the northern Saudi coast. Samples taken from southern Kuwait and from the Al Ahmadi oil terminal all showed less than 0.0015 percent total petroleum hydrocarbons (TPH). While this is higher than a baseline study published in 1986, comparisons to sample sites in Iran and Bahrain, sites unaffected by the Persian Gulf War, show much higher pollution levels there, of up to 7.24 percent TPH, the result of ongoing "localized pollution" (Greenpeace, 1992, p. 15), so that the observed levels in Kuwait might well have been the outcome of ongoing pollution rather than because of the war. Pre- and post-satellite imaging revealed that "the soft muddy intertidal flats north of . . . [Kuwait] Bay [near Mina Ash-Shuwaikh] . . . are green because of the high green algae content. A comparison of the 1986 and 1993 images indicates that the algae more or less remained in the same locations, indicating that conditions supporting their existence did not change dramatically during the seven-year interval" [http://www.kisr.edu.kw/research/environment/rs/rs3.htm#chap5 (accessed 17 April 2000)]. An IUCN mission found that fish were abundant and vibrant around Kuwaiti coral reefs with special note made of the presence of juveniles and sub-adults (that is, species replenishment was not threatened). Some decline in the number of fish species was observed, but this appears to continue a trend observed as from 1985. Regarding Kuwaiti coral reefs, in May 1992 numerous dead coral were found (tissue degradation or bleaching). But a prewar study in 1985 also found stressed coral. In Kuwaiti waters, coral live at the very edge of their natural distribution limit in very-high-salinity waters with very cold winter water temperatures so that stressed coral are to be expected. In November and December 1992, a follow-up study "showed that only limited mortalities had occurred at the reefs surrounding the islands of Kubbar, Qaru, and Um al-Maradem. At Qi'tat Urayfijan evidence of impact was observed but recovery was well advanced. The authors emphasize that although effects of the Gulf War may have contributed to the observed mortalities, they may have had only a minor influence compared to other environmental factors" [Vogt (1994, p. 65), referring to Downing and Roberts (1993)].

12. Evans (1992, p. 1).

13. 25 percent: Abdulraheem (2000, pp. 341–342). 45 percent: Evans (1992, p. 1). No sunken oil: Abuzinada and Krupp (1994, p. 7); Michel, Gundlach, and Hayes (1993, p. 109). Other sources are referred to later on.

14. Very active: Floodgate (1996, p. 75). 27 months: Smith (1996a, p. 54). Cyanobacterial mats: Höpner, et al. (1996, p. 85). Also see Hoffmann (1996, p. 96). Interestingly, in carrying out a complete survey of marine algae in the Jubail Marine Wildlife Sanctuary after the Gulf War, De Clerck and Coppejans (1996) recorded 90 taxa, including 42 species new to the Saudi Arabian coast and 15 species new to the Persian Gulf. Clean-up technique: Smith (1996b). Alterna-

tive techniques: Watt (1996, p. 116). Renewed mortality: Jones, et al. (1996, p. 138).

15. Ras as Saffaniya and Abu Ali: Barth and Niestlé (1994, p. 13). Greenpeace (1992); quote p. 14. IUCN: Price, et al. (1994); quote p. 17.

16. Abu Ali: Al-Arfaj and Alam (1993, p. 101, table 5). Comparison: Basaham and Al-Lihaibi (1993, p. 103). Subtidal: Michel, Gundlach, and Hayes (1993, p. 109). Chemical analysis: Sauer, et al. (1993, p. 117). Without spill samples, oil residue cannot be matched to a precise source. One can say only that it was not oil from the Kuwait war spill, for which spill samples were available.

17. Schneider and Kinzelbach (1994); quotes pp. 38, 34.

18. One year after: Hayes, et al. (1993, p. 135). Details vary: Jones, et al. (1994). 1994: Jones, et al. (1996, p. 138).

19. Crabs: Apel (1994); quote p. 40. Suggestion: p. 44. Follow-up study: Apel (1996, p. 327).

20. Quote: Hoffman (1994, p. 16). Mat curling: Hoffmann (1994, p. 17).

21. Böer (1994); quotes pp. 23-24; mangrove die-off: pp. 22-23. Warnken (1996); quote p. 177; destruction: p. 180. One reviewer points out that the term "extinct" in the first quote is improperly applied. "Extinct" refers to the disappearance of an entire taxon, whereas "extirpated" refers to locally lost.

22. A decade or more: Böer (1994, p. 25). Trial planting: Böer (1996, p. 186).

23. Dawhat ad Dafi: see Böer (1993, pp. 207-208). Land reclamation: Evans (1992, p. 26). Quote: Abunizada and Krupp (1994, p. 7).

24. McCain, Beard, and Fadlallah (1993, pp. 79, 80, 83, table 1).

25. One year after: Burns, et al. (1993, p. 199). NOAA: Kenworthy, et al. (1993, p. 220); quotes pp. 213, 219.

26. Initial study: De Clerck and Coppejans (1994, p. 20). Follow-on study: De Clerck and Coppejans (1996, p. 199).

27. Laboratory: Durako, et al. (1993). Zooplankton: Al-Yamani, Al-Rifaie, and Ismail (1993, p. 239).

28. 1992: Richmond (1994); quotes pp. 55, 59. 1993 and 1994: Richmond (1996, p. 159). Benthic macrofauna: Prena (1996, p. 128).

29. The physical integrity of the habitat determines the great difference between the environmental effects of this war and peacetime commercial development in the Gulf region (and to other wars). Unlike shoreline development, the war did not destroy physical habitat. This is shown and more fully discussed in the section on birds.

30. Bu-Olayan, Al-Omran, and Subramanyam (1996, p. 715).

31. Quotes from Evans (1992, p. 1) and Abunizada and Krupp (1994, p. 7).

32. Microlayer: Price (1994, p. 27). Quotes: Krupp and Müller (1994, p. 67).

33. Quote: Krupp and Almarri (1996, p. 339). IUCN: Krupp and Müller (1994). This paper suggests that the IUCN findings may have been due to the

cold temperatures that prevailed that winter rather than to oil and reduced summer temperatures due to the smoke plume.

34. Clams: Sadiq and McCain (1993, p. 163). Fish and clams: Fowler, et al. (1993, p. 171). East of Qatari: Kureishy (1993). Minimax world ranges: Abdali and Yakoob (1994, p. 99). Kuwaiti markets: Saeed, et al. (1995, p. 255); Bu-Olayan and Subramanyam (1996) conclude that "the Gulf War may have enhanced metal bioaccumulation in some fishes" (p. 758) but their use of the word "may" suggests that the evidence is not clear. In the text of their report, frequent mention is made of pollution sources such as power stations, dry docks, industries, naval bases, fertilizer plants, oil refineries, and road traffic. The Gulf War is mentioned exactly once, in the Results and Discussion section of their report. Findings are similarly ambiguous for blue crabs caught and analyzed from May 1998 to April 1999 (see Al-Mohanna and Subrahmanyam, 2001). Kuwaiti nearshore samples: Metwally, et al. (1997); quotes pp. 118, 120.

35. Order of magnitude: Price (1994, p. 35); Mathews, et al. (1993, p. 269). Long quote: Mathews, et al. (1993, p. 251).

36. Similar views: Abdulraheem (2000, p. 349); Price (1998). Comparisons: Mathews, et al. (1993, pp. 267–268). Recovered: Green Cross International (1998, p. v). An entirely different concern is that "shrimp farming ranks as one of the most resource-intensive food production systems, characterizing it as an ecologically unsustainable throughput system" (Larsson, Folke, and Kautsky, 1994, p. 663).

37. Siddiqui and Al-Mubarak (1998); liberalization: p. 105; marshland: p. 107.

38. Downing and Roberts (1993, p. 149); also Vogt (1994, p. 62). Quotes: Greenpeace (1992, p. 30).

39. NOAA: Bloom, et al. (1994); quotes pp. 57, 58. Downing and Roberts (1993, p. 152); quote p. 150.

40. Downing and Roberts (1993); all quotes p. 153.

41. First study: Vogt (1994, p. 61). Follow-up study: Vogt (1996, p. 302).

42. Heneman (1991, p. 12); quote p. 5. Environmental problems posed by fishing and fishing methods are also discussed in Esseen (1996).

43. Robineau and Fiquet (1994, p. 79). They also report that Preen counted 93 marine mammal carcasses in March and April 1991, all located at least 120 km south of Abu Ali, and not obviously related to the Gulf War oil.

44. Dugong and dolphins quote: Greenpeace (1992, p. 35). Mammalian quote: Greenpeace (1992, p. 23). Green and hawksbill turtles: Price, Sheppard, and Roberts (1993, p. 13).

45. Dugong distribution: Price, Sheppards, and Roberts (1993, p. 13). Other studies: see Bloom, et al. (1994, p. 54). Gulf of Bahrain: Bloom, et al. (1994, p. 55); also Heneman (1991, p. 3). Islands: Bloom, et al. (1994, p. 58). Greenpeace turtle: Greenpeace (1992, p. 29). Three green turtles: Evans (1992, p. 65, Table 24). Four oiled turtles: Heneman (1991, p. 9). Thomas (1995, p. 118) reports that

"hundreds of endangered turtles had been found dead in oily inshore waters," referring to a Science for Peace report of February 1992. It has not been possible to inspect the Science for Peace report and to identify any underlying scientific studies to corroborate the claim. Green and hawksbill turtles: Al-Merghani, et al. (1996, p. 351).

46. The information presented in this paragraph is based primarily on Evans (1992). Temperatures: Evans and Keijl (1993b, p. 100).

47. Bird classification: "A great many different classifications of birds have been proposed. As references to any series of bird books will make clear, there is no simple agreement" (Perrins and Middleton, 1985, p. xiv). Areas and gradients: Evans (1992, p. 4).

48. First visit: Heneman (1991); Dennis (1991). Second visit: Evans (1992); Evans and Keijl (1993b). Third visit: Harbard and Wolstencroft (1992); Evans and Keijl (1993b). Information on the war's effects on birds in Kuwait is scarce. The following is based on Pilcher and Sexton (1993), apparently the only research piece available on birds and Kuwait. A survey in May 1991 of three nature reserve areas northwest of Kuwait City came too late to observe migrating wader species who had already moved through en route to their Eurasian breeding grounds. Even though the nature reserves were heavily damaged by Iraqi military activities, Kuwaiti shorelines were only partially affected. In particular, mud flats were unaffected. Oiling of birds was moderate (p. 12, table 1). Counts around oil lakes produced "a surprisingly small number of corpses" (p. 13). The Kuwaiti Gulf islands were altogether free of oil and the bird populations were apparently entirely unaffected, with tern populations similar to those in counts undertaken in 1987 and 1990 (p. 13).

49. Prewar census: Zwarts, Felemban, and Price (1991). Dead wader counts elsewhere: Evans and Keijl (1993b, p. 87). Alternative habitats: Bloom, et al. (1994, p. 60). First quote: Bloom, et al. (1994, p. 64). The quote is from an interview with Mike Evans who conducted surveys in April and May 1991 along the Saudi coast. The interview took place in February 1992 and was revised by Evans in February 1993. Printed in Bloom et al. (1994, pp. 63–68). Second quote: Evans, Symens, and Pilcher (1993, p. 159).

50. Evans and Keijl (1993b, pp. 96–98).

51. Previous winter counts: Zwarts, Felemban, and Price (1991). Estimates: Evans and Keijl (1993b). The second ICBP team established twenty-seven count sites located around the three major previously identified bird habitats: (1) at Ras Tanaqib and Dawhat Manifah (14 April to 28 May; 13 sites), (2) the area north of Jubayl, including Dawhat al Mussalamiyah, Dawhat ad Dafi, and the Abu Ali Island areas (12 April to 28 May; 7 sites), and (3) Tarut Bay, just north of Dhahran (14 April to 28 May; 7 sites). The team counted 37,227 birds of thirty-eight species in April and May 1991. Spring migration studies carried out in Morocco and the island of Sabah (Malaysia) suggest that the actual number of birds exceeds those counted by a factor of 3 to 4.5. Thus, the number present at the twenty-seven

count sites in the Gulf may have ranged from 112,000 to 168,000, perhaps more toward the upper end of the range as the count sites primarily covered the mud and sand flats preferred by waders rather than the rocky areas that are more prominent along the southern Saudi coast.

52. 4,000 remaining: Evans and Keijl (1993b, pp. 94–95). 100,000 out of 250,000: Zwarts, Felemban, and Price (1991); Evans and Keijl (1993b, p. 95). Quote: Evans and Keijl (1993b, pp. 95–96).

53. Quote: Symens and Suhaibani (1994, p. 51). Intense observation: Zwarts, Felemban, and Price (1991); Symens and Suhaibani (1994, p. 50). Substantially re-covered: as an alternative hypothesis, a study by Symens, reported in Price (1998), notes that the 1991–1992 wader "population decline was actually the result of re-duced nutrient input into the bay, as a result of changing land-use patterns" (p. 93).

54. Symens and Evans (1993, p. 18).

55. Tern population increase: Symens and Evans (1993, table 2, p. 24). Tern chicks: Symens and Evans (1993, p. 30, table 7, and discussion on p. 34). Also see pp. 29, 33. Follow-up study: Symens and Suhaibani (1994); nests: p. 50, table 1; oiling: p. 51, table 2.

56. Interview: Heneman in Bloom, et al. (1994, pp. 53–63, here p. 61). Other information and quotes: Symens and Alsuhaibany (1996b, p. 404).

57. Dead bird counts: Symens and Suhaibani (1993, p. 39); great cormorant, 23 percent; socotra cormorant, 28 percent; great crested grebe, 21 percent; black-necked grebe, 25 percent, respectively, of all dead birds. Walking: extending this method of estimation to Kuwait, they argue that the total might rise to 30,000 birds. However, as Pilcher and Sexton (1993, p. 12) noted, 95 percent of Kuwait's coast was unoiled, and the oil spills moved relatively quickly into Saudi territory. Prewar counts: Symens and Suhaibani (1993, p. 40). On the whole, the writ-ings by ornithologists give the impression that they were embarrassed about how little was known prior to the war about bird populations, distribution, migration, feeding, breeding, and other behaviors. Indeed, the numerous postwar surveys uncovered much that was new, including three species new to Saudi Arabia and five species new to its Eastern Province (Evans, 1992, p. 32, Appendix 2). New information on wader behavior was generated (see, for instance, Evans and Keijl, 1993a), and the opportunity was used to take biometric measurements on dead socotra cormorants (Keijl and Symens, 1993).

58. Socotra cormorant mortality estimate: Symens and Suhaibani (1993, p. 41). Follow-up study: Symens and Werner (1996, p. 390). First quote: Symens and Werner (1996, p. 400). Second quote: Symens and Suhaibani (1993, p. 41).

59. Quote: Evans, Symens, and Pilcher (1993, p. 157). Shorebirds: Greenpeace (1992, p. 67). Recoveries elsewhere: Symens and Suhaibani (1994, pp. 50–51).

60. Greenpeace (1992, p. 36).

61. Evans (1992, p. 23).

62. Symens and Alsuhaibany (1996a, p. 374).

63. Possibly delayed effects: Greenpeace (1992, p. 34). Terrestrial effects: Green Cross International (1998, p. 99). Water/aquifers: Green Cross International (1998, pp. 73–75). See bibliographic note for literature on the war's effects on terrestrial and atmospheric effects in Kuwait and Saudi Arabia.

64. Quote: Green Cross International (1998, p. v). Marine protected areas: see Krupp and Khushaim (1996).

65. Abunizada and Krupp (1994, pp. 7–8).

66. Price, et al. (1993, p. 143). In more recent work Price (1998) writes: "Despite extensive damage to coastal salt marshes and mangroves, the post-war period has generally been characterised by recovery of intertidal biota . . . wintering wader populations . . . and seabird populations. . . . Post-war studies suggest that certain coastal activities unrelated to the conflict (e.g., recreation and fishing) can be equally or more damaging environmentally than war-related effects."

67. Throughout the literature on the Persian Gulf War one finds occasional comparisons to other oil spills, in particular the 1979 *Ixtoc I* blowout in the Gulf of Mexico, the 1983 *Nowruz* spill during the Iran-Iraq War, and the 1989 *Exxon Valdez* spill in Alaska. For a number of reasons, it is improper to make comparisons. See, for instance, Al-Muzaini and Jacob (1996b, pp. 373–374); Heneman (1991, p. 12); Price (1991; annex 3 in Heneman, 1991).

Civil War and Borderland Effects   **4**

Scientific literature on the effects of civil war on nature is much dispersed and extraordinarily time-intensive to gather. In the main, it is limited to the sub-Saharan African continent and there to the effects of war on large mammals such as primates, elephants, and rhinoceroses, and on the effects on national parks. The bulk of the African literature addresses Rwanda and the eastern Congo. The environmental effects of civil war in Latin American countries have rarely been examined. For Asia, Afghanistan and the effects of Afghan refugees on Pakistan are probably the best documented cases. Everything else is exceedingly limited in scope, at times no more than a single usable study for a given country.

Other literature consists of news reports or news items and single-instance anecdotes rather than scientific studies or summaries and evaluations of such studies. While emotionally powerful, the substantive quality of this literature can be poor. Assertions are made without evidentiary backing, nor reference to where the evidence might be found. This is not to say that such reports are false or that their authors are deliberately misleading, but it is to say that one cannot rely on these reports. On the plus side, from the mid-1990s more attention and funding has been given to the study of civil war and biodiversity so that a number of useful reports emerged.[1] Also on the plus side, contributors bring out issues beyond the immediacy of war. For example, civil war in financially constrained nations reduces already skimpy wildlife conservation budgets. War can thus contribute to wildlife depletion by budgetary default with regard to ongoing conservation efforts. Also, civil wars tend to produce large numbers of refugees who, to secure their own survival, pillage the flora and fauna of the lands they move through or to. These and related themes are taken up in this chapter.

The nature of the available material, briefly discussed hereunder, makes it impractical to organize the remainder of the chapter by category of ecological interest, such as by trophic level or species or biomes. Because most material is issued by country, the chapter is arranged accordingly. Section 4.1 is a case study on Rwanda and the eastern Congo. This is followed in section 4.2 with a case study on Afghanistan and Pakistan. Section 4.3 summarizes, and section 4.4 is a bibliographic note on materials available for other civil war countries.

Much of the source material regarding environmental effects of civil war is of poor quality.[2] Consider an example:

> It is very unfortunate for Uganda that the conflicts were resolved at the cost of so much destruction of the resources. It is doubtful if all the damages can be repaired. In areas like South Western Uganda, Acholi, West Nile, North Buganda (Iwero) and Soroti, to mention only a few, many forest and woodland areas were either shelled to destroy the enemy or scorched altogether by fire. Soils were also destroyed by bombs and grenades. Some rivers and lakes were either silted by physical earth transfers or soil sedimentation. The National Parks were exhausted of their wildlife and reverted to bush and were later recolonized by tsetse fly. There are no figures to confirm the damage done by the 20-year civil wars, but it will definitely have some far-reaching impact on the environment of Uganda.[3]

Strong claims are made, but there is no evidence to back up the claims. In fact, the authors state that there are "no figures to confirm the damage." All of the claimed effects are likely to have occurred to some degree, but surely it is preferable to cite numbers based on scientific studies. No one is assisted by unsubstantiated claims.

Other parts of the literature undertake great effort to locate and refer to known surveys and studies and simply come up short. For example, an extensive report on Angola by IUCN repeatedly stresses that the last substantial surveys of flora and fauna took place in the 1960s and early 1970s, that is, before the civil war began that followed Angola's independence from Portugal in 1975.[4] There is no doubt that the civil war adversely affected some aspects of Angola's wildlife, biodiversity, and conservation efforts, but it is not clear to what degree.

Another part of the literature consists of news items in environmental or scientific journals. For example, the scientific journal *Oryx* frequently publishes notes such as "Army hunts in the park" or "War and wildlife in Georgia."[5] These are one- or two-paragraph news items reprinted from various published sources. The full text of the first item reads as follows:

> On two occasions in May [1988] the Sudanese army unit stationed in Mimule National Park was ordered by the Commander to hunt in the area. Using automatic machine guns, more than 70 soldiers killed or wounded about 100 animals. The park staff were powerless to resist and have complained to the office of the Governor (CNPPA Newsletter, 43, 7).

For conservationists, this is important news but it is not usable for the larger purpose of documenting the effects of war on nature. Even the repeated occurrence of such single-instance accounts does not permit one to conclude much other than that there is some (but unspecified) effect.

On the positive side, since the mid-1990s a number of scientifically credible and serious efforts have been made to document the effects of war on nature. In a particularly instructive exercise, the U.S. Agency for International Development financed a consortium consisting of the World Wildlife Fund, the Nature Conservancy, and the World Resources Institute to establish the Biodiversity Support Program. This program in turn created a division on armed conflict and biodiversity that generated a series of useful country studies.[6] But due to the difficulty of collecting data in war zones, as outlined in chapter 1, even in this case data quality is at times deficient. The Rwandan and Afghan cases are chosen for examination in this chapter in part because data is relatively plentiful and reliable.

4.1 Rwanda and the Eastern Congo

The 1990–1994 civil war in Rwanda killed hundreds of thousands of people and generated perhaps two million refugees within Rwanda and another two million who fled south to Burundi, across the eastern border to Tanzania, or across the western border into what was then Zaire.[7] Most refugees settled in and around protected areas of great conservation value. Two years later, the war sparked a civil war in Zaire itself. The despotic ruler was deposed in 1997, and the country renamed as the Democratic Republic of the Congo. Its new leader soon was assassinated and its neighbors Uganda, Burundi, and Rwanda implicated in the continuing turmoil. For a while, Angola, Namibia, South Africa, and Zimbabwe all were enmeshed in this central African conflict as well.

Rwanda is a highly fertile country that suffers from acidic and eroding soil. It is a small country—at 26,338 km^2 it is smaller than the U.S. state of

Maryland—with a relatively large population of an estimated 10.2 million people (in 2008) and high rate of population growth (only 7.4 million people in 2002). At nearly 400 people per km^2 it has Africa's highest population density. A central plateau at elevations between 1,400 and 2,200 meters dominates the country.[8] It rises to the west, toward Congo, to heights of over 3,500 meters, and falls in elevation toward Tanzania in the east. The northwestern part, between the towns of Gisenyi and Ruhengeri, is most famous for its five volcanoes. By the 1950s, Rwanda had established two national parks and several forest reserves. Encroachment was a problem, but even in 1990 about 10–12 percent of Rwanda's land area was formally protected. The two national parks are Parc National des Volcans (Volcanoes National Park) in the west and the Akagera National Park in the east. The first covers a transboundary area known as the Virunga Volcanoes region or, simply, the Virunga. It is shared with Uganda in the north and Congo in the northwest. This region is 425 km^2 in size and lies at an altitude of 2,600 to 4,500 meters. The Congolese part, several thousand square kilometers in size, also includes lower elevations. The Rwandan part, the Volcanoes National Park, covers about 150 km^2 and was established in 1927. Most famously, Dian Fossey established a base here, the Karisoke Research Station, to support the study of mountain gorillas (*Gorilla gorilla beringei*), and gorilla tourism eventually became an important income generator for Rwanda.

The other national park, the Akagera National Park, lies in east Rwanda on the Tanzanian border. It once covered 2,500 km^2 of savannah grassland, woodland, and wetland, but since November 1998 the park's size has officially been reduced to 732 km^2.

Forest reserves in Rwanda include the Nyungwe Forest Reserve, a mountainous area of 970 km^2 in southwest Rwanda, which extends a further 400 km^2 south into Burundi (as the Kibira Forest), and the Gishwati and Mukua Forest Reserves, originally 280 km^2 and 20 km^2, respectively, in size. Both are located between the Nyungwe reserve and the volcanoes park.

Rwanda and Congo are separated by Lake Kivu. Two land bridges exist. One lies at the northern end of the lake, near the Rwandan town of Gisenyi and the Congolese town of Goma (the capital of the Congolese province of North Kivu); the other, at the southern end, is near the Rwandan town of Cyangugu and the Congolese town of Bukavu (capital of the province of South Kivu). The Congo sports a number of formally protected areas, totaling some 180,000 km^2 or nearly 8 percent of its territory.[9] In the northeastern Congo, these areas include the Garamba National Park, which borders on southern Sudan, the Okapi Faunal Reserve, the Maiko National Park, the Virunga National Park, and the Kahuzi-

Biega National Park, the last-named located due west of Lake Kivu. In contrast to Rwanda, the Congo is huge, covering about 2.4 million km^2, equal in area to the United States of America east of the Mississippi River or to the total area of all European colonizers of Africa: Belgium, Britain, France, Germany, Italy, Portugal, and Spain. With over 66 million people, the population density of the Congo is low, at about 28 people per km^2. The Congo is rich in natural resources such as cobalt, columbo-tantalite (coltan),[10] copper, diamond, gold, crude oil, timber, rubber, and coffee, and is home to spectacular large mammals. For example, the savannah Garamba National Park is home to the rare northern white rhinoceros (*Ceratotherium simum cottoni*). The okapi (*Okapia johnstoni*) is found in the Okapi Faunal Reserve and the Maiko National Park, and the eastern lowland gorilla (*Gorilla beringei graueri*) is home in the Kahuzi-Biega and Maiko National Parks. These areas are unusually rich not only in charismatic megafauna but also in other fauna, and in flora. The potential and actual effects of war are certainly of concern.

THE WAR. The Rwandan civil war of the early 1990s began when forces of the Rwandan Patriotic Front (RPF), hiding in the Ugandan part of the Virunga, crossed the border into Rwanda. The rebels, descendants of earlier wars in Rwanda, and mostly of Tutsi lineage, had bases in southern Uganda and moved freely throughout the Virunga. The Rwandan war was dispersed in time and space and did not affect the country massively or uniformly until it came to a terrible head when an airplane carrying the presidents of Rwanda and Burundi, returning from peace talks in Arusha, Tanzania, was shot down on 6 April 1994. Nearly instantly, Hutu-dominated militia groups (Interahamwe) engaged in large-scale killings, mostly of Tutsi, in Rwanda's capital, Kigali, and throughout the country. It is said that some 800,000 people lost their lives. In response, the Tutsi-dominated Rwandan Patriotic Front (RPF) launched an offensive, taking Kigali by 19 July 1994. Fearing reprisals, nearly two million people, mostly Hutu, fled the country. Among them were militia participants who then stirred up unrest from the eastern Congo. The new Rwandan rulers responded, together with Uganda and Burundi, and a civil war commenced in the Congo as well. The region remains restive.[11]

4.1.1 Rwanda

NYUNGWE FOREST RESERVE. It is best to summarize the environmental effects of the conflagration by affected area or by resource. At 970 km^2

in size, the Nyungwe Forest Reserve lies in southwest Rwanda. Administered in four management zones, according to the support received by outside agencies (French, Swiss, EU, and World Bank), it is one of Africa's largest remaining bits of afromontane forest. Even though the reserve largely escaped fighting during the war, the agencies and their expatriate staff left the country. Only unpaid junior staff remained for a few months. During the height of the war, in 1994, French troops occupied the territory. Thereafter, the new Rwandan army patrolled the area to prevent formation of potential pockets of resistance to the new government.

As a by-product of war, ecotourism faltered, and the Rwandan Office for Tourism and National Parks found itself strapped for financial resources to restaff the reserve. This opened it for poaching and agricultural encroachment, especially in its southeastern part. Snare counts and encounters with animals such as ungulates (e.g., duikers), bush pigs, porcupine (*Atherurus africanus*), and the Gambian rat (*Cricetomys gambianus*), show large numbers of the former, 300 to 400 snares a month, and declining numbers of the latter. The last elephant in Nyungwe is said to have been shot by poachers in 1999. "This leaves no large mammals in the forest to control the extent of understory herbaceous vegetation"; the likely effect of the absence of large mammals on the development of the forest is unknown. The absence of elephants would be a conservation loss but, depending on their exact ecological role, may or may not be a diversity gain. Recent experiments in Kenya show that exclusion of large herbivores can induce changes in vegetation and in insect-plant mutualism.[12]

AKAGERA NATIONAL PARK. The Akagera National Park lies adjacent to the Tanzanian border and not far from the Ugandan border in the north. Prior to the war it was huge in size, some 2,500 km², and "extremely rich in large mammals," including the aquatic duiker sitatunga (*Tragelaphus spekei*) and the roan antelope (*Hippotragus equinus*). Hosting extensive wetlands, it also served as a stopover point for migratory birds. Prior to the war, the main problem stemmed from poachers coming from Tanzania. The initial fighting in Rwanda took place in this park and involved extensive hunting to feed the troops. Conservation staff was withdrawn. After the war, Tutsi, who tend to be cattle herders, settled in the park and cleared large forested areas to prepare them for cattle grazing. In 1998, the park's boundaries were redrawn to less than one-third of its original size. "It is estimated that this reduction in size will lead to a loss of 15 percent of tree and shrub species, 20 percent of herbaceous species, and about 13 percent of bird species from the park."[13]

One can see that a reduction in numbers of individuals per species would result, but to what extent species losses would result is less clear.[14] Estimates of large-mammal densities between 1991 and 1998 suggest commensurate reductions to less than one-third of the original numbers for buffalo, impala, topi, warthog, waterbuck, reedbuck, oribi, and zebra, the combined effect of war-related hunting and postwar conversion of protected areas to grazing land. This information is supplemented by Kanyamibwa, who writes that in 1993 a research team, of which he was a part, found an estimated loss of some 90 percent of the big animals, and important losses and changes in habitat, although the nature of the losses and changes is not described. Kanyamibwa believes that the long-term impact on the park will be even worse because its animals "need large and complementary areas for seasonal migrations."[15]

THE GISHWATI AND MUKURA FOREST RESERVES. The Gishwati and Mukura Forest Reserves already had been heavily degraded by cattle herding in the 1980s. Nonetheless, they still hosted populations of chimpanzees (*Pan troglodytes*) and golden monkeys (*Cercopithecus mitis kandti*). Gishwati was subject to refugee flows and became a hideout for Interahamwe rebels after the war. Neither it nor the much smaller Mukura Forest Reserve were ever a target of concerted conservation efforts. In 2000, a survey found "only a few stands of trees of less than one hectare in size" remaining of Gishwati and "only approximately 8 square kilometers remaining" of Mukura. By 2001, the conservation community had written off these areas as complete losses.[16]

VOLCANOES NATIONAL PARK. The entire Virunga area was deemed unsafe following the RPF start of the war in October 1990. The RPF and the Rwandan Armed Forces (RAF, at that time the Rwandan army) both had laid antipersonnel land mines inside and along the perimeter of the Rwandan portion of the park. Nonetheless, park staff undertook efforts to patrol. Reminiscent of U.S. forces in Vietnam, in 1991 the RAF cut a 10-meter-wide swath through the park for ambush control. From 1990 to 1994, international and national staff working with the Karisoke gorilla research station were evacuated several times. At the height of the fighting, the facilities were looted, then destroyed. Refugees settling in the southern end of the park, in Congo, entered it to harvest firewood and poach animals for bushmeat. After the war, returning park staff were attacked by Interahamwe, leading to several deaths among staff. Still, staff organized patrols and monitored gorilla groups. Elephants were reported to have moved from the Rwandan to the Congolose part of the Virunga.[17]

A June to October 1996 study compared numbers of ungulates observed in the volcanoes park to those counted in 1988–1989. The three species of ungulates found in the park were the African buffalo (*Syncerus caffer*), the bushbuck (*Tragelaphus scriptus*), and the black-fronted duiker (*Cephalophus nigrifrons*). Of the previously sampled 160 plots, 104 could be revisited. Covering eight elevation levels, they range from lowland areas to over 3,500 meters. Census methods, essentially fecal pellet counts, are described in detail by Plumptre and co-authors.[18] In addition, two people known among the local population were employed to collect answers to questionnaires. In all, 181 people, including poachers, were interviewed. Statistically significant differences between the time periods studied were not found, at any elevation, for populations of the African buffalo. For bushbuck and black-fronted duiker, increased counts were observed at the higher elevations (without reductions in the lower elevations). The survey data further suggest that bushbuck and duiker also engaged in less crop raiding outside the park boundaries after the war (1996) than before (1989), whereas for the buffalo local residents did not perceive any difference in crop raiding frequency. A fair number of people acknowledged either having poached in the park or purchasing poached bushmeat. Relative to prewar levels, poaching apparently increased during the war but declined thereafter. Meat prices appeared constant before and during the war, and fell thereafter, except for buffalo meat, the price of which fell continuously. Poaching and selling frequency, measured as days per year, was lower during the war than after the war. (But this is based on a small sample of only twenty self-acknowledged poachers.)

In all, the data are difficult to interpret. Around the Karisoke Research Station on the east side of the park, ungulate numbers apparently did not decrease. In part, this may have been because this side was occupied by the RPF and too dangerous to enter. But this may not have deterred poachers from trying: snare removal by vigilant park staff peaked during 1992 and 1993. On the western side, decreased crop raiding may be an indication of declining numbers of animals (crop planting was about the same), but the surveys did not indicate declining animal populations. In any event, even though "fifteen gorillas [*Gorilla beringei beringei*] are known to have been killed as a direct consequence of this war," overall "few gorillas from the habituated groups were killed during the whole period of the war, although a census of the population is required to see whether this is true for the whole population. Data on nests of gorilla groups . . . indicate that the population has risen to at least 350 animals." Other researchers provide slightly higher numbers on the basis of a complete census carried out in 2000. While it is surprising, they write, that "there has been no major population decrease . . . despite the severity of human disturbance in the Virunga," they also note that "the overall increase in the Virunga population can be accounted for by the research plus Susa groups alone, and that other parts of the population have not fared so well." (The Susa group is a habituated group of gorillas accessible to tourists.) In particular, gorilla groups in the Congolese part of the Virunga appear to have suffered from armed conflict there. Also, importantly, in the 1980s the gorilla population grew at about 3 percent per year (for a theoretical population doubling time of about 23 years); in the 1990s, this dropped to only about 1 percent per year (for a doubling time of about 70 years).[19]

BEANS. Rwanda's population consists of approximately 84 percent Hutu, 15 percent Tutsi, and 1 percent Twa. Tutsi tend to be cattle herders and Hutu agriculturalists. Consequently, agriculture is of huge importance. The case of beans in Rwanda offers an instructive look at cultivated environments in war.

A study examined bean seed varieties and variety management pre- and postwar. Farmers plant between three and thirty varieties on their land, averaging ten to fifteen varieties each. The key three varieties used, however, constitute between 50 and 90 percent of the sown seed. Hundreds of phenotypes are known, and varieties differ dramatically from place to place, often as little as 15 kilometers away. Annual per capita bean consumption of 60 kilograms is the highest in the world, "contributing 65 percent of protein and 30 percent of the Rwandan caloric intake." Bean experimentation among the farmers, usually women, is dynamic and highly refined. For example, root rot and bean fly diseases have led to extensive experimentation and substitution of varieties, calibrated by growing region. Prewar scientific knowledge of Rwanda's bean culture was extensive. The study's author is aware that this is an unusual circumstance: "It is rare to find such a focused body of pre-war work with which to compare the post-war effects on varieties, seed system flows and even genetic profiles."[20]

September to January and February to June define Rwanda's two growing seasons, known as the A and B seasons. Two postwar surveys were conducted, one involving 143 households for the 1995A season (that is, the first growing season after the 1994 massacres), the other for the 1996A season, with 883 farmers. The genocide and refugee crisis took place during the 1994B season, possibly affecting the 1995A growing season. The study reports, unfortunately without source attribution, that alongside commercial market development and natural disasters, war is among the recognized stressors of crop diversity and variety erosion. But the Rwandan war was not a monolithic event occurring all at once. Instead, it was staggered over time and dispersed over space. During 1990 and 1991, only the northern provinces were affected. From 1992 to 1994, the conflict shifted to the northeast. For the remainder of the country, war meant essentially the massacre months in mid-1994.

Survey results showed that in the southeast, farmers left their fields for an average of less than four weeks. In contrast, farmers in the northeast averaged over a year's absence from their homes and fields during 1992–1994. And "in the Southwest (in Cyangugu and Gikongoro . . .), most farmers did not move at all." Even as of November 1995, that region remained relatively unpopulated. Thirty percent of farmers did not leave their home places at all, "not even for one day." In contrast, in the southeast province of Kibungo not a single interviewed farmer had stayed put during the war episodes. Surprisingly, farmers reported little physical damage to household property and seed stock. More than a third reported "no damage at all." Moreover, more than 90 percent of the interviewed people had been farming before the war in the same areas as they did after the war. This means that postwar farming took place in agro-ecozones the farmers knew well. Even during the war some 55 percent of farmers reported that they harvested most of what they sowed. Regional differences are dramatic: 85 percent in the southwest harvested successfully as compared to only 16 percent in the southeast. If at all, most farmers missed only a single growing season, the 1995A season (September 1994 to January 1995).[21]

Major seed sources came from the farmers' own stocks, market stock (usually local markets), and relief aid (stocks from northern Burundi and southern Uganda). Just under half the seed in the 1995A and 1996A seasons came from farmers' own stock. Relief aid and market stock equally shared the remainder in the 1995A season. Market seed is local seed, so it follows that about three-fourths of total seed stock was supplied from within each farmer's province of residence. By the next season, 1996A, this climbed to well over 90 percent, as relief seed supplies dropped back drastically. Market purchases of seed stock had been widespread before the war as well, with "at least a third of farmers" obtaining some seed via local markets. Overall, "bean seed use broadly paralleled pre-war patterns."[22]

Regarding seed channels, 84 percent of the interviewed farmers still sowed the same three key varieties after the war that they sowed before the war, and between 75 and 85 percent of the interviewed farmers viewed the seed components and variety mixture as equal to or better than they were before the war. Although a third of the farmers said that they had lost specific seed varieties, in nearly 90 percent of those cases they could be reaccessed via markets, friends, and neighbors, often within 100 or 200 meters distance. The "lost" varieties often were newly improved climbing bean varieties (rather than bushy beans) that tended to be provided via institutionalized agricultural services that had been hit hard during the war. These varieties frequently came premixed, which farmers in search of a single specific variety would not wish to buy. Further, market varieties were highly priced—more highly, at any rate, than farmers were willing or able to spend at the time, which due to the war was a time of relative poverty. For some, livestock, the manure source, had been stolen and needed replacing, and crucial field repairs needed to be made. But seed markets were functioning. Variety acquisition was most difficult in the more depopulated areas as friendship, kin, and neighborhood channels were more depleted there. Thus, the northeast of the country, which lost almost four growing seasons, suffered seed-stress (fewer seeds) and variety-stress (fewer available varieties). In the remainder of the country, seed-stress emerged primarily from generalized poverty, that is, lack of money to buy seed varieties in local markets.[23]

In all, "the war seems to have had few effects in terms of altering varietal profiles . . . harvests were better than first assessed; and local seed channels continued to function in most areas during the war and immediately after." Observed varietal changes were not so much the result of "erosion" as of "evolution," as farmers responded intelligently to bean fly and root rot diseases by active experimentation and variety substitution. Indeed, farmers expressed little concern about specific bean varieties. Instead, concern centered on the performance of the planted mixture of varieties. Varietal modification thus "results from farmers' positive decisions to change management strategy."[24]

Sperling's bean study is important in itself but also because it can be compared to what happened across the border at Congo's National Institute of Agronomic Studies and Research (INERA), near Bukavu, which housed an important agriculture experimental station and essentially lost all work done in the twenty years prior to the war. (The details are reported later on in this chapter.) The key to the preservation of Rwanda's bean varieties lies in the holistic integration of beans into Rwandan culture. This acquires importance when one studies the accounts of conservationists working in Rwanda and in the Congo regarding gorilla protection. Here, too, conservationists emphasize how important it was that Rwandans took pride and cultural ownership in the few remaining gorillas, whereas in the Congo, as will be shown, there was both concealed and open hostility toward park staff and its protection work in the Kahuzi-Biega park, just west of Bukavu.[25]

4.1.2 The Eastern Congo

VIRUNGA NATIONAL PARK. The Virungas straddle conservation areas of three countries, the Virunga National Park in Congo, the Volcanoes National Park in Rwanda, and the Mgahinga Gorilla National Park in Uganda. The Ugandan part is the smallest (34 km²) and is subject to heavy pressure from encroachment, illegal harvesting of trees and bamboo, and poaching. The lower reaches, below 2,500 meters, are entirely lacking in effective protection. In Rwanda, likewise, most of the lower reaches had already been lost by 1979, due to extreme human population pressures. Gorilla research and associated tourism stopped the decline and helped preserve the rest of the park. The Congolese part is the only part of the Virungas that extends below 2,500 meters and includes migration areas for large animals, including buffalo, elephants, and gorillas. The Virunga National Park in all covers some 7,900 km² in size, of which the volcano area is a small part. The eastern Congo is a long way from Kinshasa—the capital city—and institutional support for the park was and continues to be weak. In addition, poaching, cutting of wood and bamboo, and encroachment by armed rebels from Rwanda and Uganda as well as regular army groups put further pressure on the area and effectively crowded out conservation efforts.[26]

REFUGEES. The 1990–1994 war caused a variety of concerns for the Virungas—as the only wooded area between Uganda and Rwanda it assumed strategic importance—but little wildlife damage appears to have resulted from this. Mines were laid, access trails were cut, park agents were harassed and even killed, offices and lodgings were looted and destroyed, and two gorillas were reported killed. But until the massacres of mid-1994 "the protected areas in particular were not severely affected."[27] Only then, once people began fleeing through the Virungas to the Congo and settled in and near the park, did ecological problems emerge on a more drastic scale. Within a matter of days, some two million people flooded across the border, perhaps 720,000 of whom eventually settled near Goma. Five camps were established, at Kibumba, Mugunga, Katale, Lac Vert, and Kahindo, all at the southern edge of the Virungas, where nearly 750,000 people remained for two years. They moved only when, two years later, the eastern Congo itself became embroiled in war.

The first study on the effect of refugees on the environment was published in 1996. Rwandan refugees were streaming into the provinces of North Kivu (Goma) and South Kivu (Bukavu). The then-Zairean government reported that South Kivu within three weeks lost nearly 38 km² of forested areas, with Bukavu itself being denuded of every bit of greenery. Still, the authors write that the situation in South Kivu was not as dire as in North Kivu because there were fewer refugees and the camps were smaller, better provisioned with fuel wood, and farther away from forested areas. In contrast, North Kivu suffered substantial deforestation. The authors report that Mount Goma was completely denuded in three days. Literally, "not a single tree was left standing."[28]

The Congolese part of the Virungas is separated into administrative sectors. The Rugo-Kibati sector loss was estimated at 72 km² and the Mugunga sector loss at 47 km². For the Kubare-Kalengera-Katale sector no loss estimate was made but it is "probably significant." Camps were established inside the national park and in the buffer zone around the park. The Mugunga refugee camp housed a large contingent of RAF military personnel and their families. These refugees were armed and proceeded to hunt in the park for in-camp consumption and bushmeat sale, and they also established commercial woodcutting operations for the provision of charcoal and fuel wood. The safety situation was tense, and reliable estimates from this camp could not be obtained. Staff of the United Nations High Commissioner for Refugees (UNHCR), and a German aid agency, GTZ, studied deforestation at the Kibumba camp, also near the Virungas park. From 28 September to 4 October 1994, twenty main paths from the camp to the park were observed each day from 6 A.M. to 5 P.M. An average of just over 19,000 people daily used the paths (about equally divided among men, women, and children), daily carrying 406 tons of wood back to the camp, for an average load of 21.2 kg per person per trip. For all refugees, across all camps in and around the Virungas, it was estimated that deforestation amounted to 7,000 to 10,000 cubic meters per day.[29]

More important for the long term than estimating the daily cut was the observation of how refugees went about stripping the forest. Wood collection appears to have taken place in four phases: first, the collection of dead wood nearest the camp; second, the cutting of dead or live branches; third, the cutting of trunks; and fourth, the removal of tree roots. The collection or cut per unit of effort decreased steadily. This progression, together with the cut-estimates, suggests that camps should be small and widely dispersed so that small numbers of people can collect much dead wood within walking distance. Camp fuel wood and building materials need to be supplied in sufficient supplementary quantities. To accomplish this is by no means easy—not in the Congo, not even in Europe during the Balkan crises—and important lessons that should be built into emergency preparedness plans can be learned from this study. It was during the Rwandan refugee crisis that environmental protection and conservation agencies directed very sharp criticism at humanitarian relief agencies and their staff. These groups included international organizations such as UNHCR, national governmental organizations, and the dozens of nongovernmental humanitarian relief organizations that worked in Rwanda and the eastern Congo. There is now an understanding among relief, development, and conservation groups that coordination of their goals and plans is desirable (a topic taken up in chapter 5).[30]

The potential consequences of deforestation include habitat destruction, loss of biodiversity (at least locally), land-use changes, and soil erosion, especially with the onset of the rainy season. Accordingly, in the Rwandan refugee crisis, deep erosion was observed particularly in the South Kivu camps whose topography featured steeper slopes and more vulnerable alluvial soil. There, the daily trek into the protected areas initially amounted to some 40,000 people. As the camps swelled with more refugees, this increased to as many as 80,000 people a day. About two-thirds of the harvesting took place in young forests in the process of recolonizing relatively recent lava flows (pioneer species). This suggests that a second round of recolonization (succession) may be possible. It is estimated that over two years the five camps of Katale, Kahindo, Kibumba, Mugunga, and Lac Vert affected a total area of 105 km^2, of which 35 km^2 were completely denuded. This would be less than the Zairean/Congolese numbers reported earlier, but has the advantage of being based on field observations. (For comparison, recall that in the Vietnam War, forest bulldozing by U.S. armed forces amounted to 3,250 km^2, nearly two orders of magnitude higher.)[31]

The cut areas varied by camp as some received attention more readily than others. The Mugunga and Lac Vert camps were the least supervised ecologically. As mentioned, refugees there set up commercial enterprises to supply the nearby city of Goma with fuel wood harvested illegally from the protected areas. Bamboo (*Arundinaria alpina*) was harvested in higher elevations primarily by refugees from Kibumba camp. The equivalent of about half of some 19.2 km^2 of bamboo stands was cut. Regrowth rates are not known. Poaching increased but numbers are not available. As the refugee crisis wore on, aid agencies eventually began to supply fuel wood from outside the park, some of it from plantations as much as 100 km away. It is estimated that this may have prevented further park deforestation by 40 km^2.[32]

Other refugee-related environmental problems were caused by inadequate planning regarding human, medical, and solid-waste handling and removal. It appears that humanitarian aid agencies focused on ferrying in water, food, shelter, and medical supplies but had not given thought to the tail end of the emergency operations. For example, defecation areas were determined and pit latrines dug but waste removal posed a problem. At times, waste was taken and dumped in the protected park areas without thought of treatment or of the possibility of storm runoff during the rainy season that might lead to contamination of soil and water.[33] Solid waste, including disposable diapers, ended up in the park, as did medical waste. It is not known what happened to this waste or how it may have affected wildlife. One particularly unfortunate event involved a refugee camp located in and near the grounds of the aforementioned National Institute of Agronomic Studies and Research (INERA) near Bukavu. INERA is a plant genetics research and experimental station. When researchers visited in late 1994, 60,000 refugees had already denuded 60 percent of the 1 km² site. INERA lost all experimental cinchona and coffee fields developed over the 15 to 20 years prior to 1994; it also lost the results of five years' worth of soil fertility experiments. In addition, as there were no germplasm storage facilities, all genetic resource work and knowledge were lost as well. In a prescient comment, the researchers predicted that the Kahuzi-Biega National Park, just west of Bukavu, might remain unaffected so long as the refugees in South Kivu would not stay for an extended period of time. Indeed, "by negotiating with military leaders and the international aid agencies, [the park warden showed great foresight and] ensured that the refugees were settled only on one side of the park and at some distance from the park's border, unlike the earlier situation around the Virunga Volcanoes." But as we now know, many refugees stayed for two years and more. When civil war then commenced in the eastern Congo, many of the Rwandan refugees there fled back home to Rwanda. Many others fled further west, deeper into the Congo, inland toward Kahuzi-Biega National Park. There, UNHCR eventually established two camps.[34]

For a follow-up study researchers visited three sites in August 1998: the INERA station and the Kahuzi-Biega National Park in the Congo, and the Nyungwe Forest Reserve in southwestern Rwanda. From interviews it appears that INERA was eventually flooded with up to 100,000 refugees and was very nearly clearcut. UNHCR either bought cutting rights or compensated owners of nearby lands that also had been denuded, but the INERA research work was irretrievably destroyed. In principle, some species of trees can regenerate from stumps, but often the stumps were removed as well. This is what happened at INERA, which by August 1998, the time of the researchers' visit, had not seen a crop grown since 1994. Another research area about 20 km north, that housed the National Research Center for Natural Sciences (CRSN), was luckier. Its lands contained stands of eucalyptus. UNHCR bought these and supplied them as fuel wood to the refugees. Here, stumps were not removed, and a site visit showed regrowth of trees with 10–15 cm diameter and several meters in height.[35]

In contrast, the Nyungwe Forest Reserve in Rwanda appeared to be in good shape. For one thing, the war had largely bypassed this area of the country. Many Rwandans fled the country altogether rather than try to hide in Rwanda so that Nyungwe also escaped refugee-related problems. Moreover, the park was not known for large animals that might have attracted poachers, and by pointing to its conservation value the warden and guards dissuaded people and soldiers from moving through the park. This somewhat contradicts another report (which states that the warden was killed, snare counts increased, large animal counts decreased, and funding for park staff collapsed, but this apparently refers to the early to mid-1990s). In the event, by the time of the August 1998 visit, "conditions were good not only for tourism, but also for research." Trails had been improved, new facilities put up, arrears paid, guards well trained, and new projects with conservation organizations started. The proper siting of camps, channeling of refugees to these camps, combined with continuous national and international financial and administrative support of guards and wardens in protected areas appears to have been crucial to ensure minimization of the effect of war on this protected area.[36]

Despite the refugee disaster in 1994 and the stinging rebuke it received from conservation groups, UNHCR established camps in October 1996 in Kahuzi-Biega National Park and took care of refugees there until March 1997. The camps were disbanded by March 1998. The formally established camps eventually sprouted uncontrolled offshoots throughout the park as refugees set out on their own and as Congo's civil war brought armed conflict into the park. At least three major forest fires were reported in Kahuzi-Biega between 1996 and 1997. Numeric information is unavailable, but it appears that the areas affected by the fires show natural regrowth.[37] Regarding other effects, a park guard reported to researchers that at least half of the elephant population in the eastern part of the park, toward Bukavu, had been poached. For a time, park management broke down completely and tourism collapsed as well. Financial resources from outside agencies were withdrawn, as was financing from Kinshasa. Park guards went unpaid, and antipoaching patrols stopped. More recent information on Kahuzi-Biega National Park, that is, since the August 1998 field visit, is bleak, particularly with regard to the park's elephant and gorilla populations (discussed later on).

OTHER PROTECTED AREAS IN THE CONGO IN THE 1990S. A 2001 report by Hart and Mwinyihali lays out what is known. Although their language is strong ("the unprotected forests are being severely looted and trampled") they recognize that "because of continued insecurity and difficulty of access . . . there is still no way to evaluate what has been destroyed." Information is sketchy. For example, the Garamba National Park on the Congo's border with Sudan (4,900 km²) was flooded with some 80,000 southern Sudanese refugees in 1991. Firearms were plentiful and bushmeat poaching increased, first along the border areas, then farther south, encroaching on the northern white rhinoceros habitat. Park guards were sometimes supported by Kinshasa and sometimes not. At times guards were paid; at times not. At times they were disarmed, then rearmed. At times equipment was looted, including vehicles, fuel, and radios. Then the park was partially re-equipped. This is chaotic and imprecise, but is more than what we know about wildlife in the park. It is certainly not a situation conducive to conservation.[38]

The reporting on Okapi Faunal Reserve (13,400 km²) is equally indeterminate. We know that gold and coltan mining took place in the reserve, that mining camps were focal points of watercourse disturbances and of poaching, and that elephant meat showed up at area markets. This raises concern but does not amount to numbers. The Virunga National Park itself, following the Rwandan war, also was subject to further pressures. Hart and Mwinyihali report for example that the "rebels decimated essentially all of the remaining hippos on the rivers Rutshuru and Rwindi," and that the Congolese nature protection agency, the ICCN, cannot anymore protect the park from various forms of infiltration and settlement for fishing, agriculture, and pastoralism. The service's distance from Kinshasa and its lack of acceptance by the local population, as well as the continuing level of armed conflict and generalized insecurity, the absence of regional coordination, and the absence of high-level and highly visible international conservation efforts resulted, for all practical purposes, in the abandonment of the region. Even prospects for monitoring are weak. Satellite imaging may not properly capture losses, certainly not the reason for losses. For that, ground-level work would be necessary. The only wildlife surveys come when foreign groups conduct them. But most protected areas have never been visited by any outside agency at all. There "had never been baseline wildlife or plant inventories." The lack of scientific knowledge about these areas is appalling, and new surveys can produce confusing information. For example, a survey for the Itombwe Mountains (an unprotected area southwest of Bukavu), carried out in 1996, the first one done in over thirty years, found two new Grauer's gorilla populations but was unable to locate again five populations first identified in 1959. New groups are good news, but it is unclear whether the inability to locate old gorilla groups is bad news. The overall gorilla population at Itombwe was estimated at some 900 individuals. In addition, elephants, buffalo, chimpanzees, and 588 species of birds were found. But so was evidence of extensive hunting, pasture extension, and land claims for agriculture in the unprotected areas. The net effect of these changes is unknown.[39]

Regarding Garamba National Park, prewar data and new aerial population and distribution surveys suggest that its elephant population was halved (from more than 11,000 to less than 5,500) and that its buffalo population fell by two-thirds (from more than 25,000 to less than 8,000). But Garamba is savannah, where aerial surveys are possible. In contrast, in woodland parks—Kahuzi-Biega, Maiko, and Okapi—forest cover prevents aerial counts, and surveys must be carried out on the ground. The few that have been conducted suggest that elephant populations in Okapi appeared unaffected by the turmoil of the 1990s. But gorilla populations in the higher elevations of Kahuzi-Biega, the only area still patrolled, appear to have been halved and elephants appeared missing altogether (see next subsection). Snare counts had increased fourfold.[40]

THE CONTINUING CONGOLESE WAR. The Rwandan civil war took place from October 1990 to July 1994, with the genocide occurring from April to June 1994. As discussed, millions fled to what was then Zaire, from 1994 to 1996. A civil war then broke out there, lasting from October 1996 to May 1997. Zaire's ruler Mobutu Sese Seko was deposed, and a new one installed (Laurent Kabila). In August 1998, a second civil war started in the Congo. Kabila was assassinated in January 2001 and his son, Joseph Kabila, succeeded him. As of late 2008, the war has not yet ended despite peace agreements made in 2003 and in early 2008. Even as international actors have withdrawn, at least temporarily, plenty of local armed groups remain.

Much concern focuses on the Kahuzi-Biega National Park, whose warden in 1994 was able to fend off the settlement of refugees near the park.

The park is divided into a lowland and a highland portion. The highland sector, lying between 1,800 and 3,300 meters and of some 600 km² in size, was gazetted (protected on paper) in 1970; the lowland sector (elevation: 600–1,800 m; 5,400 km²) was gazetted in 1975. By 1980, the entire park, located due west of the Congo-Rwanda border, became a UNESCO World Heritage site. The nearest larger city is Bukavu, on the park's east side. As mentioned, the first Congolese civil war induced some of the Rwandan refugees to migrate back to Rwanda, but others stayed or dispersed westward into the park. By mid-2000, some 35,000 refugees were in the park, many warring with each other. Evidently, illegal mining and poaching took place in the park, and extracted resources were exported via newly built airstrips but, with few exceptions, we do not know about the extent of these activities, of the prior ecological status of the park, or of the degree of damage done.[41]

The exceptions concern coltan mining, and the gorilla and elephant populations. In the early 1990s, it was thought that between 1,350 and 3,600 elephants inhabited the lowland park area. A reliable number of 910 elephants was established in 1996 for the highland sector. Several sources mention that the park's elephant population is thought to have declined by some 95 percent between the early 1990s and the early 2000s. The onslaught appears to have occurred beginning in 1997 when international organizations left the region, the civil war continued, and Kinshasa's support for park staff evaporated exactly at the time when destitute people and armed groups moved into the park. Park services were totally suspended between August 1998 and March 1999. Illegal mining and poaching took off. The near total absence of elephant tracks, once some degree of park monitoring was reestablished in 1999, suggests that the elephants were gone. Many elephant bones were found. Elephant meat showed up at camps, and ivory was displayed, incredibly, at the Kigali airport. This evidence suggests that the elephants did not simply move, but were killed.[42]

The gorilla situation appears equally dire. A 1994–1995 census suggests that the world's total population of Grauer's gorilla (the eastern lowland gorilla, *Gorilla beringei graueri*) amounted to some 17,000 individuals. Of these, about 86 percent were thought to live in Kahuzi-Biega and the adjoining Kasese forests, with Kahuzi-Biega itself perhaps accounting for 8,000 individuals. The number of gorillas in the highland sector has been more nearly established by censuses in 1978, 1990, and 1996, at 223, 258, and 245 individuals, respectively. But a newer census, conducted June to August 2000, counted only 126 individuals, a decline of 50 percent since the 1996 census, apparently due to poaching when park operations were suspended. This poaching appears to have halted when, in September 1999, park staff "summoned" 67 suspected poachers and decided to employ 40 of them as guards.[43]

The lowland sector population of gorillas also appears to have suffered inordinately. One researcher believes that the Kahuzi-Biega and Kasese populations, formerly about 8,000 individuals, may have dropped to below 1,000, and that the overall population size of 17,000 may be down to 2,000 to 3,000 individuals, "an 80 to 90 per cent crash in only three years." Unfortunately, this researcher does not discuss the basis for his belief, but it is well established that substantial mining operations took place along the waterways within the Kahuzi-Biega park lowland sector and that miners poach for bushmeat. Park officers are in possession of maps of mining camp locations. Berggorilla und Regenwald Direkthilfe, a German conservation and advocacy group, estimates that about 10,000 miners operate in the park. Even in the best of times, only about 5 percent of the park, the highland sector, has been effectively protected by park guards. The remainder was gazetted but not actively protected in practice, leaving it open for encroachment by destitute people, armed groups, and commercial interests (coltan mining).[44]

Following a twelve-day mission in April and May 2001 to coltan mining and trading areas in Rwanda and Kahuzi-Biega, one researcher comes up with a useful list of environmental damage imposed on the park:

1. forest clearance and use of timber and poles to build camps to accommodate workers
2. forest clearance to expose substrate for mining
3. pollution of streams by silt from washing process
4. erosion of unprotected earth during rains leading to land-slips
5. cutting of firewood for warmth and cooking in camps
6. hunting of animals for bushmeat to feed miners and camp followers
7. animals maimed or dying after escaping from snares
8. debarking of trees to make panning trays for washing coltan
9. cutting of lianas to make carrying baskets for coltan
10. disturbance of animals due to large number of people resident in and moving through forest
11. silting up of streams likely to kill invertebrates and reduce photosynthesis in aquatic plants
12. reduced productivity of fish stocks in lakes and rivers affected by silt pollution

13. ecological changes due to loss of keystone species such as elephants and apes

14. long-term changes in watershed due to rapid run-off in deforested areas.[45]

No doubt, this list is qualitatively correct. Yet, as before, lack of quantitative assessment makes it impossible to put this assessment into a comparative context.

RWANDA AND CONGO IN SUM. It is probably fair to say that Rwanda, with the important exception of Akagere National Park, escaped relatively unscathed, its Gishwati and Mukura forest reserves already having been in decline. The onus is on the quality of conservation planning and action to prevent postwar threats to conservation from being realized. The situation in the eastern Congo is different. We do not know much by way of quantities. There was some cutting, and clear-cutting, in the forests following the refugee influx. Totally denuded areas are large per se, 35 km², but small relative to the entire area (the Congolese Virunga National Park alone comprises 7,900 km²), and of the deforested part only about 5 percent encroached upon mountain gorilla habitat. The numbers of mountain gorillas actually increased by 10 percent during the 1990s, but it nonetheless appears that these groups suffered disproportionately. The hippopotamus population is said to have been drastically affected, with counts in the park falling from 33,000 in 1986 to 3,000 in 1996.[46] Of even greater overall concern is the continuing civil war in Congo and its effects on Kahuzi-Biega National Park (6,000 km²), of which only a small part has been effectively protected, and only at times. The evidence is weak but nonetheless conclusive that in the unprotected parts of the park gorilla and elephant populations are nearly extirpated. It is clear that the continuing civil war in the Congo, and the lawlessness it brings, endangers their survival. What is not clear is ecosystem functioning beyond the specific conservation interests.

4.2 Afghanistan and Pakistan

4.2.1 Afghanistan

By mid-1979, just prior to the Soviet Union's invasion, the World Bank estimated Afghanistan's population at 15.5 million people. By mid-1983, it was 17.2 million, and by mid-1991, when the World Bank next published estimated population figures for the country, this had increased to 20.9 million.[47] Meanwhile, four or five million people fled the country to Iran and Pakistan. The Soviet Union withdrew by 1989 and left the country in turmoil, to be calmed, somewhat, in 1992 with the ascendance of the Taliban. That government, in turn, was toppled by U.S. forces in 2001, in a war that included U.S. bombardment of Afghan mountain ranges. Turmoil continues.

Because of the televised and much-discussed U.S. war against Taliban forces, people are familiar with the idea that the country is dominated by extremely rough and rugged terrain. Of its 650,000 km^2, about 27 percent lies above 2,500 meters in elevation. The Hindu Kush range, the westernmost outreach of the Himalaya Mountains that sweeps northeast to southwest across the country, covers about 456,000 km^2, with peaks going to 7,000 meters in height. Nonetheless, there are extensive plains in Afghanistan's northwest corner toward Turkmenistan and southwest toward Iran and Pakistan, even large sand desert areas in the central south, along the Helmand River.[48]

Little information is available on the environmental effects of Afghanistan's various wars. What little there is includes an impassioned piece on the effects of the Soviet war on Afghan agriculture. Yusufi details pre-1979 crop production (cereals, industrial crops, vegetables, fruits, and other crops) and the decline in agricultural productivity with the onslaught of the Soviet invasion. By the few accounts available, he reckons that average farm size, fertilizer use, water use, and yield declined precipitously. Among the main reasons for this is the reduction in the available labor pool as boys and men were drafted into the armed forces, fled internally to the relative safety of Kabul or to Afghanistan's mountains to join the resistance, fled to neighboring countries, or were killed. In addition, the price of draft animals rose to become unaffordable. Moreover, many instances are reported of Soviet troops demolishing agricultural installations, destroying "cultivated fields, and burn[ing] harvests, grain and houses," in addition to "bombing and destruction of irrigation dams and canals" and "cutting down of fruit trees." Killing of vast numbers of farm animals is also reported, perhaps more than half of their population. Consequently, "most of the land is uncultivated and has been bare for the last four to five years. Wild plants like camel thorn and other shrubs have replaced the cultivated crops."[49]

All this would suggest that wild flora and fauna should have experienced a resurgence. Indeed, Yusufi writes that "since most civilians have left the villages, the area looks like a desert and you can find wild animals, insects and desert birds (such as wolves, wild honey bees and other bees, partridges, etc)." In another passage, Yusufi writes that "many wild animals, birds and insects have left the mountains and deserts and occupied the villages. Wild life and natural resources such as forests and soils have deteriorated." It appears that Yusufi means to suggest that human and wildlife refugees essentially switched places: humans to the mountains, wildlife off the mountains. The extent to which this account is based on underlying quantitative information or on personal observations or personal communication with those who might have remained in the country to make such observations is unclear. That Afghanistan suffered from deforestation prior to 1979 was well known, as was the consequence for soil deterioration. This would have been furthered by people being driven into the mountains. Likewise, the depopulation of agricultural villages—and by far most of the Afghan population, some 80 percent, were agriculturally employed—would lead one to expect the sort of wildlife repopulation that Yusufi describes. But it is not clear why there should have been soil erosion on the arable land if, in fact, it was not tended and left fallow. The only hint comes from Yusufi's description of the deliberate cutting of trees in farm areas, but this possible link is not explored. Yusufi's account is evocative and, on the whole, has the right "feel" to it, but does not permit a fact-based assessment of the effect of the Soviet war on Afghan nature.[50]

A study by Skogland suggests that the pre-1979 Afghan population was ecologically well adapted. Its preference for sheep and goats over cattle, for instance, is in marked contrast to other countries with arid climate, the importance being that sheep are drought resistant and goats are flexible terrain users. Computing an "ecological stability domain," a measure that calculates the sheep-equivalent stock density of sheep, goats, and cattle per hectare of pastoral land, Skogland finds that Afghanistan lived on the upper edge of this domain, whereas neighboring Pakistan far exceeded it. In addition, Afghan traditional water management to prevent soil erosion is highly praised by both authors (Yusufi and Skogland). Skogland details how traditional water management minimized recruitment of malaria-carrying mosquitos. With the destruction of this water management system by Soviet forces, stagnant pools of water were created and malaria incidence increased sharply among the Afghan population.[51]

Few post-1979 data points are available for Afghanistan. Formoli has collected what little is known. He confirms that Soviet forces engaged in a vast and deliberate destruction of agricultural, that is, cultivated, lands. Regarding forests, he writes that Afghanistan's forested areas declined from 3.4 to 2.6 percent of land cover in ten years, largely due to bombings and associated fires, and the need for fuel wood and commercial harvesting to sustain livelihoods. "Some parts of the legendary Paktia and Kunar forests have disappeared, while erosion of topsoil is clearly visible in deforested areas." Formoli then provides an extensive list of Afghan animal wildlife adapted to its arid plains and mountain conditions. Not for a single one is there any indication as to what may or may not have happened to these populations on account of the war (among them is the snow leopard, on which more below). Among the wetland-bird and waterfowl species he lists, for only one of them—the Siberian crane (*Grus leucogeranus*)—do we learn that its count dropped from 70 individuals in 1970 to 17 in 1990.[52]

Regarding protected areas, various possible adverse effects are stipulated, but Formoli notes that "one cannot be sure [of the effects] until field visits are made and ecological surveys are performed at all of these sites." In 1994, Formoli visited one such site and "found evidence of continued egg retrieval, habitat disturbance, livestock grazing, and indiscriminate hunting," but it is not clear that this was due to the Soviet-Afghan war. By this time, the Soviets had left. (In fact, the Soviet Union had ceased to exist.) What is clear is that the manner in which the Soviet-Afghan war was conducted raises the possibility of huge adverse environmental effects throughout the country. But until studies are done, it is not possible to say much that is factually based. Moreover, even when such studies are done, "lack of sufficient baseline data [makes it impossible] to assess fully the environmental impact of the Afghan-Soviet war."[53]

To the rule that essentially no quantitative information is available with regard to Afghanistan's wildlife, there is one partial exception, which comes from a study examining conditions for the snow leopard (*Unica unica* or *Panthera unica*). The authors write that Afghanistan "has had almost no history of conservation efforts," "that essentially no wildlife research has occurred in Afghanistan in many years," and that some "seventy-five species of animals and plants found in Afghanistan have been placed on the IUCN Red List, with thirty-five species listed as either Vulnerable or Endangered." Regarding the snow leopard, poaching and killing of its prey have left, it is estimated, a mere 3,500 to 7,000 snow leopards in the world. Data for Afghanistan do not exist, but the authors believe that perhaps fewer than 100 individuals remained at the time of writing (after 11 September 2001, but before the U.S. bombing of Afghanistan began) and that perhaps no more than 1,000 ever existed in the country's high-mountain altitudes ranging from its extreme northeastern border with Pakistan to the area just north of Jalalabad and Kabul.[54]

Even as it provides a useful account of what could happen, the snow leopard study does not contain any factual information about the fate of the snow leopard in Afghanistan during the ensuing U.S.-Taliban war. Bombing might affect potential habitat, poaching pressures are likely to have increased, land mines may be harmful if they induce people to move up the mountain ranges, and refugees can encroach on the mountains as well. But hypotheticals do not substitute for data. In early 2003, UNEP released a 180-page environmental assessment study on Afghanistan. By comparing faunal, floral, habitat, and landscape accounts dating back to the 1950s and 1960s with what can now be established, it is beyond doubt that the current situation is due to thirty years of war and unrest. By mid-1977, Afghanistan's population was 14.3 million. Despite the terrible intervening years, the population very nearly doubled to 27.2 million by 2001. "Warfare, civil disorder, lack of governance, and drought have taken a major toll on Afghanistan's natural and human resources."[55] The mission is succinctly described:

> In September 2002, a month-long UNEP mission comprising twentyAfghan and international scientists and experts visited thirty-eight urban sites in four cities and thirty-five different rural locations. During the UNEP field work a total of sixty samples were collected to test air, soil and water conditions and levels of chemical contamination. State-of-the-art satellite analyses also proved to be an invaluable tool, especially in areas not accessible due to security constraints. Through the use of Landsat satellite images, land-cover analysis could look back over a twenty-five year period to investigate wetland degradation, desertification and deforestation. Due to the security situation—ongoing conflict and dangers of mines and other unexploded ordinances—the UNEP mission was not able to cover all parts of Afghanistan. For example, safe access to the Ajar Valley or the cedar forests of Kunar and Nuristan provinces was not possible due to the ongoing local fighting.[56]

Here are highlights from the findings:[57]

> Many of the country's wetlands are completely dry and no longer support wildlife populations or provide agricultural inputs. For example, UNEP found that over 99 per cent of the Sistan wetland, a critically important haven for waterfowl, was completely dry. Furthermore, wind-blown sediments were in-filling irrigation canals and reservoirs, as well as covering roads, fields and villages, with an overall effect of increasing local vulnerability to drought.

UNEP's satellite analyses revealed that conifer forests in the provinces of Nangarhar, Kunar and Nuristan have been reduced by an average of 50 per cent since 1978. Similarly, pistachio woodlands in the provinces of Badghis and Takhar were found to be highly degraded. With the loss of forests and vegetation, and excessive grazing and dry land cultivation, soils are being exposed to serious erosion from wind and rain. The productivity of the land base is declining, driving people from rural to urban areas in search of food and employment. Riverbanks are also eroding with the loss of stabilizing vegetation, and flood risks are increasing.

There are no proper landfills in any of the towns and cities, and none of the dumpsites are taking measures to prevent groundwater contamination or toxic air pollution from burning wastes. In some cases, such as in Herat, dumpsites have been located in dry riverbeds upstream from the city. The first period of sustained rainfall could wash the dump's contents back down into the city centre.

Flamingos have not bred successfully in Afghanistan for four years, and the last Siberian crane was seen in 1986. While the Wakhan Corridor contains healthy populations of endangered snow leopards and other mammals including Marco Polo sheep, active hunting is occurring in many regions of the country, either for sport, for meat, or in order to supply furs for sale to foreigners in Kabul. The legal status of all protected areas is currently in question, and no management is taking place to protect and conserve their ecological integrity and wildlife.

Note that among the bad news, there is good news regarding the snow leopard. Regarding the Siberian crane, whereas UNEP reports that it has not been seen since 1986, Formoli, citing McPherson and Fernando, reported 17 individuals in 1990. But current information on the International Crane Foundation website suggests that the so-called western and central populations have been extirpated (i.e., including those that used Afghanistan as a stop on their migration routes from Siberia to India).[58] Apart from UNEP's general findings quoted above, more qualified specific findings include the following:

1. An important wetland area, the Sistan, fed by the Helmand River, held about 150 species of migrating and nonmigrating birds in the 1970s, including eight globally threatened waterfowl species. After the wars, "the diversity of bird life in the wetlands was almost matched by nearly 140 species of fish that supported bird, mammal and human populations." This, even though after four years of drought the wetland was 99 percent dry. "UNEP obtained Landsat satellite images for the years 1976, 1987, 1998

and 2001 to verify the current condition of the wetlands and to compare it with previous years. Image analyses revealed that 99 per cent of the wetland has dried since 1998, including Hamoun-i-Puzak, Hamoun-e-Sabari and Hamoun-e-Helmand. Each of the main rivers feeding the wetland, including the Helmand, Farah Rud and Khash Rud, also appeared to be completely dry. However, the analyses also demonstrated that the wetlands have undergone significant desiccation in the past, and have recovered with the return of the rains. In 1987, for example, 73 per cent of the wetland area was completely dry. Yet by 1998 the wetlands and surrounding vegetation had almost completely recovered." Drought, it appears, is not a consequence attributable to war. Dam building in the 1970s, prior to the wars, contributed to poor water management that amplified the effects of the drought in the late 1990s.

2. Pistachio forests in Badghis and Takhar province were 55 and 37 percent of the land cover, respectively, in 1977. By 2002, satellite images do not show any detectable forest cover. The images were limited to detecting tree densities of 40 or more per hectare. Still, that none could be detected in 2002 as opposed to 55 and 37 percent cover in 1977 does suggest enormous deforestation. Further, "virtually no live seedlings were found during UNEP field missions," most probably because of increased sheep and goat grazing and nut collection by humans. Deforestation led to visible soil erosion. Moreover, riparian vegetation also has been reduced, so that soil erosion gullies now reach into the rivers.

3. Regarding juniper stands, "It was estimated that 50 per cent of the juniper cover in the Subzac pass has been lost in the last thirty years. Local sources at Kushka Kuhna in Badghis province confirmed that as much as 80 per cent of juniper woodland had been cut during the past two decades." The UNEP team had trouble even locating remaining stands.

4. As for oak and conifer forests, UNEP obtained "Landsat satellite images covering the provinces of Nuristan, Kunar and Nangarhar for 1977 and 2002. The analyses revealed that forest cover has decreased by a total of 52 per cent when the provinces are taken together." These are forests at elevations of 2,500 to 3,300 meters near the Pakistani border. Lack of access prevented UNEP from assessing remaining wildlife in these forests.

5. Regarding protected areas, most were badly affected by the drought and, for most areas, little comparative wildlife information is available so that an overall assessment of protected areas with respect to the wars' impact is difficult to make. It does appear that flamingo populations are locally nearly gone. Further, in the Ajar Valley Wildlife Reserve deforestation, hunting, and fishing with explosives appears to have depleted wildlife. "At present ibex are much reduced in number, and only a few hundred may remain. Urial have fared more poorly than ibex and only a very few survive. Bactrian deer and feral yaks no longer exist. Wolves remain, but common leopard and snow leopard may be gone."

6. Findings for the Wakhan Corridor are generally more positive. The corridor is the small strip of land in Afghanistan's extreme northeast, leading to the country's narrow border with China. A UNEP team visited the area from 20 September to 10 October 2002. Key findings include direct or indirect confirmation of the snow leopard and Marco Polo sheep, wolf, brown bear, Asian ibex, urial, red fox, cape hare, stone marten, and long-tailed marmot, but no signs of lynx. Hunting for fur (especially of the snow leopard) appears to be minor in the corridor (although apparently not in other areas of the administrative province, Badakhshan). In addition, some 50 bird species were sighted, including ten new to a list of 117 species compiled in 1978.[59]

UNEP's Afghanistan study is invaluable. Since the study covers thirty or more years of data, it is hard to argue that war is not responsible, directly or indirectly, for the observed changes. One important caveat is that during this time Afghanistan's population doubled, and that population growth alone under a typical developing-country wildlife management scenario would have led to conservation shortcomings. Still, the key insight emerging from the UNEP report is the demonstration of what prolonged war and the complete lack of effective governance can and does do, not only to people, but to the natural environment to which, after the war, they must return. An impoverished people returning to a healthy land offers hope; an impoverished people returning to an impoverished land is another matter.

4.2.2 The Effects of the Afghan Wars on Pakistan

The Rwandan/Congolese case study suggests that a major impact of war on the environment comes from the impact of refugees on the environment in which they temporarily or permanently resettle. For Pakistan, a similar observation may be made. Following the Soviet invasion of Afghanistan in 1979, about 3.5 million people fled to Pakistan (and a further one or two million to Iran). North of the Kabul-Peshawar highway, on the Afghan border, lies Pakistan's North-West Frontier Province (NWFP). Going southwest from Peshawar toward Quetta lies an area, also straddling the Afghan-Pakistani border, that is known as the Federally Administered Tribal Areas. Satellite images taken for a 1987 study suggest that "the small forest resources have disappeared in the districts between Peshawar and Quetta." This area is off limits to foreigners, so it was not possible to conduct ground-based field work. In contrast, in addition to processing satellite images, the researcher, Nigel Allan, was able to undertake field work in the summer of 1985 in NWFP. His findings are interesting, if incomplete. "The camps contain refugees from all over Afghanistan," he writes, "and their diverse former habitats reflect their use and misuse of the vegetative sources close to the camps." For example, "if the refugees came from an agricultural village in interior and northern Afghanistan the devastation of the local forest is greatest . . . in many instances, entire forests have been cleared as well as forest litter and twigs and branches used as a mulch to enhance the fertility of the soil." Agriculture-based refugees will clear forests to reestablish an agriculture-based life, even if their new environment is not suited for this type of economic activity. The consequence is visible (satellite and ground-based) widespread deforestation and soil erosion.[60]

Afghan refugees settled in camps in the eastern NWFP district of Mansehra, for instance, kept only 0.13 sheep and goats per refugee. These people came from Afghan areas completely devoid of forests, yet were resettled into heavily forested areas in Pakistan, which were then stripped to make way for agriculture. In contrast, refugees from high-altitude, above treeline, pastoral areas in Afghanistan, holding about three sheep and goats per refugee, resettled in similar environments in camps in the northwestern Chitral district. "Consequently, the impact in this district is mainly on high-altitude pastures and the forest at the treeline and not lower down where local villagers can prevent intrusions into their forests by the refugees." Allan does not provide quantitative detail on the type and degree of environmental impact on forests and high-altitude pastures, but the policy lesson in his account is clear: ideally, UNHCR, refugee-assisting NGOs, and receiving countries should have emergency plans ready that channel refugees into appropriate environments. Allan also makes the following observation: "Much spare or waste land is found in northern Pakistan but, instead of using this land, refugee officials placed camps in the prime forested areas across the entire country." Finally, Allan points out that the environmental impact of refugees is often falsely attributed to them. This occurs when unscrupulous people in the receiving country mingle among refugees and exploit natural resources using the confusion a humanitarian emergency generates, the general lack of natural resource supervision and enforcement during such crises, and their knowledge of local ways and means for their own profit, while having the consequences ascribed to refugees.[61]

A useful quantitative study was published by Lodhi, Echavarria, and Keithley in 1998. It uses satellite remote-sensing data to evaluate the impact on forested areas of about 111,000 refugees settled in a number of camps in a 618 km² area of the central part of the Siran Valley, just east of Muzzafarabad, the area that Allan said had been settled with people originating from forest-free areas in Afghanistan. The authors also collected useful, hard-to-get literature to provide background information. One bit of quantitative reference information is that the local government of the North-West Frontier Province published a study in 1991 that found approximately 850 km² of forest cover in Siran Valley in 1979 but only 470 km² in 1989, or about a 45 percent reduction. As regards their own study, the authors acquired Landsat images for 9 June 1979 and 17 June 1993 to study the valley's center. The idea was to differentiate crop, shrub, and forest areas and thus to assess land-use changes. Inevitably, some interpretative decisions had to be made as drought conditions (late monsoon arrival) in 1979 reduced land visibly used for agriculture, just as ample rainfall in 1993 resulted in visually blurred crop and forest areas ("spectral confusion"). Combining satellite-derived information with local maps, elevation data, and expert local-area knowledge, the authors find that in 1993 some 113 km² was under forest cover as compared to 203 km² in 1979, a reduction of 90 km² or roughly 44 percent, very much in line with the NWFP government's 1991 estimate of about 45 percent for the entire valley. The deforestation took place from the lower to the higher elevations. Thus, the areas nearest the populated plains and valleys were affected first and foremost. These were dominated by Chir pine forests (*Pinus roburghii*), at elevations between 900 and 1,600 meters.[62] These studies are useful not only for the specific information they yield but for the behavioral and organizational pointers they provide for anticipating and handling future crises.

4.3 In Sum

The primary destructiveness of internal war may lie with environmental lawlessness or with conservation policy by default.[63] But neither the

Rwandan nor the Afghan case fully demonstrate loss of biodiversity as a specific consequence of war. Losses or high risk of losses of a species, perhaps so: Grauer's gorilla in Kahuzi-Biega National Park in the eastern Congo and the flamingo in Afghanistan are examples. Losses of habitat aplenty: deforestation, soil erosion, water siltation. It is possible that the case could be made if, instead of disjointedly attending to one species or another, biologists and conservationists attempted a concerted effort to look systematically for evidence that would tell a complete ecological story. But that would also require studies of lands vacated by refugees and areas marked off by land mines. Are war's biological losses somehow "made up" by its biological gains? As has been learned from the Vietnam War and Persian Gulf War cases, when the guns are silent, nature does not necessarily recover because by all appearances peace (economic development) is a continuation of war on nature.

This chapter highlighted Rwanda and Afghanistan. Scientific literature on other internal/civil war cases is scant, and definitive conclusions cannot yet be drawn. (Section 4.4 lists additional studies.) But the overall reading, including reports produced by a variety of NGOs, is tantalizing in that it suggests for instance that repressive wars (e.g., Burma) may work on nature differently than cases of grievance-based civil war (e.g., Nicaragua); that short, explosive clashes (e.g., Rwanda) may carry effects different from drawn-out conflicts (e.g., Mozambique); that conflicts converted to natural-resource extraction wars (e.g, Sierra Leone) may bear upon nature differently than those in which rebels seek to stake out fiefdoms of their own (e.g., Colombia); and that violent conflict fought with outside money (e.g., Nicaragua) may reduce the incentive to raise funds by dipping into nature's treasure chest at home. Chapter 5 addresses these and other possibilities in more detail.

4.4 Bibliographic Note

Angola: Barrio Froján and Volger (1999); Global Witness (1998, 1999, 2002); IUCN (1992a; 1992b). Central African Republic: Blom and Yamindou (2001). Ethiopia: Rubenson (1991); Jacobs and Schloeder (2001). Liberia: Global Witness (2001); SAMFU Foundation (2002); Suter (n.d.); Waitkuwait (2001). Mozambique: Hatton, Couto, and Oglethorpe (2001). Niger: Ostrowski, Massalatchi, and Mamane (2001). Sierra Leone: Squire (2001). Sudan: Suliman (1993); Switzer (2002). Uganda: Smart, Hatton, and Spence (1985). Burma: Brunner, Talbott, and Elkin (1998); Harbinson (1992); and Internet-based reports, including Roger Moody

(2000); EarthRights International (www.earthrights.org/publications); and World Resources Institute (www.wri.org; search for Burma). Indonesia: Barber (2002); Barber and Talbott (2003); and www.orangutan.org.uk. Colombia: Álvarez (2003); Dávalos (2001); Kirk (2003). El Salvador and Guatemala: Gardner, Garb, and Williams (1990); Hall and Faber (1989). Nicaragua: Kaimowitz and Fauné (2003); Nietschmann (1990; 1998) [accessed 9 March 2008].

Notes

1. See, for instance, Kalpers (2001b); Blom (2000).

2. Throughout, the term "civil war" is used loosely. It can refer to outright civil war to settle political grievances, but also to natural resource extraction wars. It can refer to rebellions, insurrections, wars of secession, wars of liberation or to gain special political status, and to wars of terror and repression committed by states, nonstate agents, or both. The absence of outside troops is not a deciding factor. For example, after the conclusion of Angola's war of independence from Portugal, Cuban troops entered Angola in the follow-on civil war. In the mostly ethnically based civil war in Sri Lanka, foreign financing played a big role. The Afghan wars at times involved the Soviet Union and the United States, at times only locals. Other cases include, for instance, South Africa under apartheid; Burma; Aceh and Indonesia; Colombia; Nicaragua; El Salvador; Guatemala; Liberia; Chad; Sudan; and Mozambique. More important for the designation as a civil war is that the armed conflict is clearly not a war between two or more states (e.g., Eritrea and Ethiopia in 1998 to 2000; France and Germany; Japan and China). For a discussion see, for instance, Anderton and Carter (2009).

3. Ezaza and Othman (1989, p. 135). The piece appears in an edited volume nearly all of whose 16 contributions exhibit the same flaw of assertion without data or references to sources.

4. IUCN (1992b). For example, pp. 184, 193.

5. Volume 22, Number 4, 1988, p. 231 and Volume 30, Number 4, 1996, p. 238, respectively.

6. For a summary of findings and recommendations, see Shambaugh, et al. (2001).

7. Kanyamibwa (1998, p. 1403).

8. The following is based on Kanyamibwa (1998) and Plumptre, Masozera, and Vedder (2001).

9. The following is based on Hart and Mwinyihali (2001).

10. Also spelled as colombo-tantalite. See Redmond (2001, p. 7) and the website of the Brussels-based Tantalum-Niobium International Study Center, http://www.tanb.org [accessed 7 February 2008].

11. A useful background paper is Gasana (2002). It traces not only the political situation prior to, during, and after the war but also provides a useful case study

of how environmental, population, and policy pressures combined to precipitate the political crisis. Also see Foster (1989). Excess deaths—deaths likely due to the direct and indirect effects of war—in the Democratic Republic of the Congo are estimated at 5.4 million people between August 1998 and April 2007; see IRC (2008, p. II).

12. Poaching/encroachment: Kanyamibwa (1998, p. 1403). Since the lower-altitude sections of the park are also the most biologically diverse, Kanyamibwa foresees detrimental long-term effects (p. 1404). Snare counts: Plumptre, Masozera, and Vedder (2001, pp. 15–16). Quote: Plumptre, Masozera, and Vedder (2001, p. 15). Kenya experiments: Palmer, et al. (2008).

13. Plumptre, Masozera, and Vedder (2001); quotes p. 17.

14. See chapter 2, note 47.

15. Large-mammal densities: Plumptre, Masozera, and Vedder (2001, pp. 17–18). Kanyamibwa: Kanyamibwa (1998); habitat loss: p. 1402; quote p. 1404.

16. Plumptre, Masozera, and Vedder (2001, p. 19).

17. Plumptre, Masozera, and Vedder (2001); Kanyamibwa (1998, p. 1403).

18. The 1996 ungulate study, census methods: see Plumptre, et al. (1997); Plumptre, Masozera, and Vedder (2001). The study was conducted in part to determine the effects of snare setting on the gorilla population in the park. Gorillas do get trapped in snares and risk losing hands or feet or dying of snare-wound infection. Throughout the region researchers frequently describe gorillas with missing or crippled extremities. Two veterinarians worked in the park specifically to monitor the health of habituated gorilla groups. In April 2000, IUCN proposed a new classification of gorilla into two species, the western lowland gorilla (*Gorilla gorilla*), and the eastern mountain gorilla (*Gorilla beringei*), each with two subspecies. The latter, of interest here, is subdivided into the eastern lowland or Grauer's gorilla (*Gorilla beringei graueri*) and the mountain gorilla (*Gorilla beringei beringei*). A small, isolated population in the Bwindi Impenetrable Forest of Uganda, the Bwindi gorilla, may possibly be a distinct subspecies. As of 2006, it appears that the surviving adult population there numbers only about 300 individuals. All gorilla species—east and west—are "endangered" or "critically endangered." See www .redlist.org [accessed 16 February 2009].

19. 15 gorillas: http://www.fauna-flora.org/gorilla/gorilla_home.htm [accessed 25 February 2003]. 350 animals: Plumptre, Masozero, and Vedder (2001, p. 14). 2000 census: Kalpers, et al. (2003; p. 13 of 2002 prepublication manuscript). As of 31 January, 2001, the combined population of mountain gorillas, *Gorilla beringei beringei*, was thought to number 355, an increase of about 10 percent relative to a prewar census conducted in 1989. See http://www.fauna-flora.org/gorilla/gorilla_home.htm [accessed 25 February 2003]. Kalpers, et al. (2003) provides a detailed discussion of the story behind the numbers. By 2003, the population count increased to about 380; see http://www.iucnredlist.org/details/39994 [accessed 16 February 2009], about half of them being mature. Reproduction rates appear to be higher in the habituated, and relatively more protected, areas. For

comparison, a confirmed Ebola virus outbreak among the more numerous western lowland gorillas in the Lossi Gorilla Sanctuary in the Republic of Congo (i.e., Congo-Brazzaville) led to 139 dead or missing gorillas in November and December 2002. Autopsies of four gorillas and two chimpanzees confirmed death from Ebola. There is concern that the virus can spread to the nearby Odzala National Park, an area known for the highest western lowland gorilla densities in Africa. See http://www.ecofac.org/Divers/EbolaEN.htm [accessed 15 March 2003].

20. Sperling (2001); quotes pp. 990, 993; root rot/bean fly diseases: pp. 1003–1004.

21. Sperling (2001); quotes pp. 994, 995.

22. Sperling (2001); quotes pp. 998, 999; seed supplies dropped: p. 997, table 2.

23. Sperling (2001); sowing pre- and postwar: p. 1001, table 6; seed components/variety: p. 1001, table 5; prices/poverty: p. 1002; depleted seed channels: p. 1003.

24. Sperling (2001); quotes pp. 1004–1005.

25. See, for instance, Kalpers, et al. (2003).

26. Kalpers (2001a).

27. Kalpers (2001a); information and quote from p. 5.

28. Biswas and Tortajada-Quiroz (1996, p. 405). Zaire government report: p. 404.

29. All information from Biswas and Tortajada-Quiroz (1996); quote p. 405.

30. Biswas and Tortajada-Quiroz (1996); wood collection phases: p. 405.

31. Topography: Biswas and Tortajada-Quiroz (1996, p. 406). 40,000 people: Pearce (1994, p. 4). Denuded areas: Kalpers (2001a, p. 6). Kalpers also writes that the area of 105 km^2 amounts to 63 km^2 of "equivalent cleared area." From a biological point of view, this is not a useful measure: where something is left standing, seed sources for recolonization are available and regrowth may be possible. The cited 35 km^2 of completely denuded area is therefore a more interesting number.

32. Kalpers (2001a, p. 12).

33. Biswas and Tortajada-Quiroz (1996, p. 407). An Egyptian study of enterovirus loads of the Nile River (Ali, et al., 1996) detected significant loads of wild poliovirus strains (at 9 of 15 sampling sites, or 60 percent). Since Nile River poliovirus strains in Egypt usually come from the vaccine strains, not the wild strains, this suggests an upstream source, either Sudan or Rwanda, possibly from corpses thrown into the rivers (also suggested by Kanyamibwa, 1998, p. 1403). The samples were taken during the Rwandan war. However, being cautious, the authors write that when compared to the Danube (83 percent) or Elbe (90 percent) rivers, enterovirus detection in the Nile was low by international standards.

34. INERA and Kahuzi-Biega National Park: Biswas and Tortajada-Quiroz (1996, p. 405). Quote: Plumptre (2003, p. 81).

35. Sato, Yasui, and Byamana (2000). 10–15 cm: the authors do not report the height at which the diameter was measured.

36. Contradictions: Plumptre, Masozera, and Vedder (2001). Quote: Sato, Yasui, and Byamana (2000, p. 123).

37. UNHCR: The first UNHCR operations management guidelines to pay attention to environmental issues during and after an emergency were issued in 1996. They contained little on prevention. Even by the 1999 Kosovo crisis UNHCR appears to have had difficulties implementing its own strategies. For the updated 2005 guidelines, see UNHCR (2005). They still are short on prevention. Fires and natural regrowth: Sato, Yasui, and Byamana (2000).

38. Hart and Mwinyihali (2001); quotes p. 21.

39. First quote: Hart and Mwinyihali (2001, p. 20). A news report (*New Scientist*, 3 December 1994, p. 4) claims that between 1989 and 1994—that is, before and during the Rwandan war—Zairean soldiers took over the northern part of the Virunga park and that the population of hippopotamuses was halved by poaching to 11,000 animals, apparently in that time span. Second quote: Hart and Mwinyihali (2001, p. 25). Itombwe: Hart and Mwinyihali (2001, pp. 24–25).

40. Hart and Mwinyihali (2001, pp. 26–27).

41. UNESCO World Heritage site: http://whc.unesco.org [accessed 7 February 2008]. Other such sites in Congo include Virunga National Park (1979); Garamba National Park (1980); Salonga National Park (1984); and Okapi Wildlife Reserve (1996). Resource extraction: Hart and Mwinyihali (2001).

42. Reliable number: Yamagiwa (2003, p. 119). Park services suspended: Yamagiwa (2003, p. 126). Kigali airport: see Redmond (2001), who photographed and listed carved ivory items displayed in Kigali (literally across the street from the Commerce, Industry, and Tourism Minister's office) on 31 January 2000, and at the Kigali airport on 5 October 2000. Since elephants are rare in Rwanda, it is likely that the items came from poached elephants in eastern Congo. Ivory trade is in contravention of the Convention on International Trade in Endangered Species (CITES), to which Rwanda is a state party.

43. Grauer's world population: Yamagiwa (2003, p. 117); Redmond (2001, p. 3). Highland sector censuses: Yamagiwa (2003, p. 117). 2000 census: Yamagiwa (2003, p. 129); Redmond (2001) suggests that a population of only 126 individuals may be too small to be genetically sustainable, a concern echoed by IUCN's Redlist [accessed 16 February 2009].

44. Lowland-sector gorilla population crash: Redmond (2001, p. 3). Mining camp locations: for an example, see Redmond (2001, p. 13). Mining camp numbers: Berggorilla und Regenwald Direkthilfe, May 2001, p. 1; see http://www.berggorilla.de/kahuzie.pdf [accessed 7 February 2008].

45. Redmond (2001, pp. 9–10).

46. Mountain gorillas: Kalpers, et al. (2003). Hippopotamus: This according to the World Conservation Monitoring Centre (WCMC), Cambridge, UK. http://www.wcmc.org.uk:80/protected_areas/data/wh/virunga.html [accessed 27 February 2003].

47. See the World Bank's annual *World Development Reports* (New York: Oxford University Press).

48. A cartographic collection on Afghanistan and other countries is provided by the University of Texas, Austin, available at http://www.lib.utexas.edu/maps/ [accessed 29 April 2009].

49. Farm animal killings: this according to Formoli (1995, p. 66). Yusufi (1988, p. 200, table 15.3) counts well over 20 million sheep in 1968, as well as 3.1 million head of goat, 3.6 million cattle, 1.3 million donkeys, and about 750,000 camels, horses, and mules. Between 1989 and 1999, it is estimated, decimated flocks recovered to 24 million head of sheep and 9 million goats before collapsing again by perhaps 70 percent on account of a prolonged drought that started in 1998 (UNEP, 2003b, p. 18). The quotes are from Yusufi (1988, pp. 209, 210, 208–209).

50. Quotes: Yusufi (1988, pp. 209, 213). Pre-1979 deforestation: UNEP (2003b, p. 24, citing a 1981 FAO report). Agricultural employment: Formoli (1995, p. 66); UNEP (2003b, p. 15).

51. All information in this paragraph based on Skogland (1988).

52. Few pre-1979 data points: Formoli (1995, p. 66). Decline in forested areas: the estimates of 3.4 and 2.6 percent surely are inaccurately stated. They may refer to "closed forests" of oak, pine, and cedar that FAO in 1981 estimated at 4.5 percent of the land area. In addition, FAO counted "open woodland" of pistachio, juniper, and other species covering 48 percent of the land area (see UNEP, 2003b, p. 64, and references there). Quote: Formoli (1995, p. 66).

53. Formoli (1995); quotes pp. 67, 68.

54. Zahler and Graham (2001); quote p. 2.

55. UNEP (2003, p. 6).

56. UNEP (2003, p. 8).

57. UNEP (2003, pp. 11–12).

58. Snow leopard: Peter Zahler, co-author of the Zahler and Graham (2001) study was part of the UNEP team. Siberian crane: Formoli (1995, p. 67); McPherson and Fernando (1991). Updated information on the Siberian crane (and cranes generally) may be obtained from the International Crane Foundation at www.savingcranes.org. For migration routes and other information, also see http://www. npwrc.usgs.gov/resource/birds/cranes/grusleuc.htm [both accessed 19 February 2009]. The "eastern" population of Siberian cranes is still viable as of this writing, but is critically endangered.

59. UNEP (2003b); quotes pp. 50–52, 67, 69–70, 85.

60. Afghan refugee numbers: for a useful general background reading on Afghan refugees in Pakistan and the political, ethnic, tribal, cultural, religious, and socioeconomic, but not ecological, consequences, see, for instance, Weinbaum (1993). Quotes: Allan (1987, pp. 200, 201, 202).

61. Allan (1987); quotes p. 202.

62. Lodhi, Echavarria, and Keithley (1998).

63. Nietschmann (1990, 1998).

War and Nature in a Globalized World **5**

In 1996, Lawrence Keeley published an important book, *War before Civilization*. What distinguishes the book is the author's use of archaeological, physical evidence to make his case. By way of analogy, Keeley writes:

> In our legal system, circumstantial evidence is treated with a statutory reserve, although all law-enforcement and legal professionals know that it is actually eyewitness testimony that is notoriously unreliable and contradictory. . . . Contrary to legal statute, as evidence of "what really happens," physical circumstance is far superior to standard eyewitnesses (who could, for example, honestly proclaim the earth flat) and expert opinion (invariably contradictory). The very physicality of circumstantial evidence, while it may be and often is misinterpreted, makes it immune to dismissal and resistant to distortion.[1]

Physical evidence makes believers. It permits one to take a step back and think about patterns embedded in that evidence. Patterns allow an understanding of the past and offer insight into the design and conduct of research and policy for the future. Like Keeley's evidence regarding prehistoric warfare, the evidence for war-related environmental effects is, while incomplete, clearly far more differentiated than a simple "war is bad for the environment" statement would suggest.

Section 5.1 discusses major themes arising from the case studies in chapters 2, 3, and 4. Section 5.2 suggests where research and policy gaps exist and how they may be addressed, and section 5.3 concludes the chapter and the book.

5.1 Findings

5.1.1 Big Wars, Small Effects? Small Wars, Big Effects?

Are "big" wars associated with "small" environmental effects? With the sample size limited to two cases (the Vietnam and the Persian Gulf wars), one necessarily needs to be cautious when drawing conclusions. Regarding the war in Vietnam, recall some numbers. We have three estimates of the area sprayed by herbicides. The smallest, 13,100 km², is by Young, a larger one of 16,700 km² comes from Westing, and an even larger and more recent estimate of 26,313 km² was made by Stellman and co-authors.[2] Undisputed is that spraying killed many trees, especially among mangrove stands. Killing trees opened the canopy. Light energy reached the soil. Bamboo grasses colonized the newly opened spaces. Equally undisputed is that villagers kept the spaces open by fire and by conversion to agriculture to prevent recolonization and succession with tree species. One form of human agency (war) caused the initial damage, another form of human agency (peace) prevented reconstitution. Except for mangroves, when revegetation was not prevented, it was possible and healthy. Adverse effects were limited to humans (dioxins) or, as regards nonhuman life, remain largely unrecorded except for the forests. The density and quality of Vietnam's forests prior to the war is disputed. Most participants in the debate focus on the damage done to commercial tree stands. Regarding flora other than trees, let alone forest fauna, the available information is too thin to come to a sweeping, undifferentiated conclusion about any difference the war may have made. We cannot say that the "big" Vietnam War had a "small" effect. Neither can we say that it had a "big" effect. We just do not know what ecology-wide effects we may attribute to the Vietnam herbicide spraying. Much is suspected, but little is known. Apart from commercial tree stands and the mangrove areas, the preponderance of what evidence there is does not suggest permanent damage of natural resources due to herbicide spraying.

Ignorance is compounded by inattention. Compare the largest estimate of area sprayed, the estimate of 26,313 km², to the estimate of land areas affected by bulldozing, bombing, and shrapnel of 70,750 km² (67,500 km² for bombing and shrapnel and 3,250 km² for bulldozing).[3] Virtually nothing is known about what happened on these 70,750 km². One therefore cannot say that the war's effect was small, nor can one say that it was big. Nonetheless, it seems proper to say that the bulldozing resulted in widespread, long-term detrimental effects, but perhaps not irreversible ones. An area of 3,250 km² (325,000 hectares, 802,750 acres, or 1,250 square miles) is widespread. By definition, recolonization will take decades and hence this is a long-lasting event. Because bulldozing involved complete removal of vegetation, we may also say that the effect was severe. We do not know about the long-term ecological impact: did the bulldozing amount to disturbance, degradation, or depletion? It is not too late to find out. Bomb craters still exist, and they and the surrounding terrain can be studied for flora and fauna. Even in bulldozed areas, we can study what is there now. Are these areas recolonized or not? By which species? How would the findings compare to adjacent areas that were not bulldozed? We may yet be able to gain considerable knowledge about what the Vietnam War did to nature.

With two exceptions, the Persian Gulf War resulted in small environmentally adverse effects. One exception concerns some of the mangrove stands in the bays just west of Abu Ali Island in Saudi Arabia. Other marine and intertidal resources have recovered. Recolonization and succession worked their magic because the underlying habitat was not destroyed nor prevented, as in at least some cases in Vietnam, from being recolonized. The other exception, or so it appears, concerns the Kuwaiti desert (see bibliographic note for chapter 3). Heavily churned during the Iraqi invasion and heavily churned again during the subsequent war, the putting out of oil fires, and the reconstruction (and expansion) of oil facilities, the desert soil may be presumed to have suffered, and with it desert flora and fauna. Regrettably, few convincing studies are available to factually demonstrate the point. The unanswered question is whether the disruption amounted to disturbance, degradation, or depletion.[4]

The pattern appears to be that the more recent and the shorter is the "big" war, the smaller is its environmental impact. But a sample size of two cases does not make this a conclusive finding, only an intriguing hypothesis. Also, both cases involve exclusively or primarily the United States of America. After the Vietnam War, the United States developed the technical means to implement targeting that can with high precision discriminate among human, military, economic, environmental, and other targets. But of the industrially developed countries, none but the United States and the United Kingdom have fought a big war in recent decades, and one cannot be sure that a France or a Germany could, or would, fight an environmentally "clean" war. Yet the impression of cleanliness of recent U.S. wars derives in part from attention bias. Although the United Nations Environment Programme (UNEP) did study the environmental impact of the U.S./NATO air war on Serbia during the Kosovo war of 1999, it did not study the effect of U.S. bombing on Afghanistan's mountains (even though UNEP's Afghanistan study is excellent in other respects). Likewise, it appears that no one has fully studied the ecological effects of the 1991 and 2003 wars in and on Iraq.

Among developing countries, prolonged "big" wars, such as the 1980–1988 Iran-Iraq War, and short wars such as China's invasion of Vietnam, Vietnam's invasion of Cambodia, and secession wars such as those between East Timor and Indonesia, Ethiopia and Eritrea, Russia and Chechnya are common. Intensively studied from political and humanitarian points of view, all appear to overlook that when the warring is done, humans need to return and live in the former conflict zones. What happened to the physical habitat during these wars? The straight-up answer is, again, that for most cases we simply do not know.

If at least some big wars are associated with apparently small environmental effects, are small wars associated with big effects? To be sure, many small wars are bigger—much bigger—than most big wars. The more than fifty years of civil war in Colombia, twenty-five years in Sri Lanka, about forty years in Angola, and as many (with a ten-year respite) in Sudan, surely amount to big wars. They are small only inasmuch as news media fail to pick up on these conflicts with sufficient intensity and inasmuch as high-tech weaponry may be used sparsely. The primary weapons used in internal wars are so-called small arms, especially firearms (handguns and long guns). The dead, injured, traumatized, and displaced people in "small" wars due to firearms number in the tens of millions.[5]

The cases of Rwanda and Afghanistan studied in chapter 4 suggest that refugee streams induced by internal war can generate adverse environmental consequences. In addition, it appears from cases not explicitly presented in this book (but referred to in the bibliographic note in section 4.4) that different types of internal war result in different types of environmentally adverse effects. Findings regarding mobility, firepower, and poaching, refugees and returnees, and conservation and environmental policy in war also suggest that small wars can generate big detrimental effects. These are discussed in the following subsections.

5.1.2 Firepower and Mobility[6]
Modern weapons, combined with mobility and local, national, and global distribution networks, result in heavy poaching and resource extraction, at least locally, at least for certain species, and at least at times in apparently unsustainable ways. This is one of the major common themes arising from the civil war cases. Any single war's effects are usually comparatively small,

but the combination of many, near simultaneous, long-running wars in contiguous regions can amount to cumulative detrimental effects on nature and natural resources. This finding applies especially to African wars, such as those in the Central African Republic, the eastern part of the Democratic Republic of Congo, Liberia, Mozambique, Niger, and Uganda. While occasionally mentioned, poaching does not appear as a major concern in the Asian and Latin American cases. Why the difference? A number of answers are possible. First, the majority of larger aggregations of the remaining big animals—the elephants, rhinoceroses, hippopotamuses, and gorillas—range predominantly in African war zones.[7] They are (or were) present in relatively large numbers, they are relatively easy to locate, and they are easy to shoot. Second, researchers already had established research lines and conservation programs that focused on the large animals so that the outside world would be expected to receive more reports about their fate than for lesser known animals such as ungulates, monkeys, or birds that may be more heavily affected elsewhere. Data collection is biased in favor of the better-known animals. As a biological rule of thumb, the larger the animal, the smaller the number of offspring and the slower the rate of reproduction. The population, once decimated, is hard to reestablish. Even though this does not tell us much about ecological processes, from a species conservation point of view the focus on large animals is of course appropriate.

Third, depletion levels may already have been higher in non-African countries so that there were fewer big animals left to poach. (The human population density in Asia is much higher than in Africa.) And fourth, a genuine difference in the nature of the wars in Africa as opposed to those in Asia and Latin America may help account for the differential amount of poaching. Several reasons for this come to mind, all related to the nature of governance. Both the Burmese and Indonesian cases are/were cases of government repression and armed resistance rather than cases of outright civil war. The number of weapons available to opposing groups appears small. Their use in poaching would be limited also. The Afghan wars were, in part, international rather than internal wars (the Soviet invasion in 1979 and the U.S. bombing in 2001). And its internal wars were/are more nearly tribal rather than civil wars. Tribal wars are conflicts between established peoples who attempt to defend already existing territory, rather than wars that set out to gain control over a country as a whole. A tribal war is unlikely to result in deliberate poaching as this would undermine the people's land of which they are the already acknowledged residents. This may explain the Nicaraguan situation, especially on the Caribbean coast, where poaching was limited during the 1980s war. In contrast, African wars often aim at domination over the entire political realm of the country, even as many of them degenerate into resource extraction (for example, timber, oil, diamond, metal) to finance the wars. The Colombian case is more nearly a civil than a tribal war in that the two major rebel groups, FARC and the ELN, avowedly wished to overthrow the established government. We have only two reports on the country, one of which focuses exclusively on forest cover. The other one indeed mentions poaching as a concern.

There are varieties of poaching. At times poaching coincides with forest or park clearing, as in eastern Rwanda's Akagera Park. At other times poaching keeps people out of forests, as in the Central African Republic's Dzanga-Sangha park. A major factor facilitating poaching is the relative ease of transport, especially on the savannah or open plains. A study on the red-necked ostrich in Niger made this very clear. Motorization and guns are a deadly combination for wildlife.[8]

When does poaching not take place? The limited information on Liberia is of interest. When rebels, soldiers, and civilians are so crowded, even in forested areas, that shooting would attract attention, the level of gun-based poaching falls. It then takes the form of labor-intensive snare laying or trap setting, which tend to bind the poacher to a place and deprive him of mobility. The animal has to come to the trap instead of the poacher going to the animal. A stationary, unarmed poacher will do less damage than a mobile, armed one.

Finally, the length and financing of conflict appears of importance. Episodic war, even repeated episodic war, will allow for periods of recovery. In Nicaragua, the war did not affect the whole of the country in equal measure at each point in time. Instead, various regions were affected to various degrees at different times. The same observation was made for Rwanda, where the war moved around the country from 1990 onward before the great conflagration of April 1994 commenced, and this is true for Afghanistan as well. In contrast, it appears that many of the African wars were or are wars that affect relatively large areas of land continuously without any intervening let-up, such as in Angola and southern (and now western) Sudan.[9] When war is financed from outside, it appears that reports of natural resource extraction are muted, but when war must be financed from within, it appears that it is partly financed via the world markets to which illegally and/or unsustainably harvested resources are shipped (see section 5.2.4).

5.1.3 Refugees and Returnees

The clearest evidence of adverse environmental consequences of war, even if the magnitude is difficult to discern, comes from the impact of large numbers of refugees and returnees. In principle, refugees can be assets (e.g., a ready labor pool) rather than liabilities, but in practice the liability aspect appears to outweigh the asset aspect, at least for developing states.[10] The cases of Rwandan refugees in eastern Congo and of Afghan refugees in Pakistan are convincing, as is the lesser-developed case of Colombia. Refugees flee either to cities or to rural areas, inside or outside their state of origin. Cities become even more overcrowded than they already are, leading to environmental stresses, often mediated via inadequate water, sewage, and waste-disposal facilities, and to degradation in the immediate vicinity that mostly affects humans rather than wildlife. Alternatively, refugees flee to neighboring states that then herd refugees into huge camps from which they set out to supply or supplement their needs if these are not adequately met by relief agencies, or else they flee to somewhere within the affected country as internally displaced persons, in which case the effects on the environment would likely be dispersed instead of concentrated. The last-cited case, however, is not well studied.

Where do internally displaced persons go? What do they do on the way to where they go? How do they survive once they arrive wherever they go? And how does their survival affect the environment? There are some hints in the literature. In Ethiopia, for instance, there is a domino effect whereby one displaced group displaces another, which then displaces a third. This effect appears particularly deleterious when each displaced group moves to a territory that differs ecologically from the group's original habitat, for instance, pastoralists moving onto agricultural land or nomadic herders moving into forests. Thus, one of the studies of Afghan refugees in Pakistan showed that refugees from agricultural areas will try to reestablish agriculture: if settled in forests, they will clear forests. One study on Rwanda showed that a pastoral people (cattle herders) will bring their animals and clear forests for grazing land. Comparing different camp locations within the same country (Afghans in Pakistan, Rwandans in the eastern Congo) shows that settling refugees on undeveloped land but at considerable distance from forests will help to keep forests intact. When local natural resources are available, refugees will make use of them. Long-term refugees are likely to try to convert their camps into permanent homes. "Cities" with half a million, a million, or more people are stamped out of the surrounding patch of land, obviously destroying nature in the process. In South Vietnam, people fleeing the countryside sought shelter in Saigon (now Ho Chi Minh City), increasing the population from 250,000 to 3 million. The 500,000 Rwandans fleeing to Tanzania in 1994 created that country's "second largest urban center after Dar es Salaam."[11]

A similar appraisal derives from a biochemical assessment of the mid-1990s war in Croatia. Detailed surveys of damage to industrial installations found that the war resulted in an uncontrolled release of dangerous chemicals into the nearby environment (the effects of which we do not know) and also destroyed much of the water, sewage, and other potential treatment facilities for chemical spills. This, combined with population movements seeking refuge in larger cities, often overwhelmed the cities and exposed the population and nonhuman environment to danger.[12]

Refugee settlements can attract opportunists to profit from the confusion and lack of conservation enforcement. They extract resources on the back of humanitarian catastrophe or hold relief, conservation, and development agencies hostage by extracting rent in exchange for safe passage, guard work, and similar services.[13] The return to peace after war can also be accompanied by a rent-seeking land grab during which resource concessions are demanded and granted—even simultaneously to competing grantees for the same resource—in an unsettled policy environment as regards natural resources, biodiversity conservation, and environmental protection. In Mozambique, concessions were granted by different government agencies, influenced by corruption, without local consultation, and without coordination among government offices, granted even in protected areas that had previously been declared off limits. It was not until 1997, five years after the end of the war, that a framework environmental law was passed by the national legislature. Enforcement is another matter.[14]

While research has been carried out regarding the impact of refugees arriving at camps, the environmental, ecological, and biodiversity effects on home areas left behind does not appear to have been studied. If humans leave, wildlife should recover. That is the impression given in the Afghan case, in the Nicaraguan case, and, to a lesser degree, in the Rwandan case. For the former Yugoslavia, UNEP noted that environmental problems appeared to lessen as a result of reduced economic activity due to economic sanctions applied to the country prior to the wars there. For Angola, a researcher writes that "the war had contrary effects . . . by crippling most economic activities based on advanced [i.e., industrial] technologies. Angola's war helped curb damage to the environment from many of the effects of conventional 'development' . . . [but] where people were obliged to settle in ever-larger numbers, damage to land and vegetation intensified."[15] In the case of Colombia, however, the pattern seemed to be that paramilitary units drove people off the land to convert it to cattle-ranching land, with deforestation being the result.

Equally under-studied is the biodiversity impact of returning refugees. The Mozambique study is useful in this regard in that it appeared possible to state with some certainty that adverse wildlife effects were closely correlated with the return path of refugees. In particular, reopened highway and transportation corridors served as encroachment vectors.

5.1.4 Conservation By Default

CONSERVATION. One victim of war is countries' reduced institutional capacity to continue to protect nature and natural resources. Warfare prevents states from carrying out their normal environmental protective duties. A large number of reports point in the same direction, and the evidence is fairly clear. For example, one researcher argues that serious soil erosion in the northern Ethiopian highlands in the 1980s was caused not so much by warfare per se as by the Ethiopian government's lack of attention to the problem; efforts at rehabilitation of that environment were effectively prevented by the civil war that raged at the time.[16] Normal environmental policy, in countries that ordinarily are already short of monetary and human resources, is circumvented and becomes detrimental policy by default.

The converse observation is that war forecloses human activity from the land and therefore often protects it. This, also, is "policy" by default. For example, an IUCN report on Angola states:

> The economic paralysis caused by the war (and the depopulation of certain areas and destruction of physical infrastructure) has . . . functioned as a brake on the wholesale exploitation of certain natural resources. It is of great concern then, that instead of going forward now to repair damages caused by thirty years of war and promote sustainable patterns of natural resource use, these damages will be further compounded by a new period of rapid and unchecked economic exploitation of those resources which are still intact.[17]

Conflict prevention, conflict transformation, and postconflict environmental management all become critical conservation tasks. In practice, conservation by default means conservation neglect. Finances are redirected; staff go unpaid; habitats lose their protected status; equipment is stolen; facilities are looted; installations are destroyed; grounds are invaded; flora is trampled; animals are poached; research records are lost; achievements are reversed; and so on. However, apart from a few instances of specific threats to specific species, the exact ecological nature of these effects rarely is known. Even without war, most of Africa's protected areas are protected in name only. Although international protected areas "have grown by 50 percent or more in many areas of the world in recent years, the discouraging fact is that over 85 percent of these protected areas are little more than paper creations."[18] War exacerbates the problem.

COORDINATION AND COOPERATION. Local, national, and international human rights advocacy groups, humanitarian relief agencies, biodiversity conservation organizations, and human and economic development programs, it is now realized, can work at cross-purposes. The potential for conflict between conservation and development has been long-standing, for instance around the issue of dam building for hydropower generation. Instead of tearing down an environment for development, it may be possible to alter or relocate a project to accommodate environmental concerns. This is not a new idea. Neither is the idea of ecotourism new. For example, gorilla tourism in Rwanda helped stem forest cover decline in the Volcanoes National Park. People took pride, they earned an income, and consequently they preserved the resource that generated the income. To use potential ecosystem services, in this case ecotourism, as a form of economic development is an idea that can be developed further, but there is a downside to this strategy. As a cyclical industry, tourism depends on the discretionary spending of its customers. It is thus a risky strategy that would need to be integrated with other development offerings. The industry also requires a degree of dependable infrastructure (such as airfields, roads, communication, and hotels or camps) and security, safety, and internal stability. Ecotourism is therefore unlikely to be a priority for development planners. Still, the more relevant ideas the conservation community can generate for development planners, and the more the latter appreciate the objectives of the former, the more likely it is that some ideas can be productively pursued.

The Rwandan crisis brought another conflict to a head when representatives of conservation groups took umbrage at humanitarian relief workers who appeared oblivious to the conservation value of nonhuman life. Once an emergency has started and aid workers are overwhelmed with hundreds of thousands of people to be assisted, it is usually too late to do much about conservation. The key lies in preparedness planning. After the 1994 Rwandan crisis, UNHCR, the U.N. refugee agency, drafted new policy documents with regard to the natural environment.[19] For example, the 1998 document includes 10 principles—

1) prevention is better than cure
2) environment programs need not be complex
3) environment programs need not be costly
4) environmental management is more than providing stoves and planting trees
5) interventions should add value to environmental assets and practices
6) access rights and benefit sharing are fundamental to sound environmental management
7) coordination and implementation are vital but separate environmental roles
8) influencing policy can be as important as defining practice
9) relief and development assistance should be compatible
10) protect the environment to safeguard asylum

—but implementation appears to have been weak.

Some of this has to do with the relevant authorities in the refugee-receiving countries. They have their own location priorities. But some of it has to do with the relative lack of attention to the matter within UNHCR.

The case of Burma is instructive for a different reason. The primary connection here is not between conservation and emergency relief or economic development groups but between conservation and human rights groups. Against protests of human rights NGOs, in 1994 the Wildlife Conservation Society of New York accepted an invitation to work in Burma and become the first outside conservation organization to do so in thirty years. The concern of human rights campaigners was that Burma's military dictatorship thereby received an unwarranted degree of validation and legitimacy. But there is no reason why the human rights campaign against the Burmese government cannot be continued. Conceivably, it can even be strengthened when trustworthy ecological information might be forthcoming from within the country.

Exceptions notwithstanding, a general lack of cooperation and lack of mutual understanding and joint planning among human rights, humanitarian emergency assistance, economic development, and natural resource conservation groups still characterizes the state of affairs of nature in war. As in the case of development, conservation groups themselves can help by developing and presenting plans and offering education for those who plan, set up, and manage refugee camps in future crises. Strictly speaking, this may be viewed as lying outside the purview of conservation organizations and their donors, but it is work that needs doing nonetheless.

Another problem regards lack of knowledge of prewar biodiversity and natural resource conditions. In the absence of pertinent biodiversity knowledge, how are development planners to know what resources of conservation value to consider in their planning? Obvious errors apart, how are refugee assistance agencies and receiving governments to know where to settle refugees? The onus lies on the quality of preparation offered by conservation groups. They are the natural resource experts, they need to prepare the data and send the signals to the other groups, and they need their own emergency preparedness planning. In the late 1990s, IUCN started to exert leadership to link relief, development, and conservation together.[20] Some suggestions to address these questions are discussed in section 5.2.

5.1.5 Benefits of War, Costs of Peace

War does not always affect nature in detrimental ways. It can also offer nature a "macabre reprieve from human incursion." Bruun, in an excellent piece decrying war, praises its salutary effects on bird life: "If war is hell, and few doubt that it is, it is at least a consolation to know that some animals can take advantage of such self-destructive folly among men." Jeffrey McNeely, the IUCN's chief scientist, adds many examples. Among the best known is that of the Korean Demilitarized Zone (DMZ) and the Civilian Control Zone (CCZ), a 5–20 km wide zone south of the DMZ in which commercial encroachment is limited. This zone, and the DMZ itself, has become a haven for rare and endangered species and now constitutes a unique wildlife habitat ranging across the entire east-west landscape of the Korean peninsula.[21]

When war decimates human populations, wildlife can recuperate. When Spaniards invaded today's Panama in the 1500s, a rapid population decline ensued. "Large areas which today are covered by dense forest were in farms, grassland or low second growth in the early sixteenth century when the Spaniards arrived. At that time horses were ridden with ease through areas which today are most easily penetrated by river, so dense has the tree growth become since the Indians died away." A case of a different nature was reported in 1990, documenting that a system of extensive underground reinforced concrete tunnels in western Poland, stemming from the 1930s, houses the "largest aggregation of hibernating bats in northern Europe." The 30 km long system of connected tunnels was dug by German troops at 30 meters depth. At the time of study, the artificial bat caves hosted at least 20,000 bats of twelve species, many of them rare or endangered. There is no report on what disturbances the tunnel digging imposed or what degree of damage it may have inflicted on wildlife at the time. But modern-day threats are posed by irresponsible tourism, such as exploring the easily accessible tunnels with torch lights, in-tunnel camping, stalactite disturbances, and vandalism. These threaten to change the evolved and sensitive microclimate of the tunnels. Although a small area of tunnels is protected by law, enforcement was absent.[22]

The late Bernard Nietschmann captures another aspect in the title of a piece published in 1990, "Conservation By Conflict in Nicaragua." He writes: "Trade in gold, mahogany, cedar, animal skins, sea turtles, shrimp, and lobster nearly ceased. Forests and grasses grew over the many plantations, state farms, and ranches that had produced bananas, coffee, cotton, and cattle. Wildlife thrived, and Nicaragua began to regain its rich natural heritage." A study by Kaimowitz-Fauné, also on Nicaragua, points to the reason: for rebels to remain viable, that is, invisible, forest cover needs to be preserved. Therefore, they did not unduly exploit the forest.[23]

An important subset of the literature, not concerned with war itself, observes that the military in economically advanced countries is among the most important protectors of open land spaces. Subjecting land, sea, and airspace to exclusive military use, say for military exercises and firing ranges, the military unwittingly protects vast areas from agricultural or other forms of encroachment that have destroyed wilderness places in the past.[24]

The converse of war being beneficial for nature is that peace is often destructive of nature. An interesting juxtaposition is provided by the Vietnam War. It may have left the natural environment in Vietnam, Cambodia, and Laos in tatters, but comparisons with neighboring countries such as Burma, Indonesia, Malaysia, and Thailand that were relatively unaffected by the war show that the natural environment in the latter set of countries now is more damaged than in the former. For example, Eric Fischer, senior vice president for science and sanctuaries at the National Audubon Society in the United States, writes: "The total damage inflicted on the Earth by recent wars pales in comparison to that wrought by peacetime habitat destruction, which in itself is a kind of silent war that humans are waging against other inhabitants of the planet." Writer and critic James Fallows, no friend of war, minces no words either: "Asia's experience indicates that war can be less damaging than peace . . . war is one of the less environmentally damaging activities that people undertake . . . for now, peace is a bigger environmental problem than war."[25]

The peace that follows war is a time of high vulnerability for nature. According to field reports, bushmeat hunting in Liberia increased drastically after the war. Likewise, in Mozambique, wildlife slaughter appeared to follow the route charted by the reopening of roads. In Burma, the government's arrangements with various ethnic groups allows all of them to rape the forest. And in the Persian Gulf case, researchers noting the prewar habitat destruction expressed concern about likely postwar destruction. Worse, even traditional conservation efforts may be destructive. Thus, in the past few decades zoological gardens and aquariums have moved away from being curiosity exhibits, at which humans ogle imprisoned animals, toward an education and research mission coupled with a new conservation ethic. But an ethic that favors "nature by segregating it from humanity" is inadequate. Creating a new apartheid between humans and nonhumans will not work. Instead of merely setting public space aside for nature, where "wildlife had become an ornament of the state," private and communal spaces need to be brought jointly into the conservation fold. Naturally, this will generate new conflicts.[26]

5.2 A Way Forward

5.2.1 Perspectives and Standards Matter

MEASUREMENT, DETECTION, ASSESSMENT. Measurement is important. So is a conceptual framework that tells us what to measure and how to assess. As detection does not necessarily equal damage, assessment requires specification of threshold levels, if not quantitatively, then at least qualitatively. Scientists measure from the viewpoint of their particular discipline: an atmospheric scientist measures particulates in the Persian Gulf War smoke plume, a forester measures the extent of injury and death of trees in Vietnamese forest stands, a wildlife conservationist measures rhinoceros populations, migrations, and shifting distributions in central Africa, and a radiochemist measures radioactivity from depleted-uranium munitions in Kosovo. Even when there is a large amount of scientific evidence, as with the Persian Gulf War of 1991, the question remains how the pieces of the puzzle fit together. To answer this, an overarching framework is needed whereby environmental disruptions are graded in terms of the likelihood of ecosystem recovery and restitution (see table 1.2).

Absolute numbers are of little use. They must be put in context. Areas deforested on account of war in the eastern Congo, Pakistan, and Zimbabwe are very small as compared to the bulldozing that took place in Vietnam: partial deforestation of 105 km² in the eastern Congo, 90 km² in Pakistan's Siran Valley, and perhaps of 120 km² in Zimbabwe as compared to 3,250 km² bulldozed, let alone bombed, in Vietnam.[27] Judged purely by the numbers, deforestation associated with refugees appears small. But relative numbers also can be misleading: should Vietnam be the standard? Instead of taking the ratio of, say, Pakistan to Vietnam (90/3,250 km²), should it be the other way around (3,250/90 km²)? That is just the point made in chapter 1: there has been a curious lack of effort to set any standard of assessment, to go beyond detection of damage to meaningful measurement. Of course, no one wishes to set what might be misconstrued as a standard of destruction, but the implied zero-tolerance stance is unrealistic. Wars do occur, and their ecological impact does need to be evaluated. Not only does one need standards, one needs standards for each ecosystem. Perhaps 90 km² *is* large, not relative to Vietnam but relative to Pakistan or relative to the ecological productivity of the Siran Valley.

SOIL, WATER, AIR. In the Persian Gulf War, air pollution was quickly and widely dispersed by wind, as was water pollution by current. In contrast, soil is fairly immobile, and harm to the soil is harm that tends to stay put. As soil is the interface between nutrients and plants—the primary producers upon which all other life depends—war's effects on soil should be studied first and foremost. Yet in practice, it is the least and last studied aspect of all. In Vietnam, the focus lay on the application of defoliants to its forests. Because one of the herbicides used contained trace amounts of the highly toxic substance TCDD, a dioxin, a large amount of time, money, and research effort was spent on dioxin-related investigations. In contrast, little effort was made to document the effects of the complete eradication of large swaths of Vietnamese forests and the literal scraping off of its topsoil by means of bulldozing and the cratering and shrapnel effects due to carpet bombing that struck a surface area perhaps five times as large as that affected by herbicide spraying. As far as environmental consequences of war are concerned, the proper sequence of attention should be soil, water, and air—in that order. If the soil survives, so will nature.[28] The reversed order of study is not surprising. Potentially adverse effects carried by wind and current affect people elsewhere, even everywhere, as the case of nuclear weapons testing showed (section 1.2). They want to know if they, too, are in danger. Ecologically, however, one wants to know about the local effects for populations (including humans) that are site-bound and cannot move. Soil studies can tell us about the gradient of damage and about possibilities of recovery. If one preserves the soil and preserves seed sources, one preserves and facilitates new recruitment.

HABITAT, SPECIES, ECOSYSTEMS. Until about the mid-1990s, the literature on the environmental effects of war was dominated by lamentations—not of what has happened but of what may happen to nature in war.[29] Following the Persian Gulf War and, especially, the refugee crises in Rwanda and the eastern Congo, serious attempts were made to conduct the necessary studies and to generate the numbers. But many focused on highly visible potential effects (for instance, oil spills or those affecting charismatic species). Few related to ecosystem functioning as a whole, a critical shortcoming. Notwithstanding the study of short-term effects such as counts of individual plants or animals killed, only the long term perspective is appropriate for biological systems as a whole. This implies that we should focus on possibly systemic effects of war. However, knowledge of systemic effects, even if present, cannot carelessly be transferred from one case to another (e.g., from Prince William Sound to the Persian Gulf or from the forests of Vietnam to those of the eastern Congo). Each system is unique and needs to be studied as such. This takes time and does not help journalists and their deadlines but journalists' deadlines are not scientists' concern.

The inordinate amount of interest paid to flagship species such as tiger, elephant, and rhinoceros is understandable as they raise funds for advocacy groups more surely than do birds or small mammals, let alone microorganisms. But one cannot save species without preserving and protecting natural-range habitat. Preserving habitat without protection resulted in the near-extinction of the red-necked ostrich (*Struthio camelus camelus*) in Niger.[30] Conversely, protecting habitat without preserving it leads to cases such as eastern Congo's Kahuzi-Biega park and areas like it, where protection is limited to the funds of the day. Those who would protect nature in war must work to protect species and their habitats simultaneously.

While it is heartening to see increased application of satellite-based analysis to detect, for example, deforestation, land-use changes, and silt plumes in waterways, this distanced technology is only a complement to, not a substitute for, ground-based research and analysis. Satellite images can record changes (differences) but cannot necessarily help ascertain whether change amounts to damage. Moreover, certain damages can have occurred even when a satellite image shows no difference whatsoever. For example, species depletion underneath intact forest cover would not be detected by satellite-recorded images.

POLITICAL BORDERS; ECOLOGICAL ZONES. Another matter of per-spective arises from the observation that political borders and ecological zones rarely coincide. If we take a picture of Earth from space we can see ecological zones. We cannot see political borders. Yet borders determine much of humans' engagement. This is true even within states, where administrative borders demarcate (often overlapping) jurisdictions. So it happens that a patch of high-altitude land is set aside as a nature reserve in one district but the adjacent low-altitude land in a neighboring district is not set aside. Animals that would migrate between summer and winter forage no longer roam freely. The plant community at summer altitude cannot recover when grazers and browsers cannot move to winter pastures at another altitude. For this reason, many nature parks worldwide are not fully functional. Even the huge Yellowstone National Park in the United States does not encompass the full migratory range its species or would-be species need. By setting aside public spaces, an apartheid between hu-man and nonhuman species is created whereby the former get the choice pieces of land and the latter make do with what is left. "Public spaces are ultimately political spaces," not ecological ones. To avoid creating bio-geographic islands, nature reserves need to be ecologically, not politically, determined.[31]

War enters this discussion because violent conflict is delineated along human borders, crossing ecological zones. Byers describes how traditional peoples in Ethiopia occupy specific ecological niches. Wars there shifted people to unaccustomed regions where traditional ways of making a living clashed with what the natural environment could deliver. A similar mis-match between people's skills and their new environment was noted in the case of Afghan refugees resettled in inappropriate areas in Pakistan. One cannot do much about the legacy of colonially drawn borders in much of the world, but one can be aware of them and consider their impact when designing nature reserves. For wars to come, the lesson to be learned places the onus for the quality of crisis preparation on the conservation commu-nity. Assessment must not remain at the anthropocentric level but must be based on ecologically sensible categories.[32]

5.2.2 Continuous Biomonitoring and Rapid Assessment Matter

In the case of the Persian Gulf War, marine background data were available from 1986 for 53 specific sites along the western Persian Gulf. A small team of researchers revisited 35 sites in August 1991, and they visited 10 of those again in August 1992 and August 1993.[33] It had been decided to examine halophytes, algae, sea grasses, birds, invertebrates, and fish along the coastal ecosystem and to measure the extent of oil pollution, pollution with wood products (timber), and pollution with metals and plastics. To arrive at a rapid assessment, abundance or magnitude was rated on a 0–6 logarithmic scale. A score of 0 was assigned for a 0 observation, a score of 1 for 1 to 9 observations (floral or corals per square meter or number of individuals for fauna), a score of 2 for 10 to 99, a 3 for 100 to 999, and so on, stepping up one order of magnitude at a time. The results were averaged and compared to the 1986 data. An obvious advantage of this method is that one does not need to take meticulous measurements and therefore saves an inordinate amount of time and money. The results broadly indicate where problems may have arisen and where more intense research efforts should be focused. The results, displayed in table 5.1, show that only for birds did the oil pollution due to the war suggest a possible detrimental difference (at the oiled sites as compared to unoiled sites). Overall bird abundance, however, was greater in 1991 than in 1986. This is what the far more detailed studies confirmed later on (see chapter 3).

The rapid assessment technique needs to be integrated with ecological scaling of the disturbance. This is what the 1998 Green Cross International review study on the Persian Gulf War attempts. As explained in chapter 1, environmental risk is computed by assigning values to three factors: war's impact on a particular natural resource, the ecological and economic value of the resource, and the potential of a damaged resource to expose humans to harm.[34] If one adapts this, one would assign values only for impact values and ecological values, the former to assess short-term magnitudes, the latter to assess likely long-term effects. Instead of the low, medium, and high ranking used by Green Cross International, the scaling would be done by gradation: disturbance, degradation, depletion, destruction (table 1.2) along the soil, water, air, floral, and faunal spectra (and subcategories).

Rapid assessment and scaling are one-time efforts. To be useful beyond contemporaneous assessment, they must be employed in conjunction with prewar data and postwar monitoring. This need not be an expensive effort. An example of postwar biomonitoring is provided by efforts undertaken in Liberia's Sapo National Park. In this case, biomonitoring tracked animal abundance and distribution, not habitat per se. The reason is that habitat may be preserved in the short term even as animals are overhunted or succumb to disease. Absent certain animals, habitat changes would show up only one or more seasons later. This approach may be appropriate for Sapo but is insufficient in cases where a war's effects first show up in a habitat

Table 5.1. Rapid Survey Technique Results, Persian Gulf War, August 1991

	Coastal Ecosystems						Pollution/Impacts		
	Halophytes	Algae	Sea Grasses	Birds	Invertebrates	Fish	Oil	Wood	Other
1986									
All sites	2.47	3.33	1.77	1.06	5.31	0.63	1.77	2.11	2.29
N sites	3.23	3.69	2.06	0.65	5.53	0.33	2.24	2.65	2.65
S sites	1.71	3.00	1.47	1.44	5.11	0.93	1.33	1.61	1.94
N vs S sites	p<0.05	NS	NS	p<0.01	NS	NS	NS	NS	NS
1991									
All sites	2.54	4.97	2.06	1.46	5.45	3.63	3.20	2.15	2.68
N sites	2.65	5.29	1.82	1.12	5.12	3.65	5.00	2.50	2.69
S sites	2.44	4.67	2.28	1.78	5.78	3.61	1.50	1.83	2.67
N vs S sites	NS	NS	NS	p<0.05	NS	NS	p<0.01	NS	NS
Heavily oiled sites	3.33	5.58	1.75	0.75	5.17	3.08			
Other sites	2.13	4.65	2.22	1.83	5.61	3.91			
Heavily oiled vs. other sites	NS	NS	NS	p<0.01	NS	NS			
1986 vs 1991									
All sites	NS	p<0.01	NS	p<0.05	NS	p<0.01	p<0.01	NS	NS
N sites	NS	p<0.01	NS	NS	NS	p<0.01	p<0.01	NS	NS
S sites	NS	p<0.01	NS	NS	NS	p<0.01	NS	NS	NS

Notes: Other=metal, plastics, etc.; N, S=sites north and south of Abu Ali, respectively; NS=not statistically significant). *Source:* Adapted from Price, Wrathall, Medley, and Al-Moamens (1993, pp. 145, 147).

before affecting its flora and fauna. For example, the use of chemicals in gold mining in the Colombian Andes might well affect water quality and hence flora and fauna only later on. Thus, a complete biomonitoring program would take biotic and abiotic measurements. To create baseline data, soil, water, and air are sampled from time to time, supplemented for instance with botanical surveys and transect line monitoring of fauna (identification or by nest sites, counts, state and composition of droppings, or other means). In Liberia, an initial list of seventy popular, indicator, and keystone animal species was compiled. This was whittled down to fourteen species to be monitored monthly by hunters from local communities along several transect lines. A protocol was designed, tested, adapted, and retested, and a simple score sheet for recording data prepared. Once recorded, the data were passed on to an office in Monrovia, the capital city, for record keeping and analysis. The indicator species are selected to indicate different sorts of problems. Three monkey species were included, for instance, because they are good indicators of hunting by firearm. In contrast, duikers tend to be somewhat resilient to firearm hunting but fall prey more easily to snare-trapping and are therefore monitored for this type of hunting. The presence of certain birds indicates overall health of the forest ecosystem at Sapo. Other species indicate local disturbances rather than forest-wide disturbances.[35]

Rapid assessment, ecological scaling, and biomonitoring are relatively cheap ways of amassing a continuous stream of ground-level data that would help fulfill the objectives of perspective, standards, and evidence.

5.2.3 Preparation and Communication Matter

PREPARATION. Integrated monitoring needs to be taken further by anticipating the sorts of problems one may reasonably expect to encounter in armed conflict. For instance, to secure safe access to areas to be monitored, several of the reports in the Biodiversity Support Program series stress the importance of keeping in close contact with leaders of all (or at least various) potential adversarial groups. All should be included in the planning process, at least to some degree. Biomonitoring planning should plot gridded transect lines so that if in case of war one line in one grid sector cannot be monitored, another line in another sector may yield information from which one may make reasonable inferences about the unobserved transect. For example, if one transect cannot be observed but others show increased faunal abundance and migration, it is a reasonable guess that the line in the unobserved grid sector produces the spike in the observed sectors. This is not an absurd procedure. Recall the instances for which it was noted that internal war is mobile. Fighting moves around. A specific transect in any one grid area may be inaccessible at one time, but may be accessible a month or two later. Well-selected indicators will then yield continuous information.

The primary cost would seem to lie in the detailed setup and coordination necessary among the many local, national, and international parties involved. Because these can include governmental organizations (GOs), nongovernmental organizations (NGOs), and local, national, or international organizations, this results in a large number of combinations. There can be several GOs and NGOs operating only at the local level. All can also operate at the national level and be involved in some degree at the international level as well. For instance, the SAMFU Foundation is a private, nonprofit national NGO concerned with the rampant, uncontrolled, and often illegal logging of Liberia's forests. Its work is supported by grants from a variety of organizations overseas. Similarly, the Philadelphia Zoo acts as an international partner NGO for the Sapo National Park in Liberia, which is a local concern but also a national concern as it is the only national park in the country. The park, which is forested, obviously need not be cut for timber. Specific species in the park attract the attention of species-level organizations. The number of players involved can be large indeed. Handing off initial biomonitoring planning to an outside, independent consultant, as was done for Sapo National Park, can be a good idea. It allows each organization to carry on with its own work and, subsequently, each organization needs to adjust its own operations probably only slightly to contribute to the overarching, common monitoring goal.

Rapid assessment, ecological scaling, and biomonitoring with a view toward anticipated monitoring needs in times of war would go a long way toward avoiding situations in which the crises war may cause are compounded by ignorance and lack of field access.

Another technique for designing biomonitoring plans is to plan backward. Backward planning means to create a transboundary, ecology-centered emergency management plan, comparable to plans that exist for human emergencies. These are designed by anticipating an event of specific degree or magnitude and simulating backward the kinds of knowledge one would like to have at certain stages of the event and the personnel and equipment that would need to be available to deal with the emergency as it unfolds. These plans also specify lines of communication and delegation of authority and post-event handling. Ideally, the plans would include thoughts on interagency funding as well.

Translated from human emergencies to those involving nature in war, the key is to determine ahead of time which biotic and abiotic features need to be sampled, how often, and to what degree of specificity, to arrive at a plan for rapid assessment that would have a good probability of resulting in a reasonably uncontroversial view of the degree of damage done, if any. This plan should also include suggestions for intervention, restoration, and remediation depending on the degree of damage identified. Subplans might be developed for specific habitats, and to any desired degree of specificity, that is compatible both with the notion of ecologically scaled, rapid assessment within the biomonitoring mode and with the availability of expert teams and financing. A conservation consortium might set up an emergency fund with a "penny tax." This would tax all donations at a certain rate, say at 0.01 percent of all donations, to create an endowment. The proceeds of the endowment would be channeled to consortium members. The endowment itself would be tapped (to a limit) to fund emergency rapid assessment missions by independent conservation groups, in case governmental support is not forthcoming within five days (or some other short number of days) from the onset of a war event.

To do all this would avoid some of the data pitfalls identified in chapter 1. The requirements for the proposed emergency management plan amount to quite a list. But such plans are available already: they are human-centered emergency management plans. While the details vary by the location for which they are designed, as would ecology-centered plans, common elements generally include some type of assessment, hazard management, evacuation, welfare support, recovery plans, and the establishing of lines of authority and communication. Obviously, adjustments have to be made when the emergency is not a "natural catastrophe," but a possible *nature* catastrophe. But the idea is entirely analogous. Similarly, people working in the financial markets routinely carry out assessments of country political and economic risks. There is no reason why these ideas and experiences (especially those stemming from failures) cannot be adopted and adapted by conservation organizations to the nonhuman world.

COMMUNICATION. Another important lesson concerns the inordinate influence of politics, money, and media on the study of war's effects on nature. A free press is a capital social achievement. A commercially driven free press is a somewhat different beast. Profit-seeking shareholders of globe-spanning media conglomerates sell to paying customers what paying customers wish to buy. No doubt, environmental concerns can be big news but they tend to be big only where they affect one's own backyard.

For example, stories in the United States in the spring of 2003 about perchlorate, a component of solid rocket fuel allegedly spilled by defense contractors into the nation's waterways, were big news.[36] In contrast, at around the same time, an Ebola outbreak among gorilla populations in West Africa was barely noted, even by the scientifically interested. So it is with wars. Vietnam was of obvious interest to the United States, as was the Persian Gulf War. In contrast, untold suffering in faraway violent conflict may barely raise any media attention at all.

"What the eyes do not see, the heart does not grieve," the heart transplant surgeon Chris Barnard is reputed to have said with regard to his marital infidelities. Similarly, what the media does not report, the people do not know; and what the people do not know will not raise hackles in freely elected, democratic governments, and funds for study will not be disbursed. And so one can remain quite ignorant about war's effect on nature unless it is a war in which the West, in particular, has an interest and the study of which it will finance. Thus it is that we know a fair bit about the environmental facts of the Persian Gulf and Kosovo wars while knowing very little about the environmental facts of war elsewhere. Conservation organizations may need to rethink their media strategies.

5.2.4 Incentives in a Globalized World Matter

ACTORS AND ACTIONS IN WAR. Economists believe that although people's actions may be immoral, rarely are they irrational. However bizarre an action may appear to others, usually there is a good or bad reason for why people act the way they do. In this, incentives matter, and so do disincentives. One research team dryly notes that "economic strategies are often determined by basic survival needs at all levels."[37] If war pushes one to hide in the forest, one will have little choice but to hunt for bushmeat. A binding constraint prevents one from doing anything else. For other actors the primary consideration is not survival but doing well out of war. The task is to identify all relevant actors in war and the incentives, disincentives, constraints, and opportunities they face. Understanding this may lead to useful insights about feasible ways to intervene, prevent, or abate environmental damage in war. The list of actors would include the warring parties, their local, national, and global supporters, the local population, refugees, local and foreign governments, international organizations, a variety of nongovernmental organizations, and legitimate and illegitimate businesses that provide weaponry, supplies, transport, security, financial, and other services. And these are only the businesses that are directly engaged in the conflict. Others are indirectly affected, deliberately or inadvertently, such as foreign oil companies in Angola and the Sudan, logging companies in Sierra Leone and Liberia, and mining companies in Burma.

Examples of constraints and opportunities include cultural aspects of what is deemed permissible in ordinary life as opposed to situations of stress and crisis. They include institutional capacities (or, more likely, incapacities). They include demand factors on the part of consumers (which may be private household end-users or businesses that purchase raw materials to manufacture products for end-users), and the local, national, and international regulatory environment for business. A large array of actors and actions bear on habitat conservation in war. Jeffrey McNeely has written an instructive, although now dated (1988), text on the use of economic incentives to conserve biological resources, and this work might be usefully adapted to the case of nature in war.[38]

Consumer complicity in war, or threat of war, and related environmental change go back at least 400 years. The British (actually the "Honorable") East India Company, founded in 1600, and the Dutch East India Company, founded in 1602, both were granted state-guaranteed monopolies and assumed awesome military powers to run the trade from Southeast Asia to their respective home countries. Bringing goods such as exotic spices (pepper, nutmeg) and drink (tea, coffee) to market even if it were to involve the armed subjugation of faraway peoples and their lands is no modern-day development. Globalization, war, and nature come with a long-running history.

BUSINESS IN CONFLICT ZONES. Today, expanding coca and cattle ranching interests in Colombia contribute to the gradual degradation of its forests. Across the Pacific Ocean, in Burma and Indonesia, business interests with ties to the military log the forests in an apparently harmful and unsustainable manner. The reluctance of the respective governments and their business partners to be forthcoming with relevant information perhaps speaks for itself. In Africa, the oil interests of Sudan's rulers in southern Sudan are clear and appear as the primary cause of the dessication of the southern Sudanese marshlands. The cases of diamond mining in Sierra Leone, Liberia, and Angola have been documented as profiting from and contributing to armed conflict. Timber and mineral extraction fuels these conflicts. So did oil exploration in Angola (mostly offshore), as it still does in Nigeria where oil companies have long-standing tense relations with the communities from whose land the oil is gained. Unlike elephant poaching and ivory trading, or trading in endangered species, these activities are not necessarily illegal.

Especially when conflict has shifted from political objective to resource extraction (from grievance to greed), conservation becomes nearly impossible even when the underlying conflict is stopped: as noted before, the peace that follows war can be worse than war itself. Resource exploitation is a lucrative winner-take-all game. When warring parties come to realize that war is a costly business expense, a natural-resource exploitation cartel can make the looting even worse. This is widely recognized and lamented. But few appear to directly link warlords in developing nations to end-users in the West. Once it was the "merchants of death," the arms traders and war profiteers, who were said to immorally gain from other people's misfortunes. This is still true to a degree—the illegal firearms and ammunition trade in particular is unlikely to cease—but it overlooks the degree to which modern consumers have become part of the problem as the seemingly impersonal market for the world's raw materials turns consumers everywhere into accomplices.[39]

In the 1990s, an international conflict diamond campaign became highly successful in making consumers aware of the possibly bloody origin of the gems they may have wished to purchase. Similar efforts are made in regard to other products whose provenance may relate to war, and in this they follow other consumer-oriented awareness campaigns such as those related to environmental or international labor standards. As an economic rule of thumb, campaigning will be more successful, the more opportunities there are to substitute among products or suppliers. In the case of diamonds, in the 1990s the global supply chain was dominated by De Beers, and for all practical purposes it was the monopolist supplier. But despite De Beers's long-running "diamonds are forever" campaign, annual Valentine's Day advertisements, product placement in popular films, and other marketing techniques, consumers of course are not obliged to purchase diamonds. Discretionary dollars can be spent in other ways, and that has made De Beers, and firms in its supply and distribution chain, and companies like it, vulnerable. The so-called Kimberley Process Certification Scheme is an imperfect but nonetheless helpful outcome of a joint industry, government, and civil society effort to curtail the flow of conflict diamonds onto the world market.[40]

What is needed are not only ideas regarding economic incentives for conservation or how legitimate global businesses can profit from engaging in environmentally conscientious work. What is needed may be an equivalent to the Sullivan principles. Named after Reverend Leon Sullivan, a cleric who served on the board of directors of General Motors from 1971 to 1990, the Sullivan principles served as a human rights and equal opportunity code of conduct for companies operating in South Africa. In November 1999, Reverend Sullivan and U.N. Secretary-General Kofi Annan announced a new set of principles, called the Global Sullivan Principles, to expand this agenda from South Africa to all peoples and communities.[41] Few are now working on extending these ideas for businesses operating in conflict zones or which derive materials or profits from conflict zones.[42] To address the entire panoply of issues, the idea would have to go beyond single-issue efforts such as the Kimberley Process, which is narrowly focused on conflict diamonds only. Civil society monitoring will be important, as will public shaming of companies unwilling or unable to comply. Conservation organizations can and should be partners in such an effort, not only because they would bring natural resource expertise to the table, but also because they can mobilize tens of millions of members to enforce the principles by threat of consumer boycott or, more positively, by rewarding compliant companies with purchases.

GLOBALIZATION, CORPORATE SOCIAL RESPONSIBILITY, AND SOCIAL ENTREPRENEURS. That business can be a global force of war is well known, from the aforementioned British and Dutch trading companies to William Randolph Hearst's newspaper's role in the Spanish-American War to the Krupp family industrial concern that served as Germany's archetypical World War II armaments maker to BAE Systems, the British-headquartered but otherwise truly global defense and aerospace firm. That business can be a force for peace is, curiously, a relatively new thought. After all, if 3 percent of world income is expended on military pursuits, the other 97 percent would appear to benefit from peace. Instead of entwining political with selective commercial interests, as in the case of Krupp and others like it, the larger business community has begun to recognize that peace ultimately serves it better than does war.

The concept of corporate social responsibility (CSR) has spawned a huge literature, pro and con, and is far too voluminous to be summarized here. The basic assertion is that the legal bodies that corporations are in modern law have obligations beyond satisfying dividend-seeking shareholders. The obligations extend to employees, customers, suppliers, and society at large, for example in designing products that facilitate post-use recycling rather than clogging landfills, that promote sustainable rather than unsustainable resource use or that, indeed, consider whether raw materials originate from war-torn societies and thus help finance wars. Corporate social responsibility can be generated and driven within corporations, and its history goes back at least to the origin of the cooperative movement in the late 1700s and early 1800s.[43] Failing an internally generated and nurtured culture of social responsibility—let alone a business culture that recognizes that peace pays better than war—businesses can of course be subject to severe external scrutiny, adverse media coverage, or consumer boycotts. These can help compel corporations to create social responsibility activities and make amends with irate customers and produce a form of "good will" advertising to draw continued customer support.

For an individual person, it is costly to generate external scrutiny powerful enough to change corporate attitudes and behaviors. Thus, social entrepreneurs have emerged, people who make it their business to watch other businesses. Among the pioneer organizations was the Council on Economic Priorities, founded in the late 1960s by Alice Tepper Marlin in New York City. Its perhaps most celebrated product was a book entitled *Shopping for a Better World*, which ranked companies by criteria related to environmental stewardship and labor practices. The book sold more than one million copies. Consumers could leaf through its pages to reward "good" and punish "bad" companies or, less dramatically, sway company behavior through purchasing power.[44] At the same time, socially responsible investing became a concept on Wall Street, pioneered by, among others, Robert J. Schwartz, a successful and well-to-do Wall Streeter. He advocated creating stock and bond funds that typically excluded from their portfolios holdings related to arms-selling companies, tobacco products and, until 1994, companies investing in apartheid-ruled South Africa. At least in principle, this would redirect investors' financial resources and make the raising of capital at least marginally more difficult for certain corporations.

Nonetheless, while war and nature have featured as separate issues even within the same social entrepreneurship organization, until the 1990s it was rarely possible to directly connect war to nature as a matter of advocacy and customer awareness. This definitely changed with the aforementioned and broadly successful conflict diamonds campaign. But to link war and nature still is the exception. For example, the Sustainable Forestry Initiative and the Forest Stewardship Council both were founded in the early 1990s. The former is an industry body, the latter a body oriented toward forest products users, environmental concerns, and human rights. But both organizations simply are concerned about forests per se, regardless of the nature of threats forests face, war-related or otherwise. This facilitates focus on dangers to a particular resource emanating from multiple sources but hinders the recognition that a single source—war—may endanger multiple resources. Each set of resource-specific organizations—related to forests, land use, oceanic resources, and so on—thus must reinvent the wheel to deal with the potential and actual consequences of war, even though a concerted, overarching, joint campaign on war and nature may perhaps assist all such organizations simultaneously.

Other aspects of globalization are more hopeful. For example, advances in technology permit today's global NGOs to more easily acquire and publicize satellite images to monitor events on the ground. For another example, one London-based NGO, International Alert, recently published a highly instructive 580-page book comprising case studies of how local businesses in conflict areas can constructively assist in peacemaking processes.[45] And the Association to Advance Collegiate Schools of Business International (AACSB International), a business school association, recently created the Peace Through Commerce task force and held a conference on the subject at the Mendoza College of Business of the University of Notre Dame, one of the United States' prominent universities.[46] Other organizations have sprung up, such as Business Executives for National Security (BENS). Something is definitely afoot among advocacy groups and the business world, but the connections among war, nature, and globalization remain largely unexplored.

5.3 In Sum: Preventing War, Preserving Nature

The environmental effect of war is best discussed in terms of a compelling chain of logic: assessment, valuation, liability. Assigning liability for damage is a matter of national and international law. Claims for restitution or compensation, if fault is found and liability assigned, in turn require that an economic valuation be carried out. This valuation would rely crucially on scientific assessment of the physical damage done. The logic thus runs from assessment, which is a matter of science, to valuation, which is a matter of economics, to liability, which is a matter of law (table 5.2).

As regards economics, a huge literature exists on the economic valuation of environmental damage. But, regrettably, almost nothing is available on economic valuation of environmental damage due to war. The legal literature on war and nature is very large (see section 1.5) but legal opinion is not conclusive and enforcement presents a huge problem. This book

Table 5.2. Assessment, Valuation, Liability

• assessment	→	science
• valuation	→	economics
• liability	→	law

thus has emphasized the scientific aspects of the matter. As has been seen, even these are far less straightforward than one would wish.[47]

For the still young twenty-first century, two issues stand out. One is to further reduce the incidence of armed, violent social conflict within and among states; the other is to conserve our habitat—Earth—without which human life is impossible. To reduce violence not only among humans but violence against the rest of nature is possible. Humans are an immensely intelligent species, endowed with fantastic abilities of insight and foresight to assist their own and other species' survival and betterment. Now that nature has been so thoroughly conquered, we must live with it—not against it—even in our wars.

Notes

1. Keeley (1996, pp. 181–182). Along Keeley's line of argument, Steven LeBlanc produced a book on prehistoric warfare in the U.S. Southwest (LeBlanc, 1999; also see LeBlanc, 2003).

2. Young (1988); Westing (1976); Stellman, et al. (2003).

3. Stellman, et al. (2003); Westing (1976).

4. The 1999 Kosovo war likewise resulted in few, if any, detrimental ecological effects. Of those that did occur, all were highly localized. Notwithstanding reports about the release of dangerous chemicals from attacked sites, or the detection of depleted uranium, little by way of actual damage to the environment and to wider ecological processes has been demonstrated. UNEP and other reports are quite clear on this matter. See the UNEP reports in the list of references.

5. For documentation, see, for instance, the annual *Small Arms Survey*. Handguns are pistols and revolvers; long guns include rifles and shotguns.

6. This subsection draws on the materials listed in the bibliographic note, section 4.4.

7. Also see Hanson, et al. (2009).

8. Ostrowski, Massalatchi, and Mamane (2001). See section 4.4.

9. The use of GIS-based spatial mapping and time-linked tracking of war is a very new development in the academic literature. For an example, see Spittaels and Hilgert (2009).

10. UNHCR (2001, p. 5). Scientific refugees, of course, have made huge positive contributions to the economies of the United Kingdom and the United States in particular, especially in the immediate post–World War II period.

11. Ethiopia: Byers (1991). Vietnam: Orians and Pfeiffer (1970, p. 552); Tanzania: Paskett (1998, p. 58).

12. Richardson (1995).

13. This has become such a problem that a new literature is developing on the role of private security forces in humanitarian emergencies.

14. Hatton, Couto, and Oglethorpe (2001, pp. 64–65).

15. Sogge (1992, p. 67).

16. Ståhl (1989, p. 181).

17. IUCN (1992a, p. 1).

18. Hess (2000, p. 9, with a reference to the IUCN).

19. See, for instance, UNHCR (1996, 1998, 2001, 2005).

20. IUCN (1998; n.d.).

21. Macabre reprieve: Stone (2000, p. 21). Bruun: Bruun (1981, p. 159). IUCN: McNeely (2000); Kim (1997); Wildlife Conservation Society (1999); *Wall Street Journal* (24 August 2000, p. 1). On current efforts to establish a DMZ peace park, see, for instance, http://www.dmzforum.org/ [accessed 19 February 2009].

22. Panama: Bennett (1968, p. 101). Poland: Urbanczyck (1990, p. 30). Another example involves human population declines in the western United States. Immense tracts of land in New Mexico, Arizona, and surrounding states were later taken for military airspace and military-nuclear uses. Land was converted into "national sacrifice zones" (Kuletz, 1998), or what Adams (1990) calls "ecofascism" (cited in Byers, 1994, p. 111).

23. Nietschmann (1990, p. 42); Kaimowitz-Fauné (2003).

24. Detailed examples are provided by Owens (1990) and Hills (1991) on the United Kingdom, Vertegaal (1989) on the Netherlands, Marty (1993) on Canada, Walsh (1990)—somewhat gullible and effusive—on the case of U.S. Department of Defense forestry management, and Byers (1994, pp. 114–117) on the credible case that the U.S. Army literally rescued biodiversity from oblivion in Yellowstone National Park (the U.S. Army was given sole protective control over the park from 1886 to 1918). Also see M. Leslie, et al., *Conserving Biodiversity on Military Lands*, U.S. Department of Defense, Washington, D.C., 1996, cited in M. W. Doyle, et al. (2008). Yet even in the genuine cases of either protecting wilderness areas from civilian encroachment or of active remediation and restoration efforts (e.g., Butts, 1994, on the U.S. Department of Defense), it does not follow that military occupation or restorative activity is what protects the land, air, and seas. Owens rightly points out that normal environmental policy would (or should) accomplish the same purpose (1990, p. 500).

25. Fischer: *Audubon* (1991, p. 96); Fallows: *Audubon* (1991, pp. 94–95). Malcolm Browne, Vietnam War correspondent and later a senior science writer for the *New York Times*, raises the rhetorical level further: "I cannot imagine even a nuclear war as destructive to wildlife as the effects of unchecked human reproduction . . . the deadliest war is not between men. It is the war mankind is mindlessly waging against other living things in the name of what Nazi Germany called *Lebensraum*." (*Audubon*, 1991, p. 91).

26. Traditional conservation: see, for instance, Zimmer (2003). Quotes: Western in Hess (2000, p. 10); Hess (2000, p. 13).

27. Congo: Kalpers (2001a); Pakistan: Lodhi, Echavarria, and Keithley (1998); Zimbabwe: UNHCR (2001, p. 59); Vietnam: Westing (1976). In Nicaragua,

areas were afforested (Nietschmann, 1990, 1998). On using transborder areas to create peace parks, see for example Ali (2007).

28. Dioxin effects on humans must, of course, be studied. The argument here, as throughout the book, is not to replace studies of human populations, but to supplement them.

29. Lamentations: also see Lomborg (2001). But even since the mid-1990s, the majority of the literature debates possible violent consequences of environment-related scarcities (section 1.3), rather than the environmental impact of war itself, hence the effort to research and write this book.

30. The website of the Sahara Conservation Fund mentions nine remaining individuals in the Air Mountains of Niger. See http://www.saharaconservation.org/html/01_contenu.php?ID_menu=14722 [accessed 30 March 2008].

31. Political borders, ecological zones: Byers (1991); Hess (2000). Quote: Hess (2000, p. 8).

32. Ethiopia: Byers (1991). Nature reserves: Hill and Katarere (2002, pp. 265–266).

33. Price, Wrathall, Medley, and Al-Moamens (1993).

34. Green Cross International (1998, pp. 91–97). The codes used for quantification by extent and magnitude in terms of short-, medium-, and long-term effects are simply 1, 2, or 3 (low, medium, high) and are assigned by the study team. Once value assignments are made, a risk index is computed. The higher the index number, the more urgent the need for intervention. Unique in the literature, this is an effort not merely to measure war's impact on nature and follow-on risk, but to scale it. In a world of scarce resources, the risk index helps prioritize what to do next.

35. Sapo: Waitkuwait (2001). Droppings: droppings are very informative. For example, they can reveal the time when the animal was present, whether the animal was immature or adult, what the animal ate, and whether the animal was healthy. Record keeping: backup procedures are not reported. The experience of some conservation organizations in Africa would suggest that regular data backups to offices outside the country be part of the data protection procedures.

36. See, for instance, the *Wall Street Journal* (3 March 2003).

37. Shambaugh, et al. (2001, p. 91).

38. McNeeley (1988).

39. The peace that follows war: "In El Salvador, for example, more people have been killed in ten years of peace than died in the previous twelve years of war" (Stohl, Schroeder, and Smith, 2007, p. 56). Consumer complicity: Cooper (2002, 2006).

40. Other products: for instance, Marlin (2006) on the "no dirty gold" campaign. Environment: for instance, the Sustainable Forestry Initiative at http://www.sfiprogram.org/. International labor standards: for instance, Social Accountability International at http://www.sa-intl.org/ [both accessed 19 February 2008]. Kimberley Process: see http://www.kimberleyprocess.com/ [accessed 20 February 2008]. Also see Gold (2006).

41. Environmentally conscientious work: McNeeley (1988); Switzer (n.d.). Sullivan: first issued in 1977; see http://www.revleonsullivan.org/principled/principles.htm [accessed 12 February 2008]. Global Sullivan: see http://www.thesullivanfoundation.org/gsp/principles/gsp/default.asp [accessed 12 February 2008].

42. For example, the International Business Leaders Forum and International Alert have programs on business and conflict, but not with an emphasis on war's environmental consequences.

43. The Welshman Robert Owen (1771–1858) is frequently cited as the father of the cooperative movement, referred to by Karl Marx as "utopian socialism." The idea of forming cooperatives, working for the benefit of all employees, rather than merely for the profit-hungry business owner, caught on in England and later swept into France, Germany, the United States, and eventually all around the world. Today's employee stock-ownership plans and other forms of employee sharing in the corporation for which they work can be traced back to Owen.

44. The council was reorganized in 1996–1997 when Tepper Marlin handed operations to her successor and started a new organization, the aforementioned Social Accountability International, also in New York City.

45. Banfield, Gündüz, and Killick (2006).

46. See http://www.aacsb.edu/resource_centers/peace/default.asp [accessed 20 February 2008].

47. Economics: one important exception concerns the United Nations Compensation Commission, set up in 1991 "to process claims and pay compensation for losses and damage suffered as a direct result of Iraq's unlawful invasion and occupation of Kuwait," including environmental losses (quoted from http://www.uncc.ch/ [accessed 18 February 2009]. Law: Note that Iraq was not found to have violated international law of war or international environmental law. Instead, claims against it were made in consequences of its "unlawful invasion and occupation of Kuwait." Legal literature: the main starting point is the handy collection of papers in Austin and Bruch (2000), produced following a 1998 international conference put together by the Environmental Law Institute in Washington, D.C. Throughout this book, reference has been made to the 1999 Kosovo war and the 1990s Balkan wars in general. Many of the relevant studies are available on the United Nations Environment Programme's Post-Conflict and Disaster Management Branch's website (http://postconflict.unep.ch/).

List of References

Abdali, F., and S. Al-Yakoob. 1994. "Environmental Dimensions of the Gulf War: Potential Health Impacts," pp. 85–113 in F. El-Baz and R.M. Mahkarita, eds. *The Gulf War and the Environment*. Lausanne: Gordon and Breach Science Publishers.

Abdulraheem, M. Y. 2000. "War-Related Damage to the Marine Environment in the ROPME Sea Area," pp. 338–352 in J. E. Austin and C. E. Bruch, eds. *The Environmental Consequences of War*. Cambridge: Cambridge University Press.

Abo El-Nil, M. 1996. "Role of Plant Tissue Culture Propagation in the Rehabilitation of Desert Environment," pp. 197–205 in N. Al-Awadhi, M. T. Balba, and C. Kamizawa, eds. *Restoration and Rehabilitation of the Desert Environment*. Amsterdam: Elsevier.

Abuzinada, A. H., and F. Krupp. 1994. "Introduction: The Arabian Gulf Environment and the Consequences of the 1991 Oil Spill." *Courier Forschungsinstitut Senckenberg*. Vol. 166, pp. 3–10.

Adams, W. M. 1990. *Green Development: Environment and Sustainability in the Third World*. London: Routledge.

Al-Ajmi, D. N. 1994. "Simulation of Short Term Atmospheric Dispersion of SO_2 Resulting from the Kuwait Oil Fires," pp. 69–83 in F. El-Baz and R.M. Mahkarita, eds. *The Gulf War and the Environment*. Lausanne: Gordon and Breach Science Publishers.

Al-Ajmi, D. N., and Y. R. Marmoush. 1996. "Ground Level Concentration of Sulfur Dioxide at Kuwait's Major Population Centers During the Oil-Field Fires." *Environment International*. Vol. 22, No. 3, pp. 279–287.

Al-Ajmi, D. N., and R. Misak. 1995. "Impact of the Gulf War on the Desert Ecosystem in Kuwait," pp. 166–177 in E. Watkins, ed. *The Middle Eastern Environment: Selected Papers of the British Society for Middle Eastern Studies*. Cambridge, UK: St. Malo Press.

Al-Arfaj, A. R. A., and I. A. Alam. 1993. "Chemical Characterization of Sediments from the Gulf Area after the 1991 Oil Spill." *Marine Pollution Bulletin*. Vol. 27, pp. 97–101.

Al-Awadhi, N. 1996. "Overview of Kuwait Experience in Restoration and Rehabilitation of the Desert Environment and Introduction to Symposium Purpose and Content," pp. 13–18 in N. Al-Awadhi, M. T. Balba, and C. Kamizawa, eds. *Restoration and Rehabilitation of the Desert Environment*. Amsterdam: Elsevier.

Al-Awadhi, N., M. T. Balba, and C. Kamizawa, eds. 1996. *Restoration and Rehabilitation of the Desert Environment*. Amsterdam: Elsevier.

Al-Daher, R., N. Al-Awadhi, and A. El-Nawawy. 1998. "Bioremediation of Damaged Desert Environment Using the Windrow Soil Pile System in Kuwait." *Environment International*. Vol. 24, No. 1/2 (January), pp. 175–180.

Al-Gounaim, M. Y., A. Diab, R. Al-Abdulla, and N. Al-Zamil. 1995. "Effects of Petroleum Oil Pollution on the Microbiological Populations of the Desert Soil of Kuwait." *Arab Gulf Journal of Scientific Research*. Vol. 13, No. 3, pp. 653–672.

Al-Hassan, J. M. 1992. *The Iraqi Invasion of Kuwait: An Environmental Catastrophe*. Kuwait: Fahad Al Marzouk.

Al-Hassan, J. M. 1994. "The Gulf Marine Environment: Variations, Peculiarities and Survival," pp. 25–29 in F. El-Baz and R. M. Mahkarita, eds. *The Gulf War and the Environment*. Lausanne: Gordon and Breach Science Publishers.

Al-Houty, W., M. Abdal, and S. Zaman. 1993. "Preliminary Assessment of the Gulf War on Kuwait Desert Ecosystem." *Journal of Environmental Science and Health, Part A*. Vol. 28, No. 8, pp. 1705–1726.

Ali, A. H. 1994. "Wind Regime of the Arabian Gulf," pp. 31–48 in F. El-Baz and R. M. Mahkarita, eds. *The Gulf War and the Environment*. Lausanne: Gordon and Breach Science Publishers.

Ali, M. A., A. H. Nagwa, W. M. El-Senousy, and S. E. El-Hawaary. 1996. "Enterovirus Load of the Nile River at the Aswan As a Result of the Rwandan Civil War, 1993." *International Journal of Environmental Health Research*. Vol. 6, No. 4, pp. 331–335.

Ali, S. H., ed. 2007. *Peace Parks: Conservation and Conflict Resolution*. Cambridge, MA: MIT Press.

Allan, Nigel J. R. 1987. "Impact of Afghan Refugees on the Vegetation Resources of Pakistan's Hindukush-Himalaya." *Mountain Research and Development*. Vol. 7, No. 3, pp. 200–204.

Al-Merghani, M., J. D. Miller, A. Al-Mansi, O. Khushaim, and N. J. Pilcher. 1996. "The Marine Turtles of the Arabian Gulf. NCWCD Studies 1991–1994," p. 351 in F. Krupp, A. H. Abuzinada, and I. A. Nader, eds. *A Marine Wildlife Sanctuary for the Arabian Gulf: Environmental Research and Conservation Following the 1991 Gulf War Oil Spill*. Riyadh: NCWCD and Frankfurt am Main: Senckenberg Research Institute.

Al-Mohanna, S. Y., and M. N. V. Subrahmanyam. 2001. "Flux of Heavy Metal Accumulation in Various Organs of the Interdidal Marine Blue Crab, *Protunus pelagicus* (L.) from the Kuwait Coast after the Gulf War." *Environment International.* Vol. 27, No. 4, pp. 321–326.

Al-Muzaini, S., and P. G. Jacob. 1996a. "The Distribution of V, Ni, Cr, Cd, and Pd in Topsoils of the Shuaiba Industrial Area of Kuwait." *Environmental Toxicology and Water Quality.* Vol. 11, pp. 285–292.

Al-Muzaini, S. and P. G. Jacob. 1996b. "Marine Plants of the Arabian Gulf." *Environment International.* Vol. 22, No. 3, pp. 369–376.

Alsdirawi, F. 1994. "The Impact of the Gulf War on the Desert Environment," pp. 115–129 in F. El-Baz and R. M. Mahkarita, eds. *The Gulf War and the Environment.* Lausanne: Gordon and Breach Science Publishers.

Al-Senafy, M. N., M. N. Viswanathan, Y. Senay, and A. Sumait. 1997. "Soil Contamination from Oil Lakes in Northern Kuwait." *Journal of Soil Contamination.* Vol. 6, No. 5, pp. 481–494.

Al-Yamani, F. Y., K. Al-Rifaie, and W. Ismail. 1993. "Post-Spill Zooplankton Distribution in the NW Gulf." *Marine Pollution Bulletin.* Vol. 27, pp. 239–243.

Álvarez, M. D. 2003. "Forests in the Time of Violence: Conservation Implications of the Colombian War." *Journal of Sustainable Forestry.* Vol. 16, Nos. 3/4, pp. 49–70. [Simultaneously published under the same title, pp. 49–70, in S. V. Price, ed. *War and Tropical Forests: Conservation in Areas of Armed Conflict.* Binghamton, NY: Haworth Press, 2003.]

Anderton, C. H., and J. R. Carter. 2009. *Principles of Conflict Economics: A Primer for Social Scientists.* New York: Cambridge University Press.

Apel, M. 1994. "Effects of the 1991 Gulf War Oil Spill on the Crab Fauna of Intertidal Mudflats in the Western Arabian Gulf." *Courier Forschungsinstitut Senckenberg.* Vol. 166, pp. 40–46.

Apel, M. 1996. "Ecological Observations on Crab Communities (Crustacea: Decapoda: Brachyura) on Intertidal Mudflats in the Western Arabian Gulf and the Effect of the 1991 Oil Spill," p. 327 in F. Krupp, A. H. Abuzinada, and I. A. Nader, eds. *A Marine Wildlife Sanctuary for the Arabian Gulf: Environmental Research and Conservation Following the 1991 Gulf War Oil Spill.* Riyadh: NCWCD and Frankfurt am Main: Senckenberg Research Institute.

Arkin, W., D. Durrant, and M. Cherni. 1991. *On Impact: Modern Warfare and the Environment. A Case Study of the Gulf War.* London: Greenpeace.

Ashton, P. 1984. "Long-Term Changes in Dense and Open Inland Forests Following Herbicidal Attack," pp. 33–37 in A. H. Westing, ed. *Herbicides in War: The Long-Term Ecological and Human Consequences.* London: Taylor & Francis.

Attenborough, D. 1995. *The Private Life of Plants: A Natural History of Plant Behaviour.* Princeton, NJ: Princeton University Press.

Audubon Society. 1991 "War & the Environment." *Audubon* Vol. 93 (September), pp. 89–99. Contributions by M. W. Browne, M. Kaku, J. Fallows, and E. Fischer.

Austin, J. E., and C. E. Bruch, eds. 2000. *The Environmental Consequences of War.* Cambridge: Cambridge University Press.

Bader, M. S. H., and W. W. Clarkson. 1995. "An Overview of the Oil Lakes in Kuwait: The Problem and Remedial Methods." *Journal of Environmental Science and Health, Part A.* Vol. 30, No. 5, pp. 1039–1057.

Bakan, S., et al. 1991. "Climate Response to Smoke from the Burning Oil Wells in Kuwait." *Nature.* Vol. 351 (30 May), pp. 367–371.

Baker, R. H. 1946. "Some Effects of the War on the Wildlife of Micronesia." *Transactions of the North American Wildlife Conference.* Vol. 11, pp. 205–213.

Balba, M. T., N. Al-Awadhi, R. Al-Daher, H. Chino, and H. Tsuji. 1996. "Remediation and Rehabilitation of Oil-Lake Beds in Kuwait," pp. 21–40 in N. Al-Awadhi, M. T. Balba, and C. Kamizawa, eds. *Restoration and Rehabilitation of the Desert Environment.* Amsterdam: Elsevier.

Balba, M. T., R. Al-Daher, N. Al-Awadhi, H. Chino, and H. Tsuji. 1998. "Bioremediation of Oil-Contaminated Desert Soil: The Kuwait Experience." *Environment International.* Vol. 24, No. 1/2 (January), pp. 163–173.

Banfield, J., C. Gündüz, and N. Killick, eds. 2006. *Local Business, Local Peace: The Peacebuilding Potential of the Domestic Private Sector.* London: International Alert.

Barber, C. V. 2002. "Forests, Fires and Confrontation," pp. 99–169 in R. Matthew, M. Halle, and J. Switzer, eds. *Conserving the Peace: Resources, Livelihoods and Security.* Winnipeg, Manitoba: International Institute for Sustainable Development.

Barber, C. V., and K. Talbott. 2003. "The Chainsaw and the Gun: The Role of the Military in Deforesting Indonesia." *Journal of Sustainable Forestry.* Vol. 16, Nos. 3/4, pp. 137–166. [Simultaneously published under the same title, pp. 137–166, in S. V. Price, ed. *War and Tropical Forests: Conservation in Areas of Armed Conflict.* Binghamton, NY: Haworth Press, 2003.]

Barnaby, F. 1991. "The Environmental Impact of the Gulf War." *The Ecologist.* Vol. 21, No. 4 (July/August), pp. 166–172.

Barrio Froján, C. R. S., and A. P. Volger. 1999. "Landmine Clearance: Its Probable Effect on Angolan Biodiversity." *Oryx.* Vol. 33, No. 2, pp. 95–97.

Barth, H.-K., and A. Niestlé. 1994. "Environmental Effects of the Gulf War on Coastal Areas North of Jubail: An Overview." *Courier Forschungsinstitut Senckenberg.* Vol. 166, pp. 11–15.

Basaham, A. S., and S. S. Al-Lihaibi. 1993. "Trace Elements in Sediments of the Western Gulf." *Marine Pollution Bulletin.* Vol. 27, pp. 103–107.

Begon, M., J. Harper, and C. Townsend. 1996. *Ecology: Individuals, Populations and Communities.* 3rd ed. Oxford: Blackwell.

Bennett, C. F. 1968. *Human Influences on the Zoogeography of Panama.* [Ibero-Americana, Vol. 51.] Berkeley: University of California Press.

Benton, N., J. D. Ripley, and F. Powledge, eds. 2008. *Conserving Biodiversity on Military Lands: A Guide for Natural Resources Managers.* Available at http://www.dodbiodiversity.org. Arlington, VA: NatureServe.

Bethel, J. S., K. J.Turnbull, D. Briggs, and J. Flores. 1975a. "Military Defoliation of Vietnam Forests." *American Forests.* Vol. 81, No. 1 (January), pp. 26–30, 56, 58–61.

Bethel, J. S., K. J.Turnbull, D. Briggs, and J. Flores. 1975b. "Timber Losses from Military Use of Herbicides on the Inland Forests of South Vietnam." *Journal of Forestry*. Vol. 73, No. 4 (April), pp. 228–233.

Biswas, A. K. 2000. "Scientific Assessment of the Long-Term Environmental Consequences of War," pp. 303–315 in J. E. Austin and C. E. Bruch, eds. *The Environmental Consequences of War*. Cambridge: Cambridge University Press.

Biswas, A. K., and C. Tortajada-Quiroz. 1996. "Environmental Impacts of the Rwandan Refugees on Zaire." *Ambio*. Vol. 25, No. 6 (September), pp. 403–408.

Blackman, G. E., J. D. Fryer, A. Lang, and M. Newton. 1974. "Persistence and Disappearance of Herbicides in Tropical Soils," AD-779 025 in National Academy of Sciences. *Effects of Herbicides in South Vietnam; Part B: Working Papers*. Washington, DC: National Academy of Sciences.

Blaustein, A. R., and P. T. J. Johnson. 2003. "Explaining Frog Deformities." *Scientific American*. Vol. 288, No. 2 (February), pp. 60–65.

Blom, A., and J. Yamindou. 2001. *A Brief History of Armed Conflict and Its Impact on Biodiversity in the Central African Republic*. Washington, DC: Biodiversity Support Program.

Blom, E., ed. 2000. *Nature in War: Biodiversity Conservation during Conflict*. Mededelingen No. 37. Leiden: Netherlands Commission for International Nature Protection.

Bloom, S., J. M. Miller, J. Warner, and P. Winkler, eds. 1994. *Hidden Casualties: Environmental, Health and Political Consequences of the Persian Gulf War*. Berkeley, CA: Arms Control Research Center and North Atlantic Books. [There is also a 1991 volume of similar title, *Hidden Casualties, Volume I: The Environmental Consequences of the Persian Gulf Conflict*, published before the 1991 Persian Gulf War.]

BMU [Bundesministerium für Umwelt (Federal Ministry for the Environment, Nature Conservation and Nuclear Safety), Division G II 3]. 2002. *Climate Change and Conflict*. Berlin: BMU, November. Available at http://www.bmu.de/english/download/files/climges.pdf [accessed 18 January 2003]. In German at http://www.krium.de/upload/Texte/broschuere_klimaschutz_konflikte.pdf [accessed 4 March, 2008].

Böer, B. 1993. "Anomalous Pneumatophores and Adventitious Roots of *Avicennia marina* (Forssk.) Vierh. Mangroves Two Years after the 1991 Gulf War Oil Spill in Saudi Arabia." *Marine Pollution Bulletin*. Vol. 27, pp. 207–211.

Böer, B. 1994. "Status and Recovery of the Intertidal Vegetation after the 1991 Gulf War Oil Spill." *Courier Forschungsinstitut Senckenberg*. Vol. 166, pp. 22–26.

Böer, B. 1996. "Trial Planting of Mangroves (*Avicennia marina*) and Salt-Marsh Plants (*Salicornia europea*) in Oil-impacted Soil in the Jubail Area, Saudi Arabia," p. 186 in F. Krupp, A. H. Abuzinada, and I. A. Nader, eds. *A Marine Wildlife Sanctuary for the Arabian Gulf: Environmental Research and Conservation Following the 1991 Gulf War Oil Spill*. Riyadh: NCWCD and Frankfurt am Main: Senckenberg Research Institute.

Böer, B., and J. Warnken. 1996. "Flora of the Jubail Marine Wildlife Sanctuary, Saudi Arabia," pp. 290–295 in F. Krupp, A. H. Abuzinada, and I. A. Nader, eds. *A Marine Wildlife Sanctuary for the Arabian Gulf: Environmental Research and Conservation Following the 1991 Gulf War Oil Spill*. Riyadh: NCWCD and Frankfurt am Main: Senckenberg Research Institute.

Boffey, P. M. 1968. "Defense Issues Summary of Defoliation Study." *Science*. Vol. 159 (9 February), p. 613.

Boffey, P. M. 1971. "Herbicides in Vietnam: AAAS Study Finds Widespread Devastation." *Science*. Vol. 171 (8 January), p. 43–47.

Bouhamra, W. S., S. S. BuHamra, and M. S. Thomson. 1997. "Determination of Volatile Organic Compounds in Indoor and Ambient Air of Residences in Kuwait." *Environment International*. Vol. 23, No. 1, pp. 197–204.

Bou-Rabee, F., Y. Bakir, and H. Bem. 1995. "Contribution of Uranium to Gross Alpha Radioactivity in some Environmental Samples in Kuwait." *Environment International*. Vol. 21, No. 3, pp. 293–298.

Brashares, J. S., P. Arcese, M. K. Sam, P. B. Coppolillo, A. R. E. Sinclair, A. Balmford. 2004. "Bushmeat Hunting, Wildlife Declines, and Fish Supply in West Africa." *Science*. Vol. 306 (12 November), pp. 1180–1183.

Brauer, J. 2007. "Data, Models, Coefficients: United States Military Expenditure." *Conflict Management and Peace Science*. Vol. 24, No. 1, pp. 55–64.

Brauer, J. 2008. "International Security and Sustainable Development," pp. 249–266 in J. Fontanel and M. Chatterji, eds. *War, Peace, and Security*. Bingley, UK: Emerald Group.

Brauer, J., and H. van Tuyll. 2008. *Castles, Battles and Bombs: How Economics Explains Military History*. Chicago: University of Chicago Press.

Brown, E. T. 1998. "The Consequences of Underground Nuclear Testing in French Polynesia." *ATSE Focus*. Supplement No. 104 (November/December). [ATSE: Australian Academy of Technological Sciences and Engineering] http://www.atse.org.au/index.php?sectionid=388 [accessed 28 February, 2009].

Browning, K. A., et al. 1991. "Environmental Effects from Burning Oil Wells in Kuwait." *Nature*. Vol. 351 (30 May), pp. 363–367.

Bruch, C. E. 1998. "Addressing Environmental Consequences of War." Background paper for the First International Conference on Addressing Environmental Consequences of War: Legal, Economic, and Scientific Perspectives. June. Washington, DC: Environmental Law Institute.

Bruch, C. E., and J. E. Austin. 2000. "Epilogue: The Kosovo Conflict: A Case Study of Unresolved Issues," pp. 647–664 in J. E. Austin and C. E. Bruch, eds. *The Environmental Consequences of War*. Cambridge: Cambridge University Press.

Brunner, J., K. Talbott, and C. Elkin. 1998. *Logging Burma's Frontier Forests: Resources and the Regime*. Washington, DC: World Resources Institute.

Bruun, B. 1981. "Birds, Bombs, and Borders." *Explorers Journal*. Vol. 59, No. 4 (December), pp. 154–159.

Buckingham, W. A. 1982. *Operation Ranch Hand: The Air Force and Herbicides in Southeast Asia, 1961–1971*. Washington, DC: U.S. Government Printing Office.

Buckingham, W. A. 1983. "Operation Ranch Hand: Herbicides in Southeast Asia." *Air University Review*. Vol. 34, No. 5, pp. 42–53.

Bunge, M., L. Adrian, A. Kraus, M. Opel, W. G. Lorenz, J. R. Andreesen, H. Görisch, and U. Lechner. 2003. "Reductive Dehalogenation of Chlorinated Dioxins by an Anaerobic Bacterium." *Nature*. Vol. 421 (23 January), pp. 357–360.

Bu-Olayan, A. H., L. A. Al-Omran, and M. N. V. Subramanyam. 1996. "Trends in the Dissolution of Metals from Sediments Collected during the *Umitaka-Maru* Cruises Using the Microwave-Acid Digestion Technique." *Environment International*. Vol. 22, No. 6, pp. 711–716.

Bu-Olayan, A. H., and M. N. V. Subramanyam. 1996. "Trace Metals in Fish from the Kuwait Coast Using the Microwave Acid Digestion Technique." *Environment International*. Vol. 22, No. 6, pp. 753–758.

Burns, K., et al. 1993. "Subtidal Benthic Community Respiration and Production near the Heavily Oiled Gulf Coast of Saudi Arabia." *Marine Pollution Bulletin*. Vol. 27, pp. 199–205.

Butts, K. H. 1994. "Why the Military Is Good for the Environment," pp. 83–109 in J. Käkönen, ed. *Green Security or Militarized Environment*. Aldershot, UK: Dartmouth.

Byers, B. 1991. "Ecoregions, State Sovereignty, and Conflict." *Bulletin of Peace Proposals*. Vol. 22, No. 1, pp. 65–76.

Byers, B. A. 1994. "Armed Forces and the Conservation of Biological Diversity," pp. 111–130 in J. Käkönen, ed. *Green Security or Militarized Environment*. Aldershot, UK: Dartmouth.

Canby, T. 1991. "After the Storm." *National Geographic*. Vol. 180, No. 2 (August), pp. 2–35.

Carlson, E. A. 1983. "International Symposium on Herbicides in the Vietnam War: An Appraisal." *BioScience*. Vol. 33, No. 8 (September), pp. 507–512.

Carson, R. 1962. *Silent Spring*. Boston: Houghton Mifflin.

Cecil, P. F. 1986. *Herbicidal Warfare: The Ranch Hand Project in Vietnam*. New York: Praeger.

Cohen, S., and D. Nacci. 2002. "Effects of Dioxin-Like Compounds (DLC) Contamination on an Estuarine Fish Species: Adaptive Changes at Specific Loci." Conference paper. United States–Vietnam Scientific Conference on Human Health and Environmental Effects of Agent Orange/Dioxins, 3–6 March, 2002, Hanoi, Vietnam. [U.S. National Institute of Environmental Health Sciences] Available online at http://www.niehs.nih.gov/external/usvcrp/project1.htm [accessed 23 January, 2003].

Collier, P. 2004. "Natural Resources and Conflict in Africa." Crimes of War Project website at http://www.crimesofwar.org/africa-mag/afr_04_collier.html [accessed 5 March, 2008].

Collier, P. 2007. *The Bottom Billion: Why the Poorest Countries Are Failing and What Can Be Done About It.* New York: Oxford University Press.

Constable, J. D. 1981–1982. "Visit to Vietnam." *Oryx.* Vol. 16, pp. 249–254.

Constable, J. D., and M. Meselson. 1971. "The Ecological Impact of Large-Scale Defoliation in Vietnam." *Sierra Club Bulletin.* Vol. 56, No. 4 (April), pp. 4–9.

Cooper, N. 2002. "War Lords and Logo Warriors: The Political Economy of Postmodern Conflict," pp. 35–50 in J. Brauer and J. P. Dunne, eds. *Arming the South: The Economics of Military Expenditure, Arms Production, and Arms Trade in Developing Countries.* New York: Palgrave.

Cooper, N. 2006. "Peaceful Warriors and Warring Peacemakers." *Economics of Peace and Security Journal.* Vol. 1, No. 1, pp. 20–24.

Curry-Lindahl, K. 1972. *Let Them Live: A Worldwide Survey of Animals Threatened with Extinction.* New York: Morrow.

Dahl, A. W. 1992. "Environmental Destruction in War." *Disarmament.* Vol. 15, No. 2, pp. 113–127.

Dávalos, L. M. 2001. "The San Lucas Mountain Range in Colombia: How Much Conservation is Owed to the Violence?" *Biodiversity and Conservation.* Vol. 10, No. 1, pp. 69–78.

Davis, G. M. 1974. "Mollusks As Indicators of the Effects of Herbicides on Mangroves in South Vietnam," AD-779 020 in National Academy of Sciences. *Effects of Herbicides in South Vietnam; Part B: Working Papers.* Washington, DC: National Academy of Sciences.

De Clerck, O., and E. Coppejans. 1994. "Status of the Macroalgae and Seagrass Vegetation after the 1991 Gulf War Oil Spill." *Courier Forschungsinstitut Senckenberg.* Vol. 166, pp. 18–21.

De Clerck, O., and E. Coppejans. 1996. "Marine Algae of the Jubail Marine Wildlife Sanctuary, Saudi Arabia," p. 199 in F. Krupp, A. H. Abuzinada, and I. A. Nader, eds. *A Marine Wildlife Sanctuary for the Arabian Gulf: Environmental Research and Conservation Following the 1991 Gulf War Oil Spill.* Riyadh: NCWCD and Frankfurt am Main: Senckenberg Research Institute.

Dennis, R. 1991. "Arabian Gulf Oil Spill." Report to the International Council on Bird Preservation, March. [Reprinted as Annex 1 in Heneman, 1991.]

De Sylva, D. P., and H. B. Michel. 1974. "Effects of Mangrove Defoliation on the Estuarine Ecology and Fisheries of South Vietnam," AD-779 014 in National Academy of Sciences. *Effects of Herbicides in South Vietnam; Part B: Working Papers.* Washington, DC: National Academy of Sciences.

de Waal, F. B. M., F. Aureli, and P. G. Judge. 2000. "Coping with Crowding." *Scientific American.* Vol. 282 (May), pp. 76–81.

Diamond, J. 1999 [1997]. *Guns, Germs, and Steel: The Fates of Human Societies.* New York: W.W. Norton.

Downing, N., and C. Roberts. 1993. "Has the Gulf War Affected Coastal Reefs of the Northwest Gulf?" *Marine Pollution Bulletin.* Vol. 27, pp. 149–156.

Doyle, M. W., et al. 2008. "Aging Infrastructure and Ecosystem Restoration." *Science*. Vol. 319 (18 January), pp. 286–287.

Durako, M. J., W. J. Kenworthy, S. M. R. Fatemy, H. Valavi, and G. W. Thayer. 1993. "Assessment of the Toxicity of Kuwait Crude Oil on the Photosynthesis and Respiration of Seagrasses of the Northern Gulf." *Marine Pollution Bulletin*. Vol. 27, pp. 223–227.

Durant, R. F. 2007. *The Greening of the U.S. Military: Environmental Policy, National Security, and Organizational Change*. Washington, DC: Georgetown University Press.

Dwernychuk, L. W., et al. 2002. "Dioxin Reservoirs in Southern Viet Nam: A Legacy of Agent Orange." *Chemosphere*. Vol. 47, No. 2, pp. 117–137.

Earle, S. 1992. "Persian Gulf Pollution: Assessing the Damage One Year Later." *National Geographic*. Vol. 181 (February), pp. 122–134.

El-Baz, F. 1994. "Gulf War Disruption of the Desert Surface in Kuwait," pp. 131–161 in F. El-Baz and R. M. Mahkarita, eds. *The Gulf War and the Environment*. Lausanne: Gordon and Breach Science Publishers.

El-Baz, F., and R. M. Mahkarita, eds. 1994. *The Gulf War and the Environment*. Lausanne: Gordon and Breach Science Publishers.

El-Baz, F., et al. 1994. "Detection by Satellite Images of Environmental Change Due to the Gulf War," pp. 1–24 in F. El-Baz and R. M. Mahkarita, eds. *The Gulf War and the Environment*. Lausanne: Gordon and Breach Science Publishers.

Environmental Law Institute. 1998. "Annotated Bibliography. First International Conference on Addressing Environmental Consequences of War: Legal, Economic, and Scientific Perspectives." Research Report. June. Washington, DC: Environmental Law Institute.

Esseen, M. 1996. "A Survey of the Fisheries in the Jubail Marine Wildlife Sanctuary," p. 459 in F. Krupp, A. H. Abuzinada, and I. A. Nader, eds. *A Marine Wildlife Sanctuary for the Arabian Gulf: Environmental Research and Conservation Following the 1991 Gulf War Oil Spill*. Riyadh: NCWCD and Frankfurt am Main: Senckenberg Research Institute.

Evans, M. I. 1992. "The ICBP/NCWCD Wader Survey of the Gulf Coast of Saudi Arabia During April–May 1991." Final Report to the National Commission for Wildlife Conservation and Development and the International Council for Bird Preservation. Cambridge, UK: ICBP, 17 February.

Evans, M. I., and G. O. Keijl. 1993a. "Spring Migration of Coastal Waders through the Saudi Arabian Gulf in 1991." *Sandgrouse*. Vol. 15, pp. 56–84.

Evans, M. I., and G. O. Keijl. 1993b. "Impact of Gulf War Oil Spills on the Wader Populations of the the Saudi Arabian Gulf Coast." *Sandgrouse*. Vol. 15, pp. 85–105.

Evans, M. I., P. Symens, and C. W. T. Pilcher. 1993. "Short-term Damage to Coastal Bird Populations in Saudi Arabia and Kuwait Following the 1991 Gulf War Marine Pollution." *Marine Pollution Bulletin*. Vol. 27, pp. 157–161.

Ezaza, W. P., and H. Othman. 1989. "Political Instability and Ecological Stress in Eastern Africa," pp. 131–143 in A. Hjort af Ornäs and M. A. Mohamed Salih, eds. *Ecology and Politics: Environmental Stress and Security in Africa*. Motala, Sweden: Motala Grafiska (for the Scandinavian Institute of African Studies).

Falk, R. 2000. "The Inadequacy of the Existing Legal Approach to Environmental Protection in Wartime," pp. 137–155 in J. E. Austin and C. E. Bruch, eds. *The Environmental Consequences of War*. Cambridge: Cambridge University Press.

Ferguson, R. B. 1989. "Game Wars? Ecology and Conflict in Amazonia." *Journal of Anthropological Research*. Vol. 45 (Summer), pp. 179–206.

Fisher, F. M., et al. 2005. *Liquid Assets: An Economic Approach for Water Management and Conflict Resolution in the Middle East and Beyond*. Washington, DC: Resources for the Future.

Fisher, H. I., and P. H. Baldwin. 1946. "War and the Birds of Midway Atoll." *Condor*. Vol. 48, pp. 3–15.

Flamm, B. R., and J. H. Cravens. 1971. "Effects of War Damage on the Forest Resources of South Vietnam." *Journal of Forestry*. Vol. 69, No. 11, pp. 784–789.

Floodgate, G. D. 1996. "The Bacteriology of Oil Epuration in the Jubail Marine Wildlife Sanctuary," pp. 75–84 in F. Krupp, A. H. Abuzinada, and I. A. Nader, eds. *A Marine Wildlife Sanctuary for the Arabian Gulf: Environmental Research and Conservation Following the 1991 Gulf War Oil Spill*. Riyadh: NCWCD and Frankfurt am Main: Senckenberg Research Institute.

Formoli, T. A. 1995. "Impacts of the Afghan-Soviet War on Afghanistan's Environment." *Environmental Conservation*. Vol. 22, No. 1 (Spring), pp. 66–69.

Foster, B. E. 1989. "The Rwandese Refugees in Uganda," pp. 145–155 in A. Hjort af Ornäs and M. A. Mohamed Salih, eds. *Ecology and Politics: Environmental Stress and Security in Africa*. Motala, Sweden: Motala Grafiska (for the Scandinavian Institute of African Studies).

Fowler, S. W., et al. 1993. "Petroleum Hydrocarbons and Trace Metals in Nearshore Gulf Sediments and Biota before and after the 1991 War: An Assessment of Temporal and Spatial Trends." *Marine Pollution Bulletin*. Vol. 27, pp. 171–182.

Galston, A. W., and P. W. Richards. 1984. "Terrestrial Plant Ecology and Forestry: An Overview," pp. 39–52 in A. H. Westing, ed. *Herbicides in War: The Long-Term Ecological and Human Consequences*. London: Taylor & Francis.

Gardner, F., Y. Garb, and M. Williams. 1990. "Guatemala: A Political Ecology." Report. Earth Island Institute. San Francisco: The Environmental Project on Central America, October.

Gasana, J. K. 2002. "Natural Resource Scarcity and Violence in Rwanda," pp. 199–246 in R. Matthew, M. Halle, and J. Switzer, eds. *Conserving the Peace: Resources, Livelihoods and Security*. Winnipeg, Manitoba: International Institute for Sustainable Development.

Giesy, J. P. 2002. "Dioxin and Dioxin-Like Residues in and Their Effects on Fish and Wildlife of the North American Great Lakes." Conference paper. United

States–Vietnam Scientific Conference on Human Health and Environmental Effects of Agent Orange/Dioxins, 3–6 March, 2002, Hanoi, Vietnam. [U.S. National Institute of Environmental Health Sciences] Available online at http://www.niehs.nih.gov/external/usvcrp/project1.htm [accessed 23 January, 2003].

Glasstone, S., and P. J. Dolan. 1977. "The Effects of Nuclear Weapons." U.S. Department of Defense and Department of Energy: Defense Atomic Support Agency. 3rd edition. Washington, DC: U.S. Government Printing Office.

Gleditsch, N. P. 1998. "Armed Conflict and the Environment: A Critique of the Literature." *Journal of Peace Research*. Vol. 35, No. 4 (May), pp. 381–400.

Global Witness. 1998. *A Rough Trade: The Role of Companies and Governments in the Angolan Conflict*. Report. December. http://www.globalwitness.org/media_library_detail.php/90/en/a_rough_trade [accessed on 28 January, 2008].

Global Witness. 1999. *A Crude Awakening: The Role of the Oil and Banking Industries in Angola's Civil War and the Plunder of State Assets*. Report. December. [http://www.fatbeehive.com/globalwitness/text/campaigns/oil/downloads/cruderep.pdf; accessed on 5 April 2002].

Global Witness. 2001. *The Role of Liberia's Logging Industry on National and Regional Insecurity*. Report. January. [http://www.globalpolicy.org/security/issues/liberia/report/gwtimber.htm; accessed on 5 April, 2002].

Global Witness. 2002. *"All the President's Men": The Devastating Story of Oil and Banking in Angola's Privatised War*. Report. March. [http://www.fatbeehive.com/globalwitness/text/downloads/All_the_Presidents_men.pdf; accessed on 15 April, 2002].

Gold, D. 2006. "The Attempt to Regulate Conflict Diamonds." *The Economics of Peace and Security Journal*. Vol. 1, No. 1, pp. 49–52.

Goudie, A. 2000. *The Human Impact on the Natural Environment*. 5th ed. Cambridge, MA: MIT Press.

Green Cross International. 1998. *An Environmental Assessment of Kuwait Seven Years after the Gulf War*. Final Report. December. Geneva: Green Cross International.

Greenpeace. 1992. *The Environmental Legacy of the Gulf War*. Amsterdam: Greenpeace International.

Greenway, J. C., Jr. 1967. *Extinct and Vanishing Birds of the World*. 2nd ed. New York: Dover.

Gutter, P. 2001. "Environment and Law in Burma." *Legal Issues on Burma Journal*. No. 9 (August), pp. 1–27. http://www.ibiblio.org/obl/docs/Legal%20Issues%20on%20Burma%20Journal%209.pdf [accessed 18 March, 2003].

Hall, B., and D. Faber. 1989. "El Salvador: Ecology of Conflict." Report. Earth Island Institute. San Francisco: The Environmental Project on Central America, March.

Hamzah, R. Y. 1996. "Biochemical Aspects of Bioremediation of Oil-Contamination," pp. 83–103 in N. Al-Awadhi, M. T. Balba, and C. Kamizawa, eds. *Restoration and Rehabilitation of the Desert Environment*. Amsterdam: Elsevier.

Hanson, T., et al. 2009. "Warfare in Biodiversity Hotspots." *Conservation Biology*. Vol. 23, No. 3 (June), pp. 578–587.

Harbard, C., and C. Wolstencroft. 1992. "The ICBP/NCWCD Waterbird Survey of the Gulf Coast of Saudi Arabia During November–December 1991." Report to the International Council for Bird Preservation and the National Commission on Wildlife Conservation and Development, Kingdom of Saudi Arabia.

Harbinson, R. 1992. "Burma's Forests Fall Victim to War." *The Ecologist*. Vol. 22, No. 2 (March/April), pp. 72–73.

Harnly, C. D. 1988. *Agent Orange and Vietnam: An Annotated Bibliography*. Metuchen, NJ: Scarecrow Press.

Hart, T., and R. Mwinyihali. 2001. *Armed Conflict and Biodiversity in Sub-Saharan Africa: The Case of the Democratic Republic of Congo*. Washington, DC: Biodiversity Support Program.

Harwell, M. A., and T. C. Hutchinson, eds. 1985. *Environmental Consequences of Nuclear War. Volume II: Ecological and Agricultural Effects*. Scientific Committee on Problems of the Environment. International Council of Scientific Unions. New York: John Wiley & Sons.

Hatton, J., M. Couto, and J. Oglethorpe. 2001. *Biodiversity and War: A Case Study of Mozambique*. Washington, DC: Biodiversity Support Program.

Hayes, M. O., et al. 1993. "Distribution and Weathering of Shoreline Oil One Year after the Gulf War Oil Spill." *Marine Pollution Bulletin*. Vol. 27, pp. 135–142.

Heneman, B. 1991. "The Gulf War Oil Spills: The ICBP Survey of the Saudi Arabian Gulf Coast, March, 1991." A Report to the International Council for Bird Preservation and the National Commission on Wildlife Conservation and Development, Kingdom of Saudi Arabia. Bolinas, CA: Burr Heneman, April.

Hess, K., Jr. 2000. "Saving Space for Species: The Conservation Challenge for the 21st Century," pp. 3–25 in J. A. Baden and P. Geddes, eds. *Saving a Place: Endangered Species in the 21st Century*. London: Ashgate.

Hiêp, D. 1984a. "Long-Term Changes in Dense Inland Forest Following Herbicidal Attack," pp. 31–32 in A. H. Westing, ed. *Herbicides in War: The Long-Term Ecological and Human Consequences*. London: Taylor & Francis.

Hiêp, D. 1984b. "Long-Term Changes in the Mangrove Habitat Following Herbicidal Attack," pp. 89–90 in A. H. Westing, ed. *Herbicides in War: The Long-Term Ecological and Human Consequences*. London: Taylor & Francis.

Hill, R., and Y. Katarere. 2002. "Colonialism and Inequity in Zimbabwe," pp. 247–268 in R. Matthew, M. Halle, and J. Switzer, eds. *Conserving the Peace: Resources, Livelihoods and Security*. Winnipeg, Manitoba: International Institute for Sustainable Development.

Hills, A. 1991. "A Green Ministry." *Geographical Magazine*. Vol. 64 (May), pp. 16–20.

Hobbs, P. V., and L. F. Radke. 1992. "Airborne Studies of the Smoke from the Kuwait Oil Fires." *Science*. Vol. 256 (15 May), pp. 987–991.

Hoffmann, L. 1994. "Distribution, Species Composition and Status of the Intertidal Blue-Green Algal Mats." *Courier Forschungsinstitut Senckenberg*. Vol. 166, pp. 16–17.

Hoffmann, L. 1996. "Recolonisation of the Intertidal Flats by Microbial Mats after the Gulf War Oil Spill," p. 96 in F. Krupp, A. H. Abuzinada, and I. A. Nader, eds. *A Marine Wildlife Sanctuary for the Arabian Gulf: Environmental Research and Conservation Following the 1991 Gulf War Oil Spill*. Riyadh: NCWCD and Frankfurt am Main: Senckenberg Research Institute.

Homer-Dixon, T. F. 1994. "Environmental Scarcities and Violent Conflict." *International Security*. Vol. 19, No. 1 (Summer), pp. 5–40.

Höpner, T., M. Yousef, L. Berthe-Corti, H. Felzmann, H. Struck, and A. Al-Thukair. 1996. "Cyanobacterial Mats on Oil-Polluted Sediments: Start of a Promising Self-Remediation Process," p. 85 in F. Krupp, A. H. Abuzinada, and I. A. Nader, eds. *A Marine Wildlife Sanctuary for the Arabian Gulf: Environmental Research and Conservation Following the 1991 Gulf War Oil Spill*. Riyadh: NCWCD and Frankfurt am Main: Senckenberg Research Institute.

Huay, H. V., and N. X. Cu. 1984. "Long-Term Changes in Soil Chemistry Following Herbicidal Attack," pp. 69–73 in A. H. Westing, ed. *Herbicides in War: The Long-Term Ecological and Human Consequences*. London: Taylor & Francis.

Human Rights Watch. 2006. "Funding the 'Final War': LTTE Intimidation and Extortion in the Tamil Diaspora." *Human Rights Watch*. Vol. 18, No. 1 (C). http://hrw.org/reports/2006/ltte0306/ ltte0306webwcover.pdf [accessed 28 January, 2008].

Huynh, D. H., D. N. Can, Q. Anh, and N. V. Thang. 1984. "Long-Term Changes in the Mammalian Fauna Following Herbicidal Attack," pp. 49–52 in A. H. Westing, ed. *Herbicides in War: The Long-Term Ecological and Human Consequences*. London: Taylor & Francis.

International Atomic Energy Agency. 1998a. "The Radiological Situation at the Atolls of Mururoa and Fangataufa, Main Report." Vienna: International Atomic Energy Agency. http://www-pub.iaea.org/MTCD/publications/PDF/Pub1028_web.pdf [accessed 28 February, 2009]. A summary is available at http://www.iaea.org/Publications/Booklets/mururoabook.html [accessed 1 March, 2009].

International Atomic Energy Agency. 1998b. "Radiological Conditions at Bikini Atoll: Prospects for Resettlement." Vienna: International Atomic Energy Agency. http://www-pub.iaea.org/MTCD/publications/PDF/Pub1054_web.pdf [accessed March 1, 2009].

International Atomic Energy Agency. 2005. "Radiological Conditions at the Former French Nuclear Test Sites in Algeria: Preliminary Assessment and Recommendations." Vienna: International Atomic Energy Agency. http://www-pub.iaea.org/MTCD/publications/PDF/Pub1215_web.pdf [accessed 28 February, 2009].

International Rescue Committee. 2008. "Mortality in the Democratic Republic of Congo: An Ongoing Crisis." Report. [The report is undated but the press release announcing the report is dated January 22, 2008. The report is at http://www.theirc.org/resources/2007/2006-7_congomortalitysurvey.pdf] [accessed 16 February, 2009].

International Union for Conservation of Nature and Natural Resources. "IUCN and Conflict Resolution." Undated issue briefing. CEESP Task Force on Environment and Security. http://www.iisd.org/natres/security/publications.asp [accessed 13 January, 2003].

International Union for Conservation of Nature and Natural Resources. 1992a. "Angola: Environmental Status Quo Assessment Report. Executive Summary." Report. Harare, Zimbabwe: International Union for Conservation of Nature and Natural Resources Regional Office for Southern Africa, October.

International Union for Conservation of Nature and Natural Resources. 1992b. "Angola: Environmental Status Quo Assessment Report. Main Report." Report. Harare, Zimbabwe: International Union for Conservation of Nature and Natural Resources Regional Office for Southern Africa, October.

International Union for Conservation of Nature and Natural Resources. 1998. "Environment and Security: Identifying IUCN's Role." Workshop report and discussion paper. Gland, Switzerland: International Union for Conservation of Nature and Natural Resources, October.

Jackson, J. B. C., et al. 2001. "Historical Overfishing and the Recent Collapse of Coastal Ecosystems." *Science*. Vol. 293 (27 July), pp. 629–638.

Jacobs, M., and C. Schloeder. 2001. *Impacts of Conflict on Biodiversity and Protected Areas in Ethiopia*. Washington, DC: Biodiversity Support Program.

Johnson, B. R., and H. M. Barker. 2008. *Consequential Damages of Nuclear War: The Rongelap Report*. Walnut Creek, CA: Left Coast Press.

Jones, D. A., I. Watt, J. Plaza, T. D. Woodhouse, and M. Al-Sanei. 1996. "Natural Recovery of the Intertidal Biota within the Jubail Marine Wildlife Sanctuary after the 1991 Gulf War Oil Spill," p. 138 in F. Krupp, A. H. Abuzinada, and I. A. Nader, eds. *A Marine Wildlife Sanctuary for the Arabian Gulf: Environmental Research and Conservation Following the 1991 Gulf War Oil Spill*. Riyadh: NCWCD and Frankfurt am Main: Senckenberg Research Institute.

Jones, D. A., I. Watt, T. D. Woodhouse, and M. D. Richmond. 1994. "Intertidal Recovery in the Dawhat ad-Dafi and Dawhat al-Musallamiya Region (Saudi Arabia) after the Gulf War Oil Spill." *Courier Forschungsinstitut Senckenberg*. Vol. 166, pp. 27–33.

Kaimowitz, D., and A. Fauné. 2003. "Contras and Comandantes: Armed Movements and Forest Conservation in Nicaragua's Bosawas Biosphere Reserve." *Journal of Sustainable Forestry*. Vol. 16, Nos. 3/4, pp. 21–47. [Simultaneously published under the same title, pp. 21–47, in S. V. Price, ed. *War and Tropical Forests: Conservation in Areas of Armed Conflict*. Binghamton, NY: Haworth Press, 2003.]

Kalpers, J. 2001a. *Volcanoes under Siege: Impact of a Decade of Armed Conflict in the Virungas.* Washington, DC: Biodiversity Support Program.

Kalpers, J. 2001b. *Overview of Armed Conflict and Biodiversity in Sub-Saharan Africa: Impacts, Mechanisms and Responses.* Washington, DC: Biodiversity Support Program.

Kalpers, J., E. Williamson, M. Robbins, A. McNeilage, A. Nzamurambaho, N. Lola, and G. Mugiri. 2003. "Gorillas in the Crossfire: Assessment of Population Dynamics of the Virunga Mountain Gorillas over the Past Three Decades." *Oryx.* Vol. 37, No. 3, pp. 326–337.

Kanyamibwa, S. 1998. "Impact of War on Conservation: Rwandan Environment and Wildlife in Agony." *Biodiversity and Conservation.* Vol. 7, No. 11, pp. 1399–1406.

Keeley, L. H. 1996. *War before Civilization.* New York: Oxford University Press.

Keijl, G. O., and P. Symens. 1993. "Biometrics and Moult of Socotra Cormorant *Phalacrocorax nigrogularis.*" *Sandgrouse.* Vol. 15, pp. 44–55.

Kenworthy, W. J., M. J. Durako, S. M. R. Fatemy, H. Valavis, and G. W. Thayer. 1993. "Ecology of Seagrasses in Northeastern Saudi Arabia One Year after the Gulf War Oil Spill." *Marine Pollution Bulletin.* Vol. 27, pp. 213–222.

Kim, K. C. 1997. "Preserving Biodiversity in Korea's Demilitarized Zone." *Science.* Vol. 278 (10 October), pp. 242–243.

Kirk, R. 2003. *More Terrible Than Death: Massacres, Drugs, and America's War in Colombia.* New York: Public Affairs.

Klare, M. T. 2001. *Resource Wars: The New Landscape of Global Conflict.* New York: Metropolitan Books.

Klare, M. T. 2004. *Blood and Oil: The Dangers and Consequences of America's Growing Petroleum Dependency.* New York: Metropolitan Books.

Klare, M. T. 2008. *Rising Powers, Shrinking Planet: The New Geopolitics of Energy.* New York: Metropolitan Books.

Kock, D., and I. A. Nader. 1996. "Terrestrial Mammals of the Jubail Marine Wildlife Sanctuary," pp. 421–437 in F. Krupp, A. H. Abuzinada, and I. A. Nader, eds. *A Marine Wildlife Sanctuary for the Arabian Gulf: Environmental Research and Conservation Following the 1991 Gulf War Oil Spill.* Riyadh: NCWCD and Frankfurt am Main: Senckenberg Research Institute.

Krupp, F., A. H. Abuzinada, and I. A. Nader, eds. 1996. *A Marine Wildlife Sanctuary for the Arabian Gulf: Environmental Research and Conservation Following the 1991 Gulf War Oil Spill.* Riyadh: NCWCD and Frankfurt am Main: Senckenberg Research Institute.

Krupp, F., and M. A. Almarri. 1996. "Fishes and Fish Assemblages of the Jubail Marine Wildlife Sanctuary," pp. 339–350 in F. Krupp, A. H. Abuzinada, and I. A. Nader, eds. *A Marine Wildlife Sanctuary for the Arabian Gulf: Environmental Research and Conservation Following the 1991 Gulf War Oil Spill.* Riyadh: NCWCD and Frankfurt am Main: Senckenberg Research Institute.

Krupp, F., and O. Khushaim. 1996. "The Jubail Marine Wildlife Sanctuary," p. 17 in F. Krupp, A. H. Abuzinada, and I. A. Nader, eds. *A Marine Wildlife Sanctuary for the Arabian Gulf: Environmental Research and Conservation Following the 1991 Gulf War Oil Spill.* Riyadh: NCWCD and Frankfurt am Main: Senckenberg Research Institute.

Krupp, F., and T. Müller. 1994. "The Status of Fish Populations in the Northern Arabian Gulf Two Years after the 1991 Gulf War Oil Spill." *Courier Forschungsinstitut Senckenberg.* Vol. 166, pp. 67–75.

Kuletz, V. 1998. *The Tainted Desert: Environmental Ruin in the American West.* New York: Routledge.

Kureishy, T. W. 1993. "Concentration of Heavy Metals in Marine Organisms around Qatar before and after the Gulf War Oil Spill." *Marine Pollution Bulletin.* Vol. 27, pp. 183–186.

Kwarteng, A. Y. 1998. "Multitemporal Remote Sensing Data Analysis of Kuwait's Oil Lakes." *Environment International.* Vol. 24, No. 1/2 (January), pp. 121–137.

Lanier-Graham, S. D. 1993. *The Ecology of War: Environmental Impacts of Weaponry and Warfare.* New York: Walker and Company.

Larsson, J., C. Folke, and N. Kautsky. 1994. "Ecological Limitations and Appropriation of Ecosystem Support by Shrimp Farming in Colombia." *Environmental Management.* Vol. 18, No. 5, pp. 663–676. [Reprinted under the same title, pp. 538–551 in R. Costanza, C. Perrings, and J. C. Cutler, eds. *The Development of Ecological Economics.* Cheltenham, UK and Lyme, NH: Elgar.]

LeBlanc, S. A. 1999. *Prehistoric Warfare in the American Southwest.* Salt Lake City: University of Utah Press.

LeBlanc, S. A. 2003. *Constant Battles: The Myth of the Peaceful, Noble Savage.* With K. E. Register. New York: St. Martin's Press.

Leighton, M. 1984. "Terrestrial Animal Ecology: An Overview," pp. 53–62 in A. H. Westing, ed. *Herbicides in War: The Long-Term Ecological and Human Consequences.* London: Taylor & Francis.

Lesowitz, R. S., S. J. Berman, D. J. Gubler, C. Harinasuta, P. Guptavanij, and C. Vasavat. 1974. "Epidemiological-Ecological Effects: Studies on Intact and Deforested Mangrove Ecosystems," AD-779 023 in National Academy of Sciences. *Effects of Herbicides in South Vietnam; Part B: Working Papers.* Washington, DC: National Academy of Sciences.

Levy, B., G. Shahi, and C. Lee. 1997. "The Environmental Consequences of War," pp. 51–62 in B. S. Levy and V. W. Sidel, eds. *War and Public Health.* New York: Oxford University Press.

Lodhi, M. A., F. R. Echavarria, and C. Keithley. 1998. "Using Remote Sensing Data to Monitor Land Cover Changes near Afghan Refugee Camps in Northern Pakistan." *Geocarto International.* Vol. 13, No. 1 (March), pp. 33–39.

Lomborg, B. 2001. *The Skeptical Environmentalist: Measuring the Real State of the World.* New York: Cambridge University Press.

MacArthur, R. H., and E. O. Wilson. 1967. *The Theory of Island Biogeography.* Princeton, NJ: Princeton University Press [reissued in 2001, with a new foreword by E. O. Wilson].

Malallah, G., M. Afzal, G. Murin, A. Murin, and D. Abraham. 1997. "Genotoxicity of Oil Pollution on Some Species of Kuwait Flora." *Biologia Bratislava.* Vol. 52, No. 1, pp. 61–70.

Marlin, J. T. 2006. "The 'No Dirty Gold' Campaign: What Economists Can Learn from and Contribute to Corporate Campaigns." *The Economics of Peace and Security Journal.* Vol. 1, No. 2, pp. 58–64.

Martens, H. 1996. "A Preliminary Survey of the Terrestrial Reptiles and Sea Snakes in the Jubail Marine Wildlife Sanctuary," pp. 360–373 in F. Krupp, A. H. Abuzinada, and I. A. Nader, eds. *A Marine Wildlife Sanctuary for the Arabian Gulf: Environmental Research and Conservation Following the 1991 Gulf War Oil Spill.* Riyadh: NCWCD and Frankfurt am Main: Senckenberg Research Institute.

Marty, S. 1993. "Where the Deer and Antelope Play." *Canadian Geographic.* Vol. 113 (March/April), pp. 32–42.

Mathews, C. P., S. Kedidi, N. I. Fita, A. Al-Yahya, and K. Al-Rasheed. 1993. "Preliminary Assessment of the Effects of the 1991 Gulf War on Saudi Arabian Prawn Stocks." *Marine Pollution Bulletin.* Vol. 27, pp. 251–271.

Matthew, R., M. Halle, and J. Switzer, eds. *Conserving the Peace: Resources, Livelihoods and Security.* Winnipeg, Manitoba: International Institute for Sustainable Development.

McCain, J. C., D. W. Beard, and Y. H. Fadlallah. 1993. "The Influence of the Kuwaiti Oil Well Fires on Seawater Temperature in the Western Gulf." *Marine Pollution Bulletin.* Vol. 27, pp. 79–83. http://www.iisd.org/natres/security/publications.asp [accessed 13 January, 2003].

McNeely, J. 1988. *Economics and Biological Diversity: Developing and Using Economic Incentives to Conserve Biological Resources.* Gland, Switzerland: International Union for Conservation of Nature and Natural Resources.

McNeely, J. 2000. "War and Biodiversity: An Assessment of Impacts," pp. 353–378 in J. E. Austin and C. E. Bruch, eds. *The Environmental Consequences of War.* Cambridge: Cambridge University Press.

McNeely, J. 2002. "Biodiversity, Conflict, and Tropical Forests," pp. 33–49 in R. Matthew, M. Halle, and J. Switzer, eds. *Conserving the Peace: Resources, Livelihoods and Security.* Winnipeg, Manitoba: International Institute for Sustainable Development.

McNeely, J. 2003. "Biodiversity, War, and Tropical Forests." *Journal of Sustainable Forestry.* Vol. 16, Nos. 3/4, pp. 1–20. [Simultaneously published under the same title, pp. 1–20, in S. V. Price, ed. *War and Tropical Forests: Conservation in Areas of Armed Conflict.* Binghamton, NY: Haworth Press, 2003.]

McPherson, N., and B. K. Fernando. 1991. "Opportunities for Improved Environmental Management in Afghanistan: Report of a Mission under Contract to UNOCA." Gland, Switzerland: International Union for Conservation of Nature and Natural Resources.

Metwally, M. E.-S., S. Al-Muzaini, P. G. Jacob, M. Bahloul, Y. Urushigawa, S. Sato, and A. Matsmura. 1997. "Petroleum Hydrocarbons and Related Heavy Metals in the Near-Shore Marine Sediments of Kuwait." *Environment International.* Vol. 23, No. 1, pp. 115–121.

Michel, J., E. R. Gundlach, and M. O. Hayes. 1986. "Oil Spill Contingency Planning in the Arabian Gulf," pp. 249–262 in R. Halwagy, D. Clayton, and M. Behbehani, eds. *Marine Environment and Pollution* (Proceedings of the Arabian Gulf Conference on Environment and Pollution). Kuwait.

Michel, J., et al. 1993. "Contamination of Nearshore Subtidal Sediments of Saudi Arabia from the Gulf War Oil Spill." *Marine Pollution Bulletin.* Vol. 27, pp. 109–116.

Moody, R. 2000. "Grave Diggers: A Report on Mining in Burma." http://www.minesandcommunities.org/Country/burma1.htm [accessed 9 March, 2008].

Muller, F., and N. Vander Velde. 1999. "Overview of the Marshall Islands' Forest Resources." Republic of the Marshall Islands. Ministry of Resources, Development and Works. Agriculture Division. Edited and Updated Version of the Original Report Presented at the Pacific Sub-regional Workshop on Forest and Tree Genetic Resources. By Dr. Lex Thomson, Project Team Leader, SPRIG-2 Project, CSIRO Forestry and Forest Products, Canberra, Australia. June 2002. Available at http://www.sprep.org/att/IRC/eCOPIES/Countries/Marshall_Islands/4.pdf [accessed 2 March, 2009].

National Academy of Sciences. 1974. *Effects of Herbicides in South Vietnam; Part B: Working Papers.* Washington, DC: National Academy of Sciences.

Ney-Nifle, M., and M. Mangel. 2000. "Habitat Loss and Changes in the Species-Area Relationship." *Conservation Biology.* Vol. 14, No. 3, pp. 893–898.

Ngan, P. T. 1968. "Status of Conservation in South Vietnam," pp. 519–522 in L. M. Talbot and M. H. Talbot, eds. *Conservation in Tropical South East Asia.* Morges, Switzerland: International Union for the Conservation of Nature and Natural Resources.

Nietschmann, B. 1990. "Conservation by Conflict in Nicaragua." *Natural History.* Vol. 11, pp. 42–49.

Nietschmann, B. 1998. "The Effects of War and Peace on Nicaragua's Environments." Conference paper. First International Conference on Addressing Environmental Consequences of War: Legal, Economic and Scientific Perspectives. Washington, DC: Environmental Law Institute, June.

Norman, C. 1974. "Academy Reports on Vietnam Herbicide Damage." *Nature.* Vol. 248 (15 March), pp. 186–188.

Obuekwe, C. O., and S. S. Al-Zarban. 1998. "Bioremediation of Crude Oil Pollution in the Kuwaiti Desert: The Role of Adherent Microorganisms." *Environment International.* Vol. 24, No. 8 (November), pp. 823–834.

Olie, K. 1984. "Analysis for Dioxin in Soils of Southern Viet Nam," pp. 173–175 in A. H. Westing, ed. *Herbicides in War: The Long-Term Ecological and Human Consequences*. London: Taylor & Francis.

Omar, S. A. S., E. Briskey, R. Misak, and A. A. S. O. Asem. 2000. "The Gulf War Impact on the Terrestrial Environment of Kuwait: An Overview," pp. 316–337 in J. E. Austin and C. E. Bruch, eds. *The Environmental Consequences of War*. Cambridge: Cambridge University Press.

Omar, S. A. S., R. Misak, and S. A. Shahid. 2001. "Assessment of Oil Contamination in Oil Trenches Located in Two Contrasting Oil Types." Paper. International Conference on Contaminated Soils, Sediments, and Water. Amherst: University of Massachusetts. http://www.umasssoils.com/abstracts2001/thursday/siteassess.htm [accessed 14 February, 2003].

Orians, G. H., and E. W. Pfeiffer. 1970. "Ecoiogical Effects of the War in Vietnam." *Science*. Vol. 168, No. 3931 (1 May), pp. 544–554.

Orians, G. H., E. W. Pfeiffer, and C. Leuba. 1969. "Defoliants: Orange, White, and Blue." [Letter] *Science*. Vol. 165, No. 3892 (1 August), pp. 442–443.

Ostrowski, S., M. S. Massalatchi, and M. Mamane. 2001. "Evidence of a Dramatic Decline of the Red-Necked Ostrich, *Struthio camelus camelus*, in the Äir and Ténéré National Nature Reserve, Niger." *Oryx*. Vol. 35, No. 4 (October), pp. 349–352.

Owens, S. 1990. "Defence and the Environment: The Impact of Military Live Firing in National Parks." *Cambridge Journal of Economics*. Vol. 14, pp. 497–505.

Palmer, T. M., M. L. Stanton, T. P. Young, J. R. Goheen, R. M. Pringle, and R. Karban. 2008. "Breakdown of an Ant-Plant Mutualism Follows the Loss of Large Herbivores from an African Savanna." *Science*. Vol. 319 (11 January), pp. 192–195.

Paskett, C. J. 1998. "Refugees and Land Use: The Need for Change in a Growing Problem." *Journal of Soil and Water Conservation*. Vol. 53, No. 1, pp. 57–58.

Pearce, F. 1994. "Soldiers Lay Waste to Africa's Oldest Park." *New Scientist*. (3 December), p. 4.

Pearce, F. 1995. "Devastation in the Desert." *New Scientist*. Vol. 146, No. 1971 (1 April), pp. 40, 44. [Cited from Green Cross International, 1998, p. 55, 109.]

Perrins, C. M., and A. L. A. Middleton. 1985. *The Encyclopedia of Birds*. New York: Facts On File.

Perry Robinson, J. P. 1981. "Environmental Effects of Chemical and Biological Warfare," pp. 73–91 in W. Barnaby, ed. *War and Environment*. Environmental Advisory Council, Stockholm: Författarna och LiberFörlag.

Peterson, B. C. 1942–1943. "War's Threat to Bird Species." *Frontiers*. Vol. 7, No. 5, pp. 133–135.

Pfeiffer, E. W. 1990. "Degreening Vietnam." *Natural History*. Vol. 99, No. 11 (November), pp. 37–40.

Philips, D. J. H. 2007. "Reducing the Cost of Inter and Intrastate Conflict over Water in the Jordan River Basin." *The Economics of Peace and Security Journal.* Vol. 2, No. 2, pp. 19–25.

Pilcher, C. W. T., and D. B. Sexton. 1993. "Effects of the Gulf War Oil Spills and Wellhead Fires on the Avifauna and Environment of Kuwait." *Sandgrouse.* Vol. 15, pp. 6–17.

Pittock, A. B., T. P. Ackerman, P. J. Crutzen, M. C. MacCracken, C. S. Shapiro, and R. P. Turco. 1986. *Environmental Consequences of Nuclear War. Volume I: Physical and Atmospheric Effects.* Scientific Committee on Problems of the Environment. International Council of Scientific Unions. New York: John Wiley & Sons.

Plumptre, A. J. 2003. "Lessons Learned from On-the-Ground Conservation in Rwanda and the Democratic Republic of the Congo." *Journal of Sustainable Forestry.* Vol. 16, Nos 3/4, pp. 71–91.

Plumptre, A. J., J.-B. Bizumuremyi, F. Uwimana, and J.-D. Ndaruhebeye. 1997. "The Effects of the Rwandan Civil War on Poaching of Ungulates in the Parc National des Volcans." *Oryx.* Vol. 31, No. 4 (October), pp. 265–273.

Plumptre, A. J., M. Masozera, and A. Vedder. 2001. *The Impact of Civil War on the Conservation of Protected Areas in Rwanda.* Washington, DC: Biodiversity Support Program.

Prena, J. 1996. "The Status of the Intertidal Soft-Bottom Macrofauna Six Months after the Gulf War Oil Spill," p. 128 in F. Krupp, A. H. Abuzinada, and I. A. Nader, eds. *A Marine Wildlife Sanctuary for the Arabian Gulf: Environmental Research and Conservation Following the 1991 Gulf War Oil Spill.* Riyadh: NCWCD and Frankfurt am Main: Senckenberg Research Institute.

Price, A. R. G. 1998. "Impact of the 1991 Gulf War on the Coastal Environment and Ecosystems: Current Status and Future Prospects." *Environment International.* Vol. 24, No. 1/2 (January), pp. 91–96.

Price, A. R. G., et al. 1994. *The 1991 Gulf War: Environmental Assessments of IUCN and Collaborators.* A Marine Conservation and Development Report. Gland, Switzerland: International Union for Conservation of Nature and Natural Resources.

Price, A. R. G., and J. H. Robinson, eds. 1993. The 1991 Gulf War: Coastal and Marine Environmental Consequences. Special issue of *Marine Pollution Bulletin.* Vol. 27.

Price, A. R. G., C. R. C. Sheppard, and C. M. Roberts. 1993. "The Gulf: Its Biological Setting." *Marine Pollution Bulletin.* Vol. 27, pp. 9–15.

Price, A. R. G., T. J. Wrathall, P. A. H. Medley, and A. H. Al-Moamens. 1993. "Broadscale Changes in Coastal Ecosystems of the Western Gulf Following the 1991 Gulf War." *Marine Pollution Bulletin.* Vol. 27, pp. 143–147.

Price, S. V., ed.. *War and Tropical Forests: Conservation in Areas of Armed Conflict.* Binghamtom, NY: Haworth Press. [Simultaneously published as the *Journal of Sustainable Forestry.* Vol. 16, Nos. 3/4.]

Radwan, S. S., N. A. Sorkhoh, A. F. El-Desouky, and I. El-Nemr. 1996. "Enrichment of Kuwaiti Desert Samples with Hydrocarbon-Degrading Microorganisms during a Simulated Oil Spill," pp. 49–55 in N. Al-Awadhi, M. T. Balba, and C. Kamizawa, eds. *Restoration and Rehabilitation of the Desert Environment.* Amsterdam: Elsevier.

Radwan, S., N. Sorkhoh, and I. El-Nemr. 1995. "Oil Biodegradation Round Roots." *Nature.* Vol. 376 (27 July), p. 302.

Rappe, C. 1984. "Dioxin Chemistry: An Overview," pp. 177–182 in A. H. Westing, ed. *Herbicides in War: The Long-Term Ecological and Human Consequences.* London: Taylor & Francis.

Redmond, I. 2001. "Coltan Boom, Gorilla Bust: The Impact of Coltan Mining on Gorillas and other Wildlife in Eastern DR Congo." A Report for the Dian Fossey Gorilla Fund Europe and the Born Free Foundation. May. http://www.bornfree.org.uk/coltan/coltan.pdf [accessed 5 April, 2002].

Richards, Z. T., M. Beger, S. Pinca, and C. C. Wallace. 2008. "Bikini Atoll Coral Diversity Resilience Five Decades after Nuclear Testing." *Marine Pollution Bulletin.* Vol. 56, pp. 503–515.

Richardson, M. 1993. "Croatia. International Meeting on Effects of War on the Environment. First Mission to Croatia. Technical Report. Vienna: UNIDO.

Richardson, M. 1995. *The Effects of War on the Environment: Croatia.* London: E. & F. N. Spon.

Richmond, M. D. 1994. "Ecological Status of the Marine Subtidal Habitats and the Effects of the 1991 Gulf War Oil Spill, with Special Reference to Soft-Substrata Communities." *Courier Forschungsinstitut Senckenberg.* Vol. 166, pp. 55–60.

Richmond, M. D. 1996. "Status of Subtidal Biotopes of the Jubail Marine Wildlife Sanctuary with Special Reference to Soft-Substrata Communities," p. 159 in F. Krupp, A. H. Abuzinada, and I. A. Nader, eds. *A Marine Wildlife Sanctuary for the Arabian Gulf: Environmental Research and Conservation Following the 1991 Gulf War Oil Spill.* Riyadh: NCWCD and Frankfurt am Main: Senckenberg Research Institute.

Roberts, A. 2000. "The Law of War and Environmental Damage," pp. 47–86 in J. E. Austin and C. E. Bruch, eds. *The Environmental Consequences of War.* Cambridge: Cambridge University Press.

Robineau, D., and P. Fiquet. 1994. "Cetaceans of Dawhat ad-Dafi and Dawhat al-Musallamiya (Saudi Arabia) One Year after the Gulf War Oil Spill." *Courier Forschungsinstitut Senckenberg.* Vol. 166, pp. 76–80.

Rubenson, S. 1991. "Environmental Stress and Conflict in Ethiopian History: Looking for Correlations." *Ambio.* Vol. 20, No. 5 (August), pp. 179–182.

Sadiq, M., and J. C. McCain. 1993. "Effect of the 1991 Gulf War on Metal Bioaccumulation by the Clam (*Meretrix meretrix*). *Marine Pollution Bulletin.* Vol. 27, pp. 163–170.

Saeed, T., S. Al-Yakoob, H. Al-Hashash, and M. Al-Bahloul. 1995. "Preliminary Exposure Assessment for Kuwaiti Consumers to Polycyclic Aromatic Hydrocarbons in Seafood." *Environment International.* Vol. 21, No. 3, pp. 255–263.

Salam, A. J. A. 1996. "The Oil Lakes Environmental Disaster," pp. 117–137 in N. Al-Awadhi, M. T. Balba, and C. Kamizawa, eds. *Restoration and Rehabilitation of the Desert Environment.* Amsterdam: Elsevier.

SAMFU Foundation. 2002. "Plunder: The Silent Destruction of Liberia's Rainforest." Report. Liberia: SAMFU Foundation. September. Available at www. whitley-award.org/Articles/projects/human_rights/samfu_plunder_report_ sept_2002.pdf [accessed 24 March, 2003].

Sato, H., K. Yasui, and K. Byamana. 2000. "Follow-Up Survey of Environmental Impacts of the Rwandan Refugees on Eastern D.R. Congo." *Ambio.* Vol. 29, No. 2 (March), pp. 122–123.

Sauer, T. C., et al. 1993. "Hydrocarbon Source Identification and Weathering Characterization of Intertidal and Subtidal Sediments along the Saudi Arabian Coast after the Gulf War Oil Spill." *Marine Pollution Bulletin.* Vol. 27, pp. 117–134.

Schecter, A., L. C. Dai, O. Päpke, J. Prange, J. D. Constable, M. Matsuda, V. D. Thao, and A. L. Piskac. 2001. "Recent Dioxin Contamination from Agent Orange in Residents of a Southern Vietnam City." *Journal of Occupational and Environmental Medicine.* Vol. 43, No. 5 (May), pp. 435–443.

Schecter, A., et al. 2002. "Collaborative USA-Vietnamese Agent Orange Research from 1968 to 2002." Conference paper. United States–Vietnam Scientific Conference on Human Health and Environmental Effects of Agent Orange/Dioxins, 3–6 March, 2002, Hanoi, Vietnam. [U.S. National Institute of Environmental Health Sciences] Available online at http://www.niehs.nih. gov/external/usvcrp/project1.htm [accessed 23 January, 2003].

Schelling, T. 2006a. "Intergenerational and International Discounting," pp. 51–59 in T. Schelling, *Strategies of Commitment and Other Essays.* Cambridge, MA: Harvard University Press. First published under the same title in *Risk Analysis: An International Journal.* Vol. 20, No. 6 (2000), pp. 833–839.

Schelling, T. 2006b. "What Makes Greenhouse Sense?" pp. 27–44 in T. Schelling, *Strategies of Commitment and Other Essays.* Cambridge, MA: Harvard University Press. First published under the same title in *Indiana Law Review.* Vol. 38, No. 3 (2005), pp. 581–593.

Schmitt, M. 2000. "War and the Environment: Fault Lines in the Prescriptive Landscape," pp. 87–136 in J. E. Austin and C. E. Bruch, eds. *The Environmental Consequences of War.* Cambridge: Cambridge University Press.

Schneider, W., and R. Kinzelback. 1994. "Effects of the 1991 Oil Spill on the Supratidal Fringe." *Courier Forschungsinstitut Senckenberg.* Vol. 166, pp. 34–39.

Scholz, J. T. and B. Stiftel, eds. 2005. *Adaptive Government and Water Conflict: New Institutions for Collaborative Planning.* Washington, DC: Resources for the Future.

Scientific American. 1974. "Herbicidal Warfare." *Scientific American*. Vol. 230, No. 4 (April), pp. 49–50.

Sen Gupta, R., S. P. Fondekar, and R. Alagarsamy. 1993. "State of Oil Pollution in the Northern Arabian Sea after the 1991 Gulf Oil Spill." *Marine Pollution Bulletin*. Vol. 27, pp. 85–91.

Shambaugh, J., J. Oglethorpe, R. Ham (with contributions by S. Tognetti). 2001. *The Trampled Grass: Mitigating the Impacts of Armed Conflict on the Environment*. Washington, DC: Biodiversity Support Program.

Shapley, D. 1974. "Herbicides: Academy finds Damage in Vietnam after a Fight of Its Own." *Science*. Vol. 183, No. 4130 (22 March), pp. 1177–1180.

Siddiqui, M. S. and K. A. Al-Mubarak. 1998. "The Post-Gulf-War Shrimp Fishery Management in the Territorial Waters of Kuwait." *Environment International*. Vol. 24, Nos. 1/2, pp. 105–108.

Simon, S. L., A. Bouville, and C. E. Land. 2006. "Fallout from Nuclear Weapons Tests and Cancer Risks." *American Scientist*. Vol. 94, No. 1, pp. 48–57.

Simons, M. 2001. "Alarm Grows over Balkan Radiation: NATO Bombing Included Weapons with Uranium Tips." *The Times-Picayune* (New Orleans, LA). 7 January, p. A-14.

Skogland, T. 1988. "Ecology and the War in Afghanistan," pp. 175–196 in B. Huldt and E. Jansson, eds. *The Tragedy of Afghanistan: The Social, Cultural, and Political Impact of the Soviet Invasion*. New York: Croom Helm.

Small Arms Survey. *Small Arms Survey*. Annual. A Project of the Graduate Institute of International Studies, Geneva. [2001–2006 volumes published by Oxford University Press; 2007–present, Cambridge University Press.]

Smart, N. O. E., J. C. Hatton, and D. H. N. Spence. 1985. "The Effect of Long-term Exclusion of Large Herbivores on Vegetation in Murchison Falls National Park, Uganda." *Biological Conservation*. Vol. 33, No. 3, pp. 229–245.

Smith, G. C. 1996a. "The Concentration and Extent of Degradation of Petroleum Components from Intertidal and Subtidal Sediments in Saudi Arabia Following the Gulf War Oil Spill," p. 54 in F. Krupp, A. H. Abuzinada, and I. A. Nader, eds. *A Marine Wildlife Sanctuary for the Arabian Gulf: Environmental Research and Conservation Following the 1991 Gulf War Oil Spill*. Riyadh: NCWCD and Frankfurt am Main: Senckenberg Research Institute.

Smith, G. C. 1996b. "Hydrocarbon Concentrations in Two Intertidal Areas of Saudi Arabia Following Remediation with Mechanical Clean-up Techniques after the Gulf War Oil Spill," p. 40 in F. Krupp, A. H. Abuzinada, and I. A. Nader, eds. *A Marine Wildlife Sanctuary for the Arabian Gulf: Environmental Research and Conservation Following the 1991 Gulf War Oil Spill*. Riyadh: NCWCD and Frankfurt am Main: Senckenberg Research Institute.

Snedaker, S. C. 1984. "Coastal, Marine and Aquatic Ecology: An Overview," pp. 95–107 in A. H. Westing, ed. *Herbicides in War: The Long-Term Ecological and Human Consequences*. London: Taylor & Francis.

Sogge, D. (compiler). 1992. "Sustainable Peace: Angola's Recovery." Southern African Research and Documentation Centre. Harare, Zimbabwe.

Spektor, D. M. 1998. "A Review of the Scientific Literature as it Pertains to Gulf War Illnesses." Report MR1018/6-OSD. Santa Monica, CA: RAND.

Sperling, L. 2001. "The Effect of the Civil War on Rwanda's Bean Seed Systems and Unusual Bean Diversity." *Biodiversity and Conservation*. Vol. 10, No. 6, pp. 989–1009.

Spittaels, S., and F. Hilgert. 2009. "Are Congo's Mines the Main Target of the Armed Groups on Its Soil?" *The Economics of Peace and Security Journal*. Vol. 4, No. 2, pp. 55–61.

Squire, C. 2001. *Sierra Leone's Biodiversity and the Civil War*. Washington, DC: Biodiversity Support Program.

Ståhl, M. 1989. "Environmental Degradation and Political Constraints in Ethiopia," pp. 181–196 in A. Hjort af Ornäs and M. A. Mohamed Salih, eds. *Ecology and Politics: Environmental Stress and Security in Africa*. Motala, Sweden: Motala Grafiska (for the Scandinavian Institute of African Studies).

Stellman, J. M., S. D. Stellman, R. Christian, T. Weber, and C. Tomasallo. 2003. "The Extent and Patterns of Usage of Agent Orange and Other Herbicides in Vietnam." *Nature*. Vol. 422 (17 April), pp. 681–687.

Stellman, J. M., S. D. Stellman, R. Christian, T. Weber, C. Tomasallo, and A. Stellman. 2002. "The Extent and Usage Patterns of Military Herbicides in Vietnam, 1961–1971: A Reanalysis Based on Examination of Newly Analyzed Primary Source Materials." United States–Vietnam Scientific Conference on Human Health and Environmental Effects of Agent Orange/Dioxins March 3–6, 2002, Daewoo Hotel, Hanoi, Vietnam. Available online via http://manuel. niehs.nih.gov/diox2002/allsum.cfm [accessed 22 January, 2003].

Stellman, S. D., J. M. Stellman, R. Christian, and T. Weber. 2002. "Influence of Soil-Specific Dioxin Decay Rates on Estimates of Exposure to Residual Phenoxy Herbicides in Vietnam." United States–Vietnam Scientific Conference on Human Health and Environmental Effects of Agent Orange/Dioxins March 3–6, 2002, Daewoo Hotel, Hanoi, Vietnam. Available online via http://manuel. niehs.nih.gov/diox2002/allsum.cfm [accessed 22 January, 2003].

Stockholm International Peace Research Institute. 2007. *SIPRI Yearbook 2007: Armaments, Disarmament and International Security*. Oxford: Oxford University Press.

Stockholm International Peace Research Institute. 2008. *SIPRI Yearbook 2008: Armaments, Disarmament and International Security*. Oxford: Oxford University Press.

Stoddart, D. R. 1968. "Catastrophic Human Interference with Coral Atoll Ecosystems." *Geography*. Vol. 53, pp. 25–40.

Stohl, R., M. Schroeder, and D. Smith. 2007. *The Small Arms Trade*. Oxford: Oneworld Publications.

Stone, C. D. 2000. "The Environment in Wartime: An Overview," pp. 16–35 in J. E. Austin and C. E. Bruch, eds. *The Environmental Consequences of War.* Cambridge: Cambridge University Press.

Suliman, M. 1993. "Civil War in the Sudan: From Ethnic to Ecological Conflict." *The Ecologist.* Vol. 23, No. 3 (May/June), pp. 104–109.

Suter, J., n.d. "Report on the Workshop to Review the 1986 Integrated Management and Development Plan for Sapo National Park to Develop an Operational Plan and to Outline a Long-Term Management Plan for the Park." Cambridge, UK: Fauna & Flora International. Undated report. Available at www.fauna-flora.org/around_the_world/world_main_frame.htm [accessed 24 March, 2003].

Swanson, C. W. 1975. "Reforestation in the Republic of Vietnam." *Journal of Forestry.* Vol. 73, No. 6, pp. 367–371.

Switzer, J. 2002. "Oil and Violence in Sudan." Geneva: International Institute for Sustainable Development. 15 April. http://www.iisd.org/pdf/2002/envsec_oil_violence.pdf [accessed 9 March, 2008].

Switzer, J., n.d. "Conflicting Interests." Geneva: International Institute for Sustainable Development. http://www.iisd.org/natres/security/publications.asp [accessed 12 January, 2003].

Symens, P., and A. H. Alsuhaibany. 1996a. "The Ornithological Importance of the Jubail Marine Wildlife Sanctuary," pp. 374–389 in F. Krupp, A. H. Abuzinada, and I. A. Nader, eds. *A Marine Wildlife Sanctuary for the Arabian Gulf: Environmental Research and Conservation Following the 1991 Gulf War Oil Spill.* Riyadh: NCWCD and Frankfurt am Main: Senckenberg Research Institute.

Symens, P., and A. H. Alsuhaibany. 1996b. "Status of the Breeding Populations of Terns (Sternidae) along the Eastern Coast of Saudi Arabia Following the 1991 Gulf War," pp. 404–420 in F. Krupp, A. H. Abuzinada, and I. A. Nader, eds. *A Marine Wildlife Sanctuary for the Arabian Gulf: Environmental Research and Conservation Following the 1991 Gulf War Oil Spill.* Riyadh: NCWCD and Frankfurt am Main: Senckenberg Research Institute.

Symens, P., and M. I. Evans. 1993. "Impact of Gulf War Oil Spills on Saudi Arabian Breeding Populations of Terns Sterna in the Arabian Gulf, 1991." *Sandgrouse.* Vol. 15, pp. 18–36.

Symens, P., and A. Suhaibani. 1993. "Impact of Gulf War Oil Spills on Saudi Arabian Wintering Seabird Populations along the Northern Arabian Gulf Coast of Saudi Arabia, 1991." *Sandgrouse.* Vol. 15, pp. 37–43.

Symens, P., and A. Suhaibani. 1994. "The Impact of the 1991 Gulf War Oil Spill on Bird Populations in the Northern Arabian Gulf: A Review." *Courier Forschungsinstitut Senckenberg.* Vol. 166, pp. 47–54.

Symens, P., and M. Werner. 1996. "Status of the Socotra Cormorant in the Arabian Gulf after the 1991 Gulf War Oil Spill, with an Outline of a Standardized Census Technique," pp. 390–403 in F. Krupp, A. H. Abuzinada, and I. A. Nader, eds. *A Marine Wildlife Sanctuary for the Arabian Gulf: Environmental Re-*

search and Conservation Following the 1991 Gulf War Oil Spill. Riyadh: NCWCD and Frankfurt am Main: Senckenberg Research Institute.

Theisen, O. M. 2008. "'Blood and Soil?' Resource Scarcity and Internal Armed Conflict Revisited." *Journal of Peace Research.* Vol 45, No. 6, pp. 801–818.

Thomas, W. 1995. *Scorched Earth: The Military's Assault on the Environment.* Philadelphia: New Society Publishers.

Toon, O. B., A. Robock, R. P. Turco, C. Bardeen, L. Oman, and G. L. Stenchikov. 2007. "Consequences of Regional-Scale Nuclear Conflicts." *Science.* Vol. 315 (2 March), pp. 1224–1225.

Tschirley, F. H. 1969. "Defoliation in Vietnam: The Ecological Consequences of the Defoliation Program in Vietnam Are Assessed." *Science.* Vol. 163, No. 3869 (21 February), pp. 779–786.

United Nations Environmental Programme. 1999. *The Kosovo Conflict: Consequences for the Environment and Human Settlements.* Nairobi: United Nations Environmental Programme and United Nations Centre for Human Settlements.

United Nations Environmental Programme. 2000. *Post-Conflict Environmental Assessment: Albania.* Nairobi: United Nations Environmental Programme.

United Nations Environmental Programme. 2000a. *Albania: Analytical Results of United Nations Environmental Programme Field Samples from Industrial Hot Spots.* Technical Report. Nairobi: United Nations Environmental Programme.

United Nations Environmental Programme. 2000b. *Environmental Impacts of the Refugee Influx in the Republic of Albania.* Technical Report. Nairobi: United Nations Environmental Programme.

United Nations Environmental Programme. 2000c. *Post-Conflict Environmental Assessment: FYR of Macedonia.* Nairobi: United Nations Environmental Programme.

United Nations Environmental Programme. 2000d. *Analytical Results of United Nations Environmental Programme Field Samples from Industrial Hot Spots and Refugee Sites in the Former Yugoslav Republic of Macedonia.* Technical Report. November. Nairobi: United Nations Environmental Programme.

United Nations Environmental Programme. 2001. *Depleted Uranium in Kosovo: Post-Conflict Environmental Assessment.* Nairobi: United Nations Environmental Programme.

United Nations Environmental Programme. 2002. *Depleted Uranium in Serbia and Montenegro: Post-Conflict Environmental Assessment in the Federal Republic of Yugoslavia.* Nairobi: United Nations Environmental Programme.

United Nations Environmental Programme. 2003a. *Depleted Uranium in in Bosnia and Herzegovina: Post-Conflict Environmental Assessment.* Nairobi: United Nations Environmental Programme.

United Nations Environmental Programme. 2003b. *Afghanistan: Post-Conflict Environmental Assessment.* Nairobi: United Nations Environmental Programme.

United Nations Environmental Programme. 2003c. *Desk Study on the Environment in Iraq.* Nairobi: United Nations Environmental Programme.

United Nations Environmental Programme and H. Partow. 2001. *The Mesopotamian Marshlands: Demise of an Ecosystem*. Division of Early Warning and Assessment (DEWA). Technical Report. UNEP/DEWA/TR.01-3 Rev. 1. Nairobi: United Nations Environmental Programme. http://www.grid.unep.ch/activities/sustainable/tigris/marshlands/ [accessed 15 January, 2003].

United Nations High Commissioner for Refugees. 1998. *Refugee Operations and Environmental Management Key Principles for Decision-making*. Geneva: United Nations High Commissioner for Refugees. http://www.unhcr.ch/cgi-bin/texis/vtx/home/+bwwBmeDz_w_wwwwnwwwwwwwxFqzvxK6q6sx6mFqA72Z-R0gRfZNhFqA72ZR0gRfZNtFqrpGdBnqBzFqmRbZAFqA72ZR0-gRfZNDzmxwwwwwww5Fqw1FqmRbZ/opendoc.pdf [accessed 19 May, 2003].

United Nations High Commissioner for Refugees. 2001. *Refugee Operations and Environmental Management: Selected Lessons Learned*. Geneva: United Nations High Commissioner for Refugees. http://www.rmi.org/images/other/Con-UNHCR_SelLesLrn.pdf, via http://www.rmi.org/sitepages/art7206.php [accessed 17 April, 2002].

United Nations High Commissioner for Refugees. 2005. *UNHCR Environmental Guidelines*. Geneva: United Nations High Commissioner for Refugees. http://www.unhcr.org/protect/PROTECTION/3b03b2a04.pdf [accessed 7 February, 2008]. This is an update for guidelines first issued in 1996.

United States Department of Energy. 2000. "United States Nuclear Tests: July 1945 through September 1992." U.S. Department of Energy. Nevada Operations Office. Document DOE/NV--209-REV 15. December 2000. See http://www.cfo.doe.gov/me70/manhattan/library.htm#usnuclear [accessed 26 February, 2009].

United States General Accounting Office. 1992. "International Environment: Kuwaiti Oil Fires: Chronic Health Risks Unknown but Assessments are Underway." Briefing Report to the Chairman, Legislation and National Security Subcommittee, Committee on Government Operations, House of Representatives. GAO/RCED-92-80BR. Washington, DC: United States General Accounting Office, January. http://archive.gao.gov/d31t10/146058.pdf [accessed 11 February, 2003].

United States Senate. 2005. "Nuclear Testing Program in the Marshall Islands." Hearing before the Committee on Energy and Natural Resources. United States Senate. One Hundred Ninth Congress. First Session on Effects of U.S. Nuclear Testing Program in the Marshall Islands. 19 July, 2005. Washington, DC: U.S. Government Printing Office.

Urbanczyk, Z. 1990. "Northern Europe's Most Important Bat Hibernation Site." *Oryx*. Vol. 24, No. 1 (January), pp. 30–34.

Uvin, P. 1996. "Tragedy in Rwanda: The Political Ecology of Conflict." *Environment*. Vol. 38, No. 3, pp. 7–29.

Van den Berg, M., B. A. T. C. Bosveld, J. P. Giesy, R. Letcher, and T. Sanderson. 2002. "Effects on Dioxinlike Compounds and PCBs on Wildlife: Is

There (Still) a Global Problem?" Conference paper. United States–Vietnam Scientific Conference on Human Health and Environmental Effects of Agent Orange/Dioxins, 3–6 March, 2002, Hanoi, Vietnam. [U.S. National Institute of Environmental Health Sciences] Available online at http://www.niehs.nih. gov/external/usvcrp/project1.htm [accessed 23 January, 2003].

Vertegaal, P. J. M. 1989. "Environmental Impact of Dutch Military Activities." *Environmental Conservation*. Vol. 16, No. 1, pp. 54–64.

Vogt, H. 1994. "Status of the Coral Reefs after the Gulf War." *Courier Forschungsinstitut Senckenberg*. Vol. 166, pp. 61–66.

Vogt, H. 1996. "Investigations on Coral Reefs in the Jubail Marine Wildlife Sanctuary Using Underwater Video Recordings and Digital Image Analysis," p. 302 in F. Krupp, A. H. Abuzinada, and I. A. Nader, eds. *A Marine Wildlife Sanctuary for the Arabian Gulf: Environmental Research and Conservation Following the 1991 Gulf War Oil Spill*. Riyadh: NCWCD and Frankfurt am Main: Senckenberg Research Institute.

Waitkuwait, W. E. 2001. "Report on the Establishment of a Community-Based Biomonitoring Programme in and around Sapo National Park, Sinoe County, Liberia." Report. Cambridge, UK: Fauna & Flora International. September. Available at www.fauna-flora.org/around_the_world/world_main_frame.htm [accessed 24 March, 2003].

Walsh, B. W. 1990. "War Games and Multiple Use." *American Forests*. Vol. 96 (November/December), pp. 21–23 and 74–75.

Warnken, J. 1996. "Salt-Marshes and Intertidal Habitats of the Jubail Marine Wildlife Sanctuary: Extent of Oil-Impacted Areas and Estimated Losses of Above-Ground Plant Biomass Following the 1991 Gulf War Oil Spill," pp. 177–185 in F. Krupp, A. H. Abuzinada, and I. A. Nader, eds. *A Marine Wildlife Sanctuary for the Arabian Gulf: Environmental Research and Conservation Following the 1991 Gulf War Oil Spill*. Riyadh: NCWCD and Frankfurt am Main: Senckenberg Research Institute.

Watt, I. 1996. "A Summary of the Clean-up Techniques Used in the Jubail Marine Wildlife Sanctuary after the Gulf War Oil Spill and an Assessment of their Benefits to Intertidal Recovery," p. 116 in F. Krupp, A. H. Abuzinada, and I. A. Nader, eds. *A Marine Wildlife Sanctuary for the Arabian Gulf: Environmental Research and Conservation Following the 1991 Gulf War Oil Spill*. Riyadh: NCWCD and Frankfurt am Main: Senckenberg Research Institute.

Weinbaum, M. G. 1993. "The Impact and Legacy of the Afghan Refugees in Pakistan," pp. 125–146 in J. H. Korson, ed. *Contemporary Problems of Pakistan*. Boulder, CO: Westview Press.

Westing, A. H. 1971. "Forestry and the War in South Vietnam." *Journal of Forestry*. Vol. 69, No. 11, pp. 777–783.

Westing, A. H. 1972. "Herbicidal Damage to Cambodia," pp. 177–205 in J. B. Neilands, et al., eds. *Harvest of Death: Chemical Warfare in Vietnam and Cambodia*. New York: Free Press.

Westing, A. H. 1974. "Postwar Forestry in North Vietnam." *Journal of Forestry.* Vol. 72, No. 3, pp. 153–156.

Westing, A. H. 1975. "Letters." *Journal of Forestry.* Vol. 73, No. 12, p. 755.

Westing, A. H. 1976. *Ecological Consequences of the Second Indochina War.* Stockholm: Almqvist & Wiksell.

Westing, A. H. 1978. "Ecological Considerations Regarding Massive Environmental Contamination with 2,3,7,8-Tetrachlorodibenzo-*para*-Dioxin." *Ecological Bulletin.* Vol. 27, pp. 285–294.

Westing, A. H. 1980. *Warfare in a Fragile World: Military Impact on the Human Environment.* London: Taylor & Francis.

Westing, A. H. 1981a. "Laotian Postscript." *Nature.* Vol. 294, p. 606.

Westing, A. H. 1981b. "Crop Destruction as a Means of War." *Bulletin of the Atomic Scientists.* Vol. 37, No. 2, pp. 38–42.

Westing, A. H. 1981c. "Environmental Impact of Conventional Warfare," pp. 58–72 in W. Barnaby, ed. *War and Environment.* Ministry of Agriculture Environmental Advisory Council. Stockholm: Författarna och LiberFörlag.

Westing, A. H. 1983. "The Environmental Aftermath of Warfare in Viet Nam." *Natural Resources Journal.* Vol. 23, No. 2 (April), pp. 365–389.

Westing, A. H. 1984. "Herbicides in War: Past and Present," pp. 3–24 in A. H. Westing, ed. *Herbicides in War: The Long-Term Ecological and Human Consequences.* London: Taylor & Francis.

Westing, A. H., ed. 1985. *Explosive Remnants of War: Mitigating the Environmental Effects.* London: Taylor & Francis.

Westing, A. H. 1989. "Herbicides in Warfare: The Case of Indochina," pp. 337–357 in P. Bourdeau, J. A. Haines, W. Klein, and C. R. Krishna Murti, eds. *Ecotoxicology and Climate.* Chichester, UK: John Wiley & Sons.

Westing, A. H. 1993. "The Environmental Modification Convention," pp. 947–954 in R. D. Burns, ed. *Encyclopedia of Arms Control and Disarmament.* New York: Scribner.

Westing, A. H. 2000. "In Furtherance of Environmental Guidelines for Armed Forces during Peace and War," pp. 171–181 in J. E. Austin and C. E. Bruch, eds. *The Environmental Consequences of War.* Cambridge: Cambridge University Press.

Westing, A. H. 2003. "Environmental Dimension of the Gulf War of 1991," pp. 523–534 in H. G. Brauch, et al., eds. *Security and Environment in the Mediterranean: Conceptualizing Security and Environmental Conflict.* Berlin: Springer.

Westing, A. H., and E. W. Pfeiffer. 1972. "The Cratering of Indochina." *Scientific American.* Vol. 226, No. 5, pp. 20–29.

Westing, A. H., and C. Westing. 1981. "Endangered Species and Habitats of Viet Nam." *Environmental Conservation.* Vol. 8, No. 1, pp. 59–62.

Westing, A. H., et al. 2002. "Long-term Consequences of the Vietnam War: Ecosystems." Report to the Environmental Conference on Cambodia, Laos, Vietnam. Stockholm: Föreningen Levande Framtid. Available online at http://www.nnn.se/environ/ecology.pdf [accessed 17 February, 2009].

Wildlife Conservation Society. 1999. "Amid Land Mines and Barbed Wire, Rare Species Abound." http://www.wcs.org/news/breakingnews/international/ 990323.dmz.html [accessed 18 April, 2000].

Williams, J. 1997. "Land Mines: Dealing with the Environmental Impact." *Environment and Security*. Vol. 1, No. 2, pp. 107–124.

Wolf, A. T. 1997. "'Water Wars' and Water Reality: Conflict and Cooperation along International Waterways," pp. 251–265 in S.C. Lonergan, ed. *Environmental Change, Adaption, and Security*. Boston: Kluwer.

Yamagiwa, J. 2003. "Bushmeat Poaching and the Conservation Crisis in Kahuzi-Biega National Park, Democratic Republic of the Congo." *Journal of Sustainable Forestry*. Vol. 16, Nos. 3/4, pp. 115–135.

Yateem, A., M. T. Balba, N. Al-Awadhi, and A. S. El-Nawawy. 1998. "White Rot Fungi and Their Role in Remediating Oil-Contaminated Soil." *Environment International*. Vol. 24, No. 1/2 (January), pp. 181–187.

Yen, M. D., and N. X. Quynh. 1984. "Long-Term Changes in the Freshwater Fish Fauna Following Herbicidal Attack," pp. 91–93 in A. H. Westing, ed. *Herbicides in War: The Long-Term Ecological and Human Consequences*. London: Taylor & Francis.

Young, A. L. 1988. "The Military Use of Herbicides in Vietnam," chapter 2, pp. 9–30 in A. L. Young and G. M. Reggiani, eds. *Agent Orange and Its Associated Dioxin: Assessment of a Controversy*. Amsterdam: Elsevier.

Yusufi, M. Q. 1988. "Effects of the War on Agriculture," pp. 197–216 in B. Huldt and E. Jansson, eds. *The Tragedy of Afghanistan: The Social, Cultural, and Political Impact of the Soviet Invasion*. New York: Croom Helm.

Zahler, P., and P. Graham. 2001. "War and Wildlife The Afghanistan Conflict and Its Effects on the Environment." Special Report. International Snow Leopard Trust. http://www.snowleopard.org/islt/pdf_bin/war.pdf [accessed 17 January, 2002].

Zimmer, C. 2003. "Rapid Evolution Can Foil Even the Best-Laid Plans." *Science*. Vol. 300 (9 May), p. 895.

Zinke, P. J. 1974. "Effect of Herbicides on Soils of South Vietnam," AD-779 024 in National Academy of Sciences. *Effects of Herbicides in South Vietnam; Part B: Working Papers*. Washington, DC: National Academy of Sciences.

Zinke, P. J. 1984. "Soil Ecology: An Overview," pp. 75–81 in A. H. Westing, ed. *Herbicides in War: The Long-Term Ecological and Human Consequences*. London: Taylor & Francis.

Zwarts, L., H. Felemban, and A. R. G. Price. 1991. "Wader Counts along the Saudi Arabian Gulf Coast Suggest That the Gulf Harbours Millions of Waders." *Wader Study Group Bulletin*. Vol. 63, pp. 25–32.

Index

Other Works by Jurgen Brauer

Economic Issues of Disarmament: Contributions from Peace Economics and Peace Science. With Manas Chatterji. London: Macmillan and New York: New York University Press, 1993.

Public Economics III: Public Choice, Political Economy, Peace and War. With Ronald Friesen and Edward Tower. Chapel Hill, NC: Eno River Press, 1995.

Economics of Conflict and Peace. With William Gissy. Burlington, VT: Avebury, 1997.

The Economics of Regional Security: NATO, the Mediterranean, and Southern Africa. With Keith Hartley. Amsterdam: Harwood, 2000.

Arming the South: The Economics of Military Expenditure, Arms Production, and Arms Trade in Developing Countries. With J. Paul Dunne. New York: Palgrave, 2002.

Economics of Peace and Security. With Lucy L. Webster and James K. Galbraith. A volume in the *Encyclopedia of Life Support Systems.* Developed under the Auspices of the United Nations Educational, Scientific, and Cultural Organization (UNESCO). Oxford, UK: EOLSS Publishers, 2003 www.eolss.net).

Arms Trade and Economic Development: Theory, Policy, and Cases in Arms Trade Offsets. With J. Paul Dunne. London: Routledge, 2004.

Castles, Battles, and Bombs: How Economics Explains Military History. With Hubert van Tuyll. Chicago: University of Chicago Press, 2008.

About the Author

Jurgen Brauer is a professor of economics at Augusta State University's James M. Hull College of Business in Augusta, Georgia. His research interests lie with economic and other aspects of conflict, war, and peace. He coedits the peer-reviewed *Economics of Peace and Security Journal* (www. epsjournal.org.uk), coedits the Studies in Defense and Peace Economics book series with Routledge (London), and has published a number of books, most recently *Castles, Battles, and Bombs: How Economics Explains Military History*. Widely published in prominent academic journals such as *Economic Development and Cultural Change*, the *Journal of Economic Education*, the *Journal of Economic Surveys*, the *European Journal of Political Economy*, and the *Journal of Economic Perspectives*, Dr. Brauer is a former vice-chair of the board of directors of *Economists for Peace and Security* and serves on the editorial boards of *Defence and Peace Economics*, the *International Journal of Applied Econometrics and Quantitative Studies*, and *Nação e Defesa*, an international journal of Portugal's National Defense Institute. In private life, he enjoys backpacking, motorcycle touring, scuba diving, and outdoor photography. He is a published underwater photographer.